GORDON STO...
P.O. Box 15901
Nashville, Tennessee...

The Jordanaires have been very fortunate t...
greatest entertainers the world has known.
Gospel, Country, Blues, Rock & Roll.. you ...
business is the kind of business where it ... ... the best out in someone or it can go the other way. Not long ago we received a recorded tape from
Johnny Earl, he seemed very sincere and had an honest approach in portraying
his music.

We toured with Johnny in England, and from then on a bond was formed in
friendship. Neal Matthews, second tenor singer and arranger for the
Jordanaires, and Johnny wrote songs together, and we had a ball on the
recording sessions we did with Johnny.

Johnny came to Nashville, where Carl Perkins a long standing friend of
ours joined in on a recording session, along with Scotty Moore and
D.J. Fontana ... Elvis' former band members for many years.

The Jordanaires have had the joy of recording several songs with Johnny,
and its great to know he writes a lot of his material which stands tall
in our opinion, and protrays the Artist   that Neal, Duane West, Ray Walker,
and myself have come to admire.

On and off stage THANKS JOHNNY for being our friend and we shall always
treaure your friendship.

Gordon Stoker

Gordon Stoker

Group Manager & First Tenor
The Jordanaires

All The King's Men

Photo © JEMusic

There's no reason to be
lonesome tonight! Put on
your blue suede shoes and
book a room at the
Heartbreak Hotel...

To
Christina x

" *The Party Girls* " *Holly*

JOHNNY EARL

BLUE SUEDE DREAMS

MY STORY, MY JOURNEY
1965 – 1999

Love & Best Wishes

A NOTE FROM PATRICIA RECORDS

This autobiography is written by Johnny Earl in his own words.
Any spelling mistakes, grammar failings or people feeling they have
been mildly (or cleverly) insulted, whether it be justified or otherwise,
please always look on the bright side of life. Any new terms or phrases
unknown to the English dictionary, man or womankind then please throw
the first stone unless oneself is perfect. Try not to lend (or borrow) your
copy of "Blue Suede Dreams" – you might never see it again! Tell them to
purchase their own copy. As Ray Walker from the "Jordanaires" said
"Life is short and the grave is deep."

You now have the book in your hands. Enjoy your
musical roller coaster ride on a "Blue Suede Dream."

Blue Suede Dreams

First released in Great Britain by Blue Suede Dreams Limited, UK 2019

Copyright © Johnny Earl

Currently unpublished

The right of Johnny Earl to be identified as the author of this work has been asserted in accordance
with sections 77 and 78 of the Copyright, Designs and Patents Act, 1988.

This book is copyright under the Berne convention.

ISBN 978-1-78808-363-8 (Hardback):

A CIP catalogue record for this book is available from the British Library

First Edition 2019

Book design & layout by Angelfire Creative Ltd.

Printed by CPI Colour Ltd.

FOREWORD

Ray Walker... The Jordanaires
20/05/2014

"When the Jordanaires met, and worked with Johnny Earl
the first time, we knew that Elvis would have liked him
and his work, and I told Johnny so at the time.

Johnny is sincere, properly aggressive, one of the best voices we have
encountered, and above all, respectful of all with whom he comes in
contact. Gordon, Neal, and Duane have passed on, but loved him until
they left us. I love and respect him 'till this day.
God bless John. Keep up the good work."

Sincerely,
Ray Walker
Bass singer of The Jordanaires
54 Years, 365 Days.

Johnny Earl - Rock 'n' Roll Legend

FOREWORD INTRODUCTION

A Note from Noel 'Razor' Smith – Author

If anyone can be described as a modern rock 'n' roll legend it is the great Johnny Earl. As an Elvis man, he is simply unsurpassable and has played with The Jordanaires and Scotty Moore, amongst others. As a songwriter, he has proved his versatility, penning Elvis-style ballads as well as dance-floor filling jivers that have become classics of the rock 'n' roll / rockabilly scene. A man of warmth and humour who always has time for his fans. I am proud to be involved, even in a small way, in the release of his autobiography. This is a story that is begging to be told.

Noel 'Razor' Smith

CONTENTS

1

COUNTRY BOY HEADS FOR LONDON

I was a restless young rocker. It was September 1984, and there was only one thing on my mind – destination London. I gave my mum a teary hug, she was sad to see me go like any mother would be. I was 19 years of age but for the last three years she knew my ambitions had grown and I yearned to join showbiz at whatever level. Mum knew that I was itching to go to lands afar and time and time again I kept telling her there was a band in London who were waiting for me, and I was not going to let them down.

I carried my suitcases with all my worldly belongings down the steep hill of Orchard Gardens, Dawlish, Devon and strangely enough as fate would have it, when I reached the bottom of the hill I came face to face with my brother David. He stopped in his tracks 'Where you off to then buy?' (I have spelt the word buy right, that is how we say 'boy' in Devon). 'I'm off to London to live', I replied. 'Just be careful, they are a crafty lot', he replied. I said, 'I have got to know a few of them quite well, and I get on great with them'. 'Okay John just look after yourself, I'll see you soon'. I think he said that because it was a Thursday and he thought I would be back on the first train the following Monday morning. Off I went and made my way to the train station.

I had an hour to spare so where better to spend it than having my last drink at the bar of the Grand Hotel which had been my destination on a few weekend pub crawls. The Grand Hotel was aptly situated right next to the train station. As I sat there with my two suitcases, it was quite obvious to one and all I was not going on a picnic and it was not long before one of the locals came up to me and said 'Off on holiday then?' 'No, I'm off to London to live'. He said 'Got a good job then?' 'Yeah I'm going to be a rock 'n' roll singer'. He gave me a funny look but then realized I was deadly serious. The man took a sip of his pint 'Have you thought long and hard of what you are about to do?' 'Oh yes', I replied 'In fact I'm on the next train to London, Paddington in about 45 minutes with a one-way ticket'.

I didn't let on, but my nerves were a fusion of anxiety, great expectation, but I had a one-track mind; nothing was going to stop me now! The guy finally said, 'Look why don't you go home and sleep on it, you won't like the people, they are not that friendly'. I finished my drink, took a long look around the lounge and bar area and nodded to my old friend the pool table, gazing a goodbye to one and all, and thinking oh well the pool table was the one thing in here tonight that was a pleasure to see. 'See ya', I said to one and all, and anyone who cared to listen, and made my way to the train platform.

There I sat contemplating my future in the few minutes I had left before my train arrived. I was only 19. I looked straight ahead at the tunnel where I knew the train would appear and take me to my new life.

I was very brave now when I think about it, but ambition and age were on my side, so that 'Train, Train is comin' round, round the bend and it's taking Johnny to the bright lights of London's West End'.

2

ROCK 'N' ROLL MUSIC

Growing up I was always surprised how when you mentioned the term rock 'n' roll music to Americans they would throw into the pot the likes of Elton John, The Rolling Stones along with Credence Clearwater Revival etc. To me, being British, rock 'n' roll music does what it says on the tin – music spanning the 1950's & early 1960's; a mixture of blues, country and swing. And once you have the Rock 'n' Roll bug you have it for life. When you hear that beat, you'll start tapping your feet and begin to sway to the rhythm. It really is a musical potion that to this very day works on me, so if you have rock 'n' roll in your soul basically it's got you hook, line and sinker.

Some people just can't understand it because when they were young they could have been either hippies, punk rockers, soul boys, mods, skinheads, smoothies or just plain square. To them they have their memories and most feel they have finished living the music and fashion they loved from all those years ago, and now they've moved on with their lives, which often leaves them struggling to understand why rock 'n' rollers just keep rockin' 'n' rollin' and really are in it till the very end.

All I can tell you is play me Little Richard, Elvis Presley, Eddie Cochran, Gene Vincent, Buddy Holly, Bill Haley, Carl Perkins, and a transition starts taking place. It makes one forget those unpaid bills, unhappy girlfriends, and whatever the modern music of the day may be, it all fades away and becomes a distant memory. Yes, I am a rock 'n' roll addict. I want more and more, and if rock 'n' roll is the devil's music I'm going down, down, down in a burning ring of fire. If anyone reading this thinks I'm overreacting or exaggerating then take a trip to a rock 'n' roll event, or one of the many popular themed weekenders anywhere in the UK or Europe and all will become very clear – that rock 'n' roll to a lot of people is a way of life. God bless rock 'n' roll and all who sails in her.

But what lights the fuse to this rock 'n' roll musical way of life? We all have our stories, so I'll tell you mine.

It's August 1977, I'm sitting in the passenger seat of a black Ford Cortina estate MK11 with big wide wheels – a tiger tank of its day. At the steering wheel the person who I loved but also sometimes feared, depending on how the world was treating him at the time, was my father (Stuart). He led a very busy life being the man in charge of what became most probably Exeter City's biggest plant and machinery company, Star Contractors. In my father's youth, he was a leather-clad rocker riding his pride and joy, a Triumph Bonneville. He then joined the Merchant Navy, a family tradition, as my granddad was in the Royal Navy. My father after his years of naval service left to become a postman and my beautiful mother (Patricia) always told me how my father had nothing against being a postman but wanted a more financially secure future, so he worked long days and nights building his way up in the plant and machinery business learning how to drive, maintain and fix a JCB Loader, HYMAC etc., from top to bottom.

Although very busy in his work life, he loved his music and that was why he was my mentor for rock 'n' roll. We had family weekends away mainly to Weston-super-Mare, and there would be music in the car all the way there and back supplied by none other than the eight-track tape cartridge (the forebear of the cassette), which had pictures of the album title and the artist stuck on its side. The eight-track was shaped like two pieces of thick sliced bread, buttered together, which you rammed into the opening fitted in the dashboard of the car, and then the show was on the road.

August 1977: I'm now a twelve-year old boy full of excitement and always eager to travel in my dad's car because I could listen to anything my father decided to play, which I just loved. On this August day as he put the key in the ignition, he slowly turned the key and as he started the car he moved his hand towards the eight-track player, but this time he slowly passed over it and went to put the radio on instead. Strange, I thought. I noticed he hesitated as he did so, I knew something was on his mind, but being twelve and knowing how strict my father could be I kept my lip buttoned.

My father was no different from most people who had their radio tuned in to their favourite radio station. It was always tuned into the same station, a little turn, click, and the radio lit up, but on this occasion I remember an advert was playing followed by the disc jockey, his words like a slow sobering Sir Winston Churchill speech intoned... 'There will never be another. I, like millions of people all over the world are in mourning at the loss and the unfortunate death of Elvis Presley, the king of rock 'n' roll, who last night passed away at his Graceland home in Memphis, Tennessee. God Bless The King.'

This was immediately followed by the Jordanaires distinctive intro... ooh ooh ooh wah o wah ooh then Elvis's mesmerizing vocal croons "Are You Lonesome Tonight..." Now for the first time in my life I witnessed my father raise his hands to his face covering his eyes, and then helplessly start to wipe away tears. This man was my rock of Gibraltar, tough-as-nails father, who I adored, and I am watching him sobbing and wiping tears from his face. With a low tone in his voice he raised his head gazed straight ahead through the car windscreen saying the words 'Music will never be the same, the DJ is right, there'll never be another'. I was quite taken back and started to get a little choked up and emotional myself. We sat there right through the song until the last haunting renditions where the King – as only he could do – finished the song with 'Tell me dear are you lonesome too-oo night'. My father was paying his last respects to his greatest music idol, Elvis Presley.

All of my boyhood years until that moment were mostly spent playing soccer, judo, hit (tag), kiss chase (which always meant I got caught by the girls on purpose, as I loved kissing girls on the cheek even at that age) and fishing, but at the tender age of twelve, three minutes of my father's uncontrollable emotions had changed me forever.

In August of 1977 if you were a true rock 'n' roller your King and music idol had just died, and the world of music would never be the same because Elvis left behind a legacy which will forever crown him the King of rock 'n' roll. That was the defining moment for me. I now needed to know all about this guy Elvis Presley, especially as all the press and media of the day were full of nothing else. All through the school holidays and for the next few years, Elvis movies were on T.V. and to me I was reliving my father's teenage years and loving it. For me nobody came any cooler than the characters Danny Fisher or Vince Everett who Elvis played in the early movies *King Creole* and *Jailhouse Rock*. My father let me have all his rock 'n' roll records and even bought me new ones which meant as soon as I came home from school I played those records till the grooves came out. Elvis, Buddy Holly, Gene Vincent, Jerry lee Lewis, Roy Orbison – these guys to me were gods that sang through whichever two speakers were in front of me. I also adored the record labels RCA, Columbia, H.M.V, London, MGM, Parlophone. I was collecting antiques without knowing it.

My father realized by the time I was thirteen a rock 'n' roller was emerging. Aged fourteen I was pestering for a Teddy Boy suit. We were living in Teignmouth in Devon now and on my fourteenth birthday he asked me what I wanted – He knew exactly what I wanted, and off to the tailors in the City of Exeter we went.

Remember my father was an original rocker who wore smart Teddy Boy suits; only the best hung in his closet. Not one to mince his words he strongly said to me 'Forget all that Showaddywaddy rubbish; you are going to have a proper tailor-made Teddy Boy suit'. I listened, soaking in every word and of course whether I agreed or not this car wasn't turning back for anything. I remember thinking Joseph's amazing technicolor dream coat is just jumble-sale fodder compared to my awaiting splendour. Today I'm going to be inducted properly into the rock 'n' roll world with my all-new Teddy Boy suit.

We walked through the tailor's front door. A middle-aged man approached us, 'Can I help you sir?' My Dad replied, 'I'd like a Teddy Boy suit for my son'. 'Follow me sir', said the tailor. We walked to a long table where he took out roll after roll of fabric. 'Can I suggest gabardine sir?' My father felt the cloth. 'What do you think?' He grinned and looked at me, 'Yeah I like it'. 'What colour sir?' said the tailor. My father stepped in, 'I'll let my son choose the colour, he's the one who will be wearing it'. I was confronted with all these cloths – dark blue, black and varying shades of grey (there could have been up to 50), not the slightest hint of any fluorescent Showaddywaddy colours in sight, and right here at my fingertips was this beautiful gabardine material. I then pointed at what looked to me to be a confederate grey colour 'That's the one', I gasped. 'Come this way sir and we will get some measurements'. It was all new to me AND I WAS LOVING IT!

After he took my measurements, 'How many pockets sir?' my reply 'Pockets?' This is where my father stepped in 'Two at the bottom and a half moon breast pocket'. Half moon, wow! I'm now in half moon heaven. The trousers were not totally drain pipes but were going to fit well over my new suede shoes. On the way home I was completely full of excitement and elation and my dad could see it, and as if the whole experience wasn't enough, he said 'This weekend you're going to a rock 'n' roll concert at The Paignton Festival Theatre'. I didn't even ask who was on the bill, all I knew was that I was ready to start rocking 'n' rolling. I had been to a few rock 'n' roll record hops, one being the regular at the R.A.O.B. club in Newton Abbott where the disc jockey was the legendary Devon's own Eddie Falcon, who was also spinning the discs every Sunday at the Grasshopper Hotel in Ashburton. Now a record hop is one thing, but this was to be my very first rock 'n' roll concert.

On the bill at this concert was Heinz, Screaming Lord Sutch, and Ricky Valance. Even though a coffin came on stage and Lord Sutch pranced about in what looked like Robin Hood tights, the whole night was a huge success for me. Let's put it this way... rock 'n' roll music had now fully embraced me. From that day way back in 1979 I was in all the way - hook, line and sinker.

3

GROWING UP IN DEVON

I was born in Exeter, Devon, and the youngest of three children. I had a sister June and brother David. I had a (very strict) father, Stuart and the person I adore more than anyone, my beautiful mummy Patricia. My first memory was somewhere between the age of 2 and 3. I can remember being in a pram at Exeter bus station and women were taking turns pinching my cheek. They had big smiley faces, talking baby language to me in a way that only women can do. Those early years of my life were spent living in Sandford Street, Exeter, from there we moved to 100 Mount Pleasant Road. I was a pupil attending Ladysmith infants then junior school. I enjoyed my infant and junior school days, lots of kiss chase and football. In each year, you had what were called houses (which were teams), each house having a colour; yellow, green, blue and I was in the red. When you were in the 5th year (the last year of juniors) each house had 4 prefects, 16 in all, and these prefects were all commanded by the highest-ranking pupil of the whole school: This person was called the monitor. Yes, the field marshal of pupils, and even teachers would use the monitor to watch over their classes in emergency situations.

I quite enjoyed being monitor. It had its advantages, and I would take classes of pupils and escort them around the school until the teacher arrived back. I would send a pupil to look out for when the teacher was arriving and until then let the class all have a good old chin wag with one another, making sure they all knew not to be too loud or else I would warn them 'Johnny might administer the cane'.

Ladysmith was a good laugh, but my family then decided to leave Exeter when I was the ripe old age of 12, which was my last year of juniors. In this year I enjoyed being in the school soccer team and loved playing the position of midfield, as I could attack and score goals as well as defend when needed.

My family moved to 21 Ferndale Road in Teignmouth, about 15 miles away from Exeter on the coast, and my Nan and Granddad from my father's side came with us as well. My new educational quarters was now Teignmouth Secondary Modern, where I tried to get on with a lot of the other pupils in my first year. When you move to a new school however, a lot of the groups already have their mates and are not too keen on new members. Where I was blessed was my love of rock 'n' roll music, which drew all the rockers together. It was at this age of 12-13 where I was surprised to find out that whatever type of music you liked dictated who was going to like you.

Being a rock 'n' roller was pretty good really because all the parents generally liked your music and a lot of the teachers too. They all joined in with the not-very-punk-rocker-friendly attitude which was rife at the time. At school in the year above me was a guy named Neil Leggett who was a very close friend, and we rock 'n' rolled right up until I moved to London. We both had early morning paper rounds and some of those stormy Devonshire mornings it was not unusual to have a couple of your papers fly up the road and have pages wrapped around trees and ending up in peoples' gardens, so when you had collected all the pages you would try your best to put back together the paper in the original format. Quite often the pages did not always run in the proper order. By the time, you came to deliver your papers, instead of being nice and flat with all pages in the correct order, there was a good possibility that through the letter box would arrive a newspaper looking more like something that could have been wrapped around fish and chips the night before. I can tell you on mornings like this when it was freezing cold and you were up at 5.30am to return home for 8am to get ready for school, if you could do this, it certainly set you up to be able to do anything that came your way in the future.

While we are on the topic of newspapers a dear friend of mine who I was very close with (but unfortunately is no longer with us) was Sean Thomas, a great mate who really was instrumental for me in moving to London. He was born in Camden Town, London, in the pub his family owned. His mother Sheila told us that when they celebrated his birth, an alcohol induced mistake led a family member to wrap up this young rocker in a newspaper and throw him in the bin. On hearing of his arrival I sang to Sean *"Welcome to the world, won't you come on in, wrapped like fish and chips, and then thrown into the bin".* Sean brought down to Devon some of his London friends, among them a double bass rockabilly player Paul Maitland (who became a very close friend). They heard me sing a couple of songs upon which Paul told Sean he wanted me as the lead singer for his London band.

Through my early teens, I realized to be able to rock 'n' roll and go out at weekends, and of course to buy my vinyl records, money was required – and it had to be earned. When I was 14, I worked my way into unloading two local trawlers, The Thistle, and The Peggy. This was not easy work but as they mainly trawled for sardines and herring they also caught in the nets mackerel, pollock, and whiting which were given to us as payment. Both these trawlers I went out to sea on, to see if this was a career I wanted to pursue, because at school you could get time off from lessons if you went to the careers teacher with what you thought was the career for you, and they would give you as much help as possible.

I therefore went to see the careers teacher as much as I could; though I remember it did not start well. On my first session, he asked me what I wanted to do when I left school and I told him in no uncertain terms 'I'm going to be a rock 'n' roll singer'. He just stared at me and a few minutes later I found myself walking back to class.

I went back to the careers teacher with a change of tact, this time to pursue my ambition of being a trawler man, and this led me to the position of being able to go out on the trawlers on numerous occasions. This in turn required me to go to the fish quay most nights after school to help to unload the trawlers. I suppose in terms of becoming a trawler man, I was nearly halfway there. I made a fish barrel at my woodwork classes at school, it was a sort of elongated tea chest with handles, and I finished it off with go cart wheels. It held about 200 mackerel. I had regular customers, mainly on the route back to my home – which unfortunately was mostly uphill – so by the time I came to the last customers I tried to make sure they were guest houses or hotels, so I could sell all that I had left. Financially it was great; I even sold a lot of fish to my school teachers. I remember Mr. Taylor who lived down the bottom end of Ferndale Road, who was also a big record collector. He along with other teachers was surprised to find out I had not even left school yet and earned as much as they did, some weeks more. The big difference being they had mortgages and families to look after while I had amusement arcades, rock 'n' roll records and girlfriends to spend my earnings on (..not much changed there then).

In my teens, the punks, skinheads, mods and smoothies all sort of hung around their own fraternity. My mates were rockers which included bikers, teds, and rockabillies. Not much fighting and falling out with one another went on in Teignmouth as we were in the same classes at school, but when you travelled to Exeter or Torquay you had to take care. I mean it as well.. even in friendly old Devon, end up in the wrong club or the wrong place with a different music cultured gang before you; it could be very likely that bandages and large plasters were soon needed.

We had great games of tag all along the sea front and down the fish quay, and like you do, all us school kids decided one night to have a massive egg fight all around the town. Some of the streets of Teignmouth looked like an omelette after this escapade, and we even made the local papers on that one!

We had the local town rock 'n' roll discos at the Carlton Theatre and they were good fun. The central hub for all groups of teenagers at the time in Teignmouth was the triangle which was in the centre of town. (When any teenager was bored, all they would say was 'I'm off to the triangle').

The house in Ferndale Road that we lived in backed onto the local convent which had a tennis court, and one night a friend and I decided to try and have a go at playing tennis. We made amateurs look brilliant but without us realising a couple of nuns appeared out of nowhere. One came up and asked who we were. I pointed out my house to her and told her that was where I lived and she had a quick discussion with the other nun then said, 'Do you go to Teignmouth Grammar School?' I replied, 'No we go to Teignmouth Secondary Modern'. Straight faced the Nun then replied, 'Then I'm sorry, you will have to leave'. We were gutted, and for the first time I realized posh people didn't really like people like me. Night after night we returned to play, and then legged it when we saw the nuns. In the end, they called the police and wanted us dealt with firmly. Rather unfortunately for the nuns, one of the policemen who took me aside was one of my regular fish customers and he knew how hard I worked each night at the fish quay. I told him they said we could not play because we went to the wrong school, so he just told us to leave quietly and come back on Sunday mornings when they are all at prayer! To be honest tennis was not for me; I preferred football and rugby.

A life changing point was when I was 16 years of age, walking down that steep Teignmouth hill to my house. It was a Thursday and unusually my brother was sat on the wall with his girlfriend and I noticed he was crying. His girlfriend looked at me and said, 'Oh no it's John', and ran off. 'What on earth is wrong with her?' I asked my brother. He looked at me with the saddest look a person could give, took a deep breath and cried as he said, 'Dad died today'. I was stunned, I stood there in shock, walked backwards repeatedly saying 'No! No! No!' Emotions got the better of me. I just ran as fast as I could to the house, bolted through the back door, ran into my Nan and Granddad's room, and standing there torn apart with grief, were my grandparents and my beautiful mummy. I have had sad times in my life, personal grief I would wish on no one, but at this moment in time, I was so heartbroken at the loss of my father I could hardly stand. I just held my mother and we sobbed in each other's arms. Anyone who has lost a loved one will know the grief I am talking about and I believe to this day that because my father died at the age of 38 it planted a seed in me to try to enjoy every day that I open my eyes to – as you really never know what is around the corner. Had my father lived I very much doubt I would have ever moved to London, but a lasting promise and tribute I gave to him was recording his favourite Elvis song *"It's So Strange"* with Elvis's band backing me. Now tell me that's not the ultimate Blue Suede Dream.

I had an apprenticeship at Torquay Technical College as a painter and decorator and worked my way to receive my City and Guilds. I worked for a company called Richcraft that had offices in a quaint little village called Star Cross, on the coastal road just before Dawlish Warren. The boss was a fabulous Irish guy called Paddy who worked hard and played hard and was good enough to help me get my apprenticeship. A lot of days I would work in the office in the back room filling the paint shelves and spend most of the day crying with laughter with Paddy, telling him jokes. His son Steve and all the other decorators could never understand why we laughed so much together, but when an Irishman like Paddy kept telling me jokes about Devonshire people, I would respond with machine gun fire, one-after-the-other jokes about the Irish. They were good days.

I moved to Dawlish with my mother when I was 16. We stayed at my auntie Lyn's for about 6 months before moving to 13 Orchard Gardens, Dawlish, Devon. These were the last three years I lived in Devon, but the defining moment for me which I will never forget, was when I was coming back into shore from being at sea working a day on the trawlers. As we came into the harbour, I looked at the whole of Teignmouth from the sea and said to myself as beautiful as it is, you are not going far being a rock 'n' roll singer there, I pulled in the fish nets for the last time, a new sun set on my life that day. As I stepped back onto shore, a voice in my mind over and over kept telling me - it's time to go!

4

MANAGERS

Should you be an artiste or a band with the potential to procure fame and fortune and can be seen to be a viable and sellable product, you can only go so far in the music and entertainment world without having the right representation. As legally clever as you might think you are, or personally able to take control of one's business and personal affairs, the music and entertainment business is after all a BUSINESS.

I found out very early on in my career that this business is mostly run by very clever and educated people from all levels of society, who in a lot of cases do not necessarily care about the artiste or whoever they are representing. All that matters is making sure that in every conceivable way possible – every euro, dollar and yen, in fact every currency that's available at a bureau de change – yes, every penny that they can procure is indeed earned. One day a light turns on in your mind and the time comes when you realise you cannot do everything yourself; someone else has to take the helm. Whether you like it or not, to that someone else you will pretty much have to give almost total autonomy – and should they require it – the air you breathe, your entire schedule and time for an agreed period of your life, which can be years in some cases. Yes, he or she will come to the fore and will be the newly appointed headmaster of everything you do! Your soul will belong to neither God nor the Devil but to 'THE MANAGER'!

There is a saying in the music business when you are looking for a good manager that there are none available, as they are already managing successful artistes and stars of the day. Just take Colonel Tom Parker, Elvis's manager, who was already managing two of the world's biggest country music stars (Eddie Arnold and Hank Snow) and dropped them like a stone to manage The King... the rest is history. Don King, the boxing manager legend, walks in to a world heavyweight fight with one boxer, who goes on to lose, and walks out becoming the new manager of, you've guessed it, the winner (Oh how the worm turns). Yes, I might be talking about the highest level of the management world but at all levels, the right manager is imperative. In most cases however, when you start off and throw into the pot you are pretty much green; unfortunately there is no way of telling who is the right person for the job. A good friend of mine and co-songwriter Chris Skornia (who I might add also hails from Devon) had me thinking very early on how important managers could be with his experiences. He had success with a punk band in his earlier days called The Truth. Now I have always looked at Chris as a good competent keyboard player as well as a very talented and clever individual. One of those musicians who saw a lot of things others couldn't, so in my book worth taking notice of.

He told me he remembered very well when The Truth were the warm up band for none other than Blondie at the height of their career, and at the time The Truth were represented by a very famous manager of the day. Chris reminisced on more than one occasion how things could have been so different and how much more successful the group could have been had the management spent as much time on them as they did with the other major stars they were managing - Rod Stewart being one.

So, let's get things right. A lot of people wear a lot of hats in the music and entertainment business and although they say they are a manager, often they are the person financing the whole project and so they trust absolutely no one. Thus they become the stand-in manager, which never really works, or alternatively the person at the helm is really a promoter or an agent which is an entirely different job altogether. If you look at the very top end of the music business the stars of the day will have a number of managers, for instance one taking care of all the touring (and that is all he or she will deal with). The artiste will also have a personal manager who will deal direct with them on all his or her affairs, and then another manager again will take care of all the TV and press and media. The normal process of having a manager though is much like what I have experienced: Starting from the bottom rung and in some cases working your way downwards. You cause a little ripple in the music world as I did when starting out, and then out of the fog you are approached by a person introducing themselves and telling you they are a manager; or the person willing to take you (and the whole project) under their wings and guide the whole package to the stars!

I can personally say I have had 3 people representing me solely, whose job it was to manage. And so enter manager number one, Chris Emo.

Chris was quite famous in his own right in the rock 'n' roll world as the bass player for a well-known band called Whirlwind. He was a likeable guy who lived in a flat in Hayes, Middlesex with his wife and newly born daughter and at the time he helped me find lodgings with his mother Barbara who was also living in Hayes – Chatsworth Road to be precise. This was not far from him which made it quick and easy to get hold of one another. At this time I had not long moved from Devon to London, so it helped a great deal for me to have a roof over my head for a year (Thank you Barbara). Chris had good ideas and a lot of enthusiasm but not all the funds needed to carry out all his ideas. One night at his flat it was agreed the time had come for a career and band discussion about the way forward, only this time two non-band members were to be present: his wife who was holding their new born baby. (Uh oh, not the usual group of people that attend such meetings but hey, we are all on the same side, plus they too can enjoy the success if it works).

Chris anchored himself on the corner of the settee and after a minute or two of Chris's CEO management ideas – which I may add I thought were very constructive and exciting, and good ways to go forward – I said very little but listened intently. His wife waited for the right moment to interject and when that moment came she exclaimed 'Sounds great Chris but where is all the financing coming from?' She took one look at me and realized I had limited funds so Chris intervened saying 'Well I thought I could, Aghhh!..' and like a professional American baseball pitcher Chris's wife threw the hardest looking pet dog ball right at Chris's chops which knocked him right off the side of the settee (I thought she's definitely won a big cuddly toy for that one). Boy it must have hurt! Sometimes strategic action is needed to get one's point over, however she was embarrassed and swiftly apologized – to me I must add – and that was the start of the end of Chris's management endeavours, with me anyway. Credit where it was due, Chris was a stickler and as well as embarking on management he was also doing karate at the time (he did become a black belt) but as far as the management was concerned he knew his obligations lay elsewhere and within a couple of weeks manager number one was no more. Now just like a jack-in-the-box up popped manager number two... Emerging through the fog enter Mr. Kevin Allen.

Ten years was to be the length of time Kevin Allen and I worked as Manager & Artiste and of course people would always liken us to the Colonel and Elvis, except neither of us had much showbiz experience. Kevin had some experience working with a couple of the best known rock 'n' roll acts of the day, The Stargazers being one, and hung around other bands like The Deltas who were another well-known act on the r 'n' r circuit. Both had UK chart success and although Kevin associated himself with them, he was more of a friend than having any managerial capacity, but the fuse was lit and he obviously decided management was for him. He was at the time also quite a credible Disc Jockey as well.

Our manager/artiste relationship was very heated at times to say the least and I do regret the way I spoke and treated him on a few occasions, but if ever there was an artiste running way too fast for their own good it was me! To say we were both green is an understatement. In our working relationship it went along the lines of every time something good or successful happened we took all the glory and smiled like Cheshire cats, but when disaster struck Kevin took the blame.

Kevin looked a bit like Elvis – even to the extent that when we were in Nashville, one man we had a meeting with introduced himself to Kevin and he then sat himself down and started ranting how good Kevin looked and he could take him all the way, not realizing he was speaking to the manager (nor even asking who Johnny Earl was). Kevin had previously sent this guy a full package which he obviously took no notice of, so he cooked his goose before he'd started. Kevin looked at me and I just told them to carry on while I went to get a coffee and when I returned this guy was still explaining to Kevin how much he could make him a star. I thought 'good homework my friend' and needless to say we never saw him again.

Kevin just like myself was a big Elvis fan but in our association Kevin had to take the role of the Colonel. Very often he took quite a liking to it as it gave him a bit of power and the final say in a lot of situations. The day came when it dawned on Kevin that to be able to properly put his plans into effect it was going to take money and lots of it, so he started by looking for an angel (this is the name given in the music business to someone who puts the finances into musical ventures). Unfortunately for us the angels had all flown away and Kevin soon came to the realisation there were literally thousands of people with ventures and ideas and sadly very few angels. (In fact was there even such a thing?)

First lesson learnt. When you put your hand out and look for financing in the music business you often find yourself alone in the wilderness speaking only to yourself. In time the realisation finally hits home: If you are using all your own ideas – well, you can pay for them too. And so Kevin concluded that he needed to work two jobs. One job he obtained was as a mini-cab driver for a company called Al cars in Hillingdon, and the other was working as a bus driver stationed at the Hounslow depot.

My input was to keep the band rehearsing and performing which meant most of the monies we procured from shows went straight back into the next tour that we were planning, or the next recording venture, so basically we both just kept on reinvesting all our earnings back into the whole project. What we were actually aiming for, or where we were going, to be honest both of us never had a clue and so when the gigging monies dried up we went without. Yes, we were in it up to our quiffs, and soon learned it was going to be one tedious and long hard slog in a world we knew very little about. Most frightening was the business side which had to be conquered, and it was very apparent that we had to learn ..and quick!

In the beginning of our manager artiste relationship, all that mattered as far as we were concerned, was we had all the tools along with all the ambition you could wish for. We thought not much else was needed to create a music empire, so the business side for the moment ..well that was just a minor blip and tended to get in the way of the music.

Kevin Allen was more than dedicated and learned as he went along, so found out the hard way how to be a manager. Very quickly he came to learn it was not all about the bright lights and fun with women and drink – oh no Mr. Allen! The more unprofessional and incompetent you are as a manager the more difficult and expensive the world becomes. Rule number one: You earn a lot more being sober. In the early days of working with Kevin we both enjoyed a pint down the pub because that was how we grew up and like most people in their late teens and early twenties we were raised living a social British life.

In the beginning, as the strains of our dreams piled upon us, Kevin fought many a round with one hand tied behind his back, sometimes winning but mostly going back to square one. Sinking in gradually for Kevin was that no one gives you a helping hand, you have to do it all yourselves until you get recognized. Only then do certain people help a little (for their own gain) and if it's in their favour, and then you reach that stage where the question is asked 'What am I doing it for?' So after ten years Kevin finally worked out he was much more aligned to being an agent rather than a manager. (Nothing wrong with that). He will not be the first and certainly not the last person to join the music world with a certain aim or a goal in mind only to find the tide took you in another direction. Throughout this book, Kevin will appear in various events and situations, some hilarious, and some that will take you to the depths of the cynical and callous world that the music business can be.

To sum up my decade with Kevin, we had a lot of laughs, a lot of falling outs, but for a guy who managed to pull off bringing all of Elvis's original band to the UK and Europe, he did what he set out to do. And as anyone will know when you have big ambitions in this world and start from the bottom, especially in the music world, you take on that poisoned chalice until the sobering reality hits you in the face.. what are you actually trying to do? Well Kevin experienced all of this and even when confronted with the scale of what was before him he still relentlessly carried on, despite the endless criticism and barracking from musicians and friends. Although he probably does not know it, he is respected for what he achieved. I for one was there and I saw first-hand the utmost pressures he dealt with; there was no help, just the greed the music business desired. The Jordanaires found Kevin hard-working and respected him, as well as finding him hilarious at times as they knew Colonel Tom Parker so well and always remarked to Kevin 'The Colonel wouldn't have done it like that' – but I know they respected him. I may not have shown it at the time, I certainly take my hat off to Mr Allen for his achievements while we were manager/artiste, and I can tell you for sure very few people had the tenacity Kevin did, especially through our ten years together.

Let me give you an example. When we promoted our first big show in 1986 at 'The Academy Rooms' at the Brunel University, Uxbridge, West London, to promote this event we both fly posted – and what I mean by that is we took 1,000 A1 sized posters – and with bucket and paste, plastered them all over Soho, the Kings Road, north, south, east and west London, alongside all the other people's posters who were touring and having hits at the time like Sting, Elton John, Bryan Adams, Madonna. So what would have cost us tens of thousands of pounds in promotion we took care of and did ourselves from midnight to four, five, six, in the morning, night after night, in snow and rain. We stood alongside the professional fly poster people (taking good care not to go over theirs) and we made it work.

It was unfortunate when the day arrived that I had to tell Kevin 'let's put our cards on the table'. I in no way belittled him, just expressed how in my mind he was much better at being an agent than a manager and we had really come to the end of the line. He was a bit upset because he knew what I was really saying was I did not want to sign another contract, and like any manager when you have been together through so much for such a long period of time it was hard to take. After a short period of time I'm pretty sure he would have agreed it was for the best. Although walking in the steps of Colonel Tom Parker I openly say Kevin Allen fulfilled his Blue Suede Dream and can hold his head up higher than most who failed where he achieved. 'LONG LIVE COLONEL KEV'.

Enter manager number three... Please step up and take your turn Mr. Peter Oakman (none other than the man who co-wrote Joe Brown's biggest hit *"Picture of You"*, a UK number 1 hit in the summer of 1962). Peter was the bass player for The Bruvvers who backed an array of legends, not only Joe Brown but Gene Vincent on his first UK tour. Peter never forgets to remind his audiences that in his early days when starting out, the band they used as a warm up act - we know them today as The Beatles... that's right, the real ones. To Peter's own pleasure he has a recorded version of the fab four performing his hit *"Picture of You"* with lead vocals by George Harrison. Pete's list of who he has worked with includes not only Gene Vincent, The Beatles, but also Chet Atkins, Guy Mitchell, Marvin Rainwater, Don Gibson.. Basically it's a stellar list of 1950's and 1960's legends.

At the time of Pete becoming my third manager, I was working with the band Skiffabilly. Up until that moment Skiffabilly was mainly run by myself with fellow band members Robbie Mac and Annie Watts, but even with our enthusiasm the whole Skiffabilly project now needed proper management. After a few discussions it was evident there were too many egos and too many ideas holding the Skiffabilly project back so someone had to take the helm. This was the first and only time I was under management while being in a band. The other bands I was in – The Louisiana Hayriders and Southern Star – were never going to be managed as they didn't really need it, but with Skiffabilly it was a unanimous decision with all involved the time had come for management representation. Peter Oakman wanted a month's trial period to see how it worked, as a clause in the management contract, and true to his word a month later we were all summoned to a band and management meeting where the band sat there with baited breath to hear how Pete's plans were going to take effect and enable Skiffabilly to rocket to showbiz glory. Pete stood up and in one sentence informed every one present 'I can't manage what can't be managed'. Goodbye manager number three.

To finish the showbiz manager section let me share the conversations I had with the Jordanaires, because when you are an Elvis fan you cannot help at some point to be amazed with the success Colonel Tom Parker had as Elvis's personal manager and what was achieved. Whether you agreed or not with all the Colonel did, I recall Gordon Stoker shared his experiences with me regarding the Colonel. One such story being on the film set while Elvis was filming *Blue Hawaii*. Elvis and everyone was messing around on the beach until along came the Colonel and immediately the fooling around stopped. Gordon told me, 'Johnny the respect that man commanded was unreal, when he appeared on the film set not a sound could be heard, nobody dared to cross him. The one thing the Colonel knew about me was that I hated the smell of tobacco and on this occasion, he told everyone to get on with their jobs and to start filming, as time was money. He then strolled over to me and can you believe it, put a handful of cigars in the top of my Hawaiian shirt pocket and told me, Gordon when I want one I'll shout.' I could tell by the tone of Gordon's voice the Colonel at times was not one of the most pleasant of guys to be around. Ray Walker said to me 'Johnny would you believe one day a reporter who was some sort of critic walked up to the Colonel and said, 'Colonel, you keep being bad to people on your way up and you are going to have hell to pay on the way down'. The Colonel drew a puff on his cigar and replied 'Sir, I ain't ever coming down'.

The Colonel had respect from all corners of society. He was always in touch directly with the police in whichever town or city in the U.S. Elvis performed and many a rumour of links with crime bosses surrounded him.

Even the head of security of the White House thought it was incredible how protected Elvis was at his performances with the security stage pass system put in place by the Colonel to allow different people into different zones, so he approached the Colonel for advice on protecting the U.S. President. With the police in one pocket and the mafia in the other you have to say Colonel Tom Parker was pretty much the biggest heavyweight of music business managers of all time.

I thought it was fabulous when I was informed that when Elvis filmed the motion picture *Jailhouse Rock*, the Colonel made sure all the props e.g. the tables, chairs and ornaments could easily just be picked up in the space of ten minutes and taken immediately to another film studio in the event he fell out with the current film producer, thus making sure all on the film set knew who was the boss. If anybody thinks Elvis was mistreated by the Colonel I can totally understand that, but as David Stanley personally told me (David Stanley being Elvis's step brother – his mother married Elvis's father, Vernon Presley), Elvis was given the chance to leave the Colonel on many occasions but stayed with him as he knew there was no one else better for the job.

With all the experiences I have had with managers you come to understand that you don't necessarily need to have one, unless you really think it is essential. That is why some of the successful artistes you see today do not have managers, just good lawyers who take care of what needs to be done legally. If the day arrives where all the business gets on top of you and the artistry is being halted, then you need to start looking for representation, but take on-board a good piece of advice I was given regarding managers... only one thing is for certain in this business: When it comes to management there is one word you must live and die by – Trust. (TRUST NO ONE)!!!

5

CO-WRITING THE OFFICIAL
SOCCER WORLD CUP SONG

I have found that in the music business, to gain success of any nature, you generally need one good project to follow another. I had just finished working on the film movie soundtrack *Private Elvis* which myself and Chris Skornia had co-written the songs for, and it was a successful project for the world-renowned film company Lumiere Pictures. The man in charge of that whole project was Gary Shoefield, a well-respected entrepreneur from the glory days of the music and film world.

Gary was the manager for a short time of Patrick McGoohan, star of 'The Prisoner' and the actor who had played the film role of Longshanks in Mel Gibson's 'Braveheart'. You might remember Gary being portrayed in the 2006 film 'Alien Autopsy' - not that he looked like one, that was more Ray Santilli's role. (In the movie Gary and Ray were portrayed by none other than Ant and Dec).

What worked well in the movie *Private Elvis* was that Gary really loved the songs that Chris and I wrote and said it was like listening to out-takes from the motion picture *G.I. Blues*. This led Gary to speak to an associate of his called Rick Blaskey, creator of the England football song *"Three Lions"*, who was also heavily involved with the rugby world cup song *"World in Union"*. Rick was president for Arista in America and EMI in Europe producing artists like Whitney Houston, Barry Manilow and Tina Turner.

Gary knew Rick was now in the process of putting together his music campaign for the 1994 Soccer World Cup, so he chatted with Rick explaining, as it was going to be held in Atlanta U.S.A. (the first time the biggest sporting event on the planet was going to be held on their shores), an idea that he thought might work. This was the collaboration of Rick and his writer associate Charlie Skarbek (who wrote the lyrics for "World In Union") to join forces with myself and Chris Skornia and, who knows, as a team we could write the official soccer world cup song. A meeting was set at Rick's offices in Gloucester Road, West London which went very well. I could see Rick was certainly on top of his game but unfortunately, he was not convinced by my and Chris's demos of what we thought was right for the project. After three visits, Chris said to me 'John I don't know what they want, and if it does not work this time let's move on'. Unfortunately, Rick did not like what we brought to the table and so once more we got rejected, and myself and Chris once again made our way home on the tube.

Not to be beaten I locked myself away in my room in Ruislip Manor and worked by candlelight day and night. I knew one of the most important ingredients of the project in hand would be to get the right title; it had to say everything that was America and had to encompass the world's biggest sporting event, the Soccer World Cup.

I am a great believer in the shorter the title the more impact it has. I finally rang Chris and I told him 'Chris I think I've got it - the title is "Gloryland" and I have some lyrics as well. Put the kettle on mate, I'm coming around'. Chris waited for me in his flat in Harefield, Middlesex, a quaint little village just outside Uxbridge, West London. Although I was excited I had not forgotten Chris was getting a bit browned-off with the whole project, so when I arrived I told him 'If this doesn't work this time Chris, then I've had it with the whole thing as well'. I left Chris to carry on with some more lyrical input and the following day I set up a meeting with Rick telling him this was our last attempt, but I think we have it this time. I knew the title was strong and "Gloryland" was very American. The tune was going to be pretty much along the lines of the battle hymn of the republic, you could say sort of Elvis's *"American Trilogy"*. I knew this was our last tube excursion to Gloucester Road for the Soccer World Cup project; this was it - all or nothing.

Rick greeted us once more, we sat down, and I said to Rick 'I think we have it this time'. 'Well let's see'. He started to play the song and looked at the lyrics I gave him. 'Gloryland, emm', he said. 'Gloryland, eh', he paused, I could tell he knew there was something in it. He said, 'I'll pass it on to Charlie Skarbeck and see what he makes of it'. 'That's great Rick', I replied. The game was on and I knew it. I could tell Chris was not so confident when we said our goodbyes. On the tube home Chris said, 'John they don't really need us anyway'. I agreed with him, but I also told him in no uncertain terms 'Well Chris, if Gloryland does not work, I'm definitely moving on'.

I knew Rick was working tirelessly on the project and a month before the start of the soccer world cup I got a call from Chris, 'Have you read the newspapers?' 'No', I replied, 'Well our song is there in print - *'Gloryland'*. I told Chris I would call him back. I went running up to the newsagents. It was official, right there in black and white in the tabloids. I stood there like a waxwork dummy, motionless, gazing at the half a page in one of the major tabloids, absolutely gobsmacked. I could not help myself, 'Yes!' I exclaimed. I was WH Smith's happiest customer of the day. I drew a deep breath, well done Rick I thought, you've gone and done it. Before my very eyes I'm reading Gloryland with all the lyrics written to give the effect of being on a scroll, then underneath stating this is going to be the official soccer world cup song for 1994, to be performed by Darryl Hall and The Sounds of Blackness.

Now everything was in place except for the contracts. Rick had been so busy securing the project he forgot about my and Chris's involvement. I made a quick phone call to Rick's office, we had a little bit of deliberation on who actually did what, which led unfortunately to both sides seeking music lawyers and this was followed by two weeks of music lawyer's banter as only they can do, and here we are, a week before the biggest sporting event on planet earth and only now were contracts being put before myself and Chris to sign. Yes that's right, a week before the Soccer World Cup was actually going to start.

Now contracts are a funny thing in the music business and please take my advice anyone who is thinking of signing a contract in this business at any level: Take the contract to a music solicitor or the musicians union and they will thoroughly check all is okay. I had signed a few contracts in the music world to date, managerial as well as music publishing, and song-writing contracts, but with co-writing the official Soccer World Cup theme I could not believe the scale of all the parties involved.

This was not my normal 2-4 page contract – believe me when I say this, it was 3 inches thick, like the old yellow pages. I got bored reading the small print because after the tenth page, all I can tell you is it was full of every

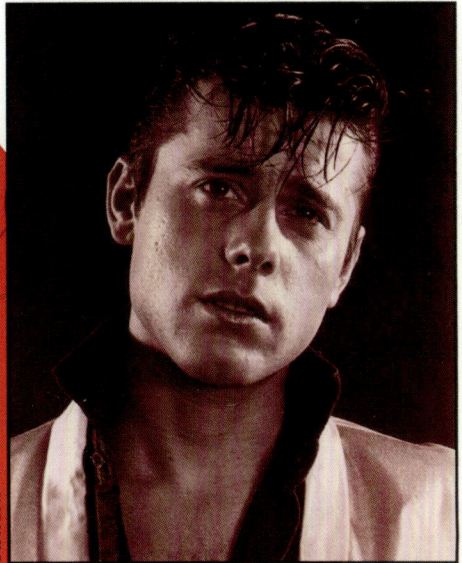

KEVIN ALLEN & HENRY SELLERS
present
THE GOOD ROCKIN' TONITE TOUR UK 1991

JOHNNY *Earl*

and ELVIS PRESLEY'S LEGENDARY GROUP

THE JORDANAIRES

01 Programme cover from the Good Rockin' Tonite Tour

02 ©The Jordanaires (from the film *"Loving You"*)
03 ©The Jordanaires (from the film *"King Creole"*)

ELVIS PRESLEY'S LEGENDARY GROUP

THE JORDANAIRES

MR. ROCK 'N' ROLL

quotes LISA MARIE PRESLEY

"NEAREST THING TO BEING BACK ON STAGE WITH ELVIS"
THE JORDANAIRES

Johnny Earl

FORMERLY
JOHNNY
DUMPER

"THE VERY BEST THERE IS"
DAVID STANLEY
(Elvis Stepbrother)

KEVIN ALLEN PROMOTIONS *present*

★ IN CONCERT ★

FRIDAY AUGUST 10th:
BECK THEATRE
GRANGE ROAD, HAYES. AT 8.00 pm
BOX OFFICE: 081 561 8371

05 Concert poster

06, 09 (**opposite page**) My very first publicity photograph taken at the Purple Penny amusement arcade in Teignmouth Devon,1980. Standing next to me my very close friend Sean Thomas. I was a mere fifteen years of age and Sean sixteen. This was for the magazine 'The Young Photographer' and was titled 'Teds and fruit machines' - the magazine was sold worldwide.

07, 08 (**opposite page**) Two of the very first Louisiana Hayride flyers

NOT TO BE
MISSED

LIVE ON
STAGE

FRIDAY
JUNE 29

HEADSTONE
OPPOSITE NORTH HARROW TUBE

DELLS HOP
8 - 11.00

£1.50

The
Louisiana
Hayride

THE
LOUISIANA
HAYRIDE

PLUS DELL'S RECORD HOP
at
8 -11pm   THE CLAY PIGEON
FIELD END ROAD,
EASTCOTE.
date SUN 2nd JUNE

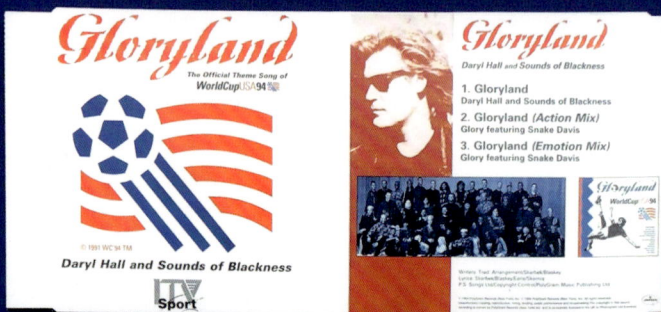

10 *"Gloryland"* disc

The Uxbridge

informer

PRATTS MOTOR INSURANCE
CAN WE SAVE YOU MONEY?
OPEN
Non-8pm weekdays
☎ (0895) 232212
40 LONG LANE, HILLINGDON

SONGWRITING DUO SCORE A WINNER

Lads write World Cup hit

By DAVE PETERS

NEVER mind the footballers, Hillingdon songwriters Johnny Earl and Chris Skornia will be flying the flag for England at this year's World Cup.

DELIGHTED: Johnny Earl, co-writer of Gloryland

Gloryland

WorldCupUSA 94

FEATURING:
Jon Bon Jovi
Fleetwood Mac
Daryl Hall and
Sounds of Blackness
James
The Moody Blues
Queen
Santana
Scorpions
Tears for Fears
Tina Turner
... And More

SUNDAY INDEPENDENT, JULY 10, 1994   25

Duo score at World Cup – they wrote hit theme song!

TWO lads from the West Country have scored at this summer's World Cup finals – by writing the official song.

Singer Johnny Earle and songwriting partner Chris Skornia have penned the song Gloryland – a Top 40 hit for superstar Daryl Hall and the Sounds of Blackness.

The pair, who come from Exeter, had their song chosen from dozens of others by the official World Cup committee in the USA.

Gloryland was also chosen by ITV as the theme tune for its coverage of the finals.

And now Johnny and Chris are waiting to find out if the record – on sale in record shops all over the world – will net them a fortune.

Chance

'I always knew I would be in the charts one day,' said 29-year-old Johnny, who shot to fame playing Elvis Presley in musicals.

'But I thought it would be for something I'd sang – not something I'd written.

'It all started when I wrote the sound track to the movie Private Elvis,' he explained.

'The film company gave me the chance to submit a song to the World Cup committee – so I got together with Chris and came up with Gloryland.

'I couldn't believe it when it was accepted as the official song – it beat entries from Queen, Gary Glitter and the Scorpions. Now every time it comes on the TV or radio I think about how I wrote it in my bedroom.

'It could be the biggest song this year. It's being played a lot in America, Germany, Holland and Italy and is on every night in the ITV coverage of the finals. The World Cup is on 460,000 television networks so the song is being heard all over the world.

'And there isn't a record shop anywhere that isn't selling it. I never thought I'd write such a world wide hit.

'Now I have to wait for the royalty cheques – Chris and I still don't know how much money we'll make after the record companies take their slice.

Celebrate

'I just hope I'm not only remembered as the man who wrote the World Cup song. I'd like this to be just the beginning of my career,' said Exeter City fan Johnny.

'I've been in show business for ten years now – it's a nice way to celebrate the decade but I want to go on and do more.

'I've got an agent in the USA and I've started performing New Country music, a bit like Garth Brooks.

'I've been following the World Cup on TV. It's been excellent,' he added. 'I could have gone out there to watch some games but decided I needed to stay home and work.

'But if England had been there I'd have probably gone.'

WORLD CUP WINNER: Songwriter Johnny Earle.

JOHNNY EARLE

BILLY RAY CYRUS AND FRIENDS
HEARTLAND LIVE

BILLY RAY CYRUS
LIVE

Signature Series
· M · U · S · I · C · I · N · T · H · E · C · A · N ·

BILLY RAY CYRUS & FRIENDS Heartland - Live

1. **Intro** (B.R. Cyrus) C C	0'46
2. **Heartland** (T. Teely) Rondor MV GmbH	4'41
3. **The Thunder Rolls**	5'40
(G. Brooks / P. Alger) Rondor MV GmbH / Global MV	
4. **Friends In Low Places**	5'46
(D. Blackwell / L. E. Bud) Kronen MV, Michael Holm KG	
5. **A Healing Fire** (S. Ewing / D. R. Sampson) Edition Opry-Rose, Neue Welt MV GmbH	4'56
6. **Crying** (R. Orbison / J. Melson) Edition Opry-Rose, Neue Welt MV GmbH	4'16
7. **Sign Of The Dotted Line**	4'54
(S. Ewing) Edition Opry-Rose, Neue Welt MV GmbH	
8. **Johnny Come Lately** (S. Earle) Neue Welt MV GmbH	4'24
9. **The Will To Love** *	4'21
(S. Ewing / D.R. Sampson) Edition Opry-Rose, Neue Welt MV GmbH	
10. **Indian Man** * (J. Earle) Neue Welt MV GmbH	4'36
11. **Losing You** * (J. Earle) Neue Welt MV GmbH	1'09
12. **Cry Out** * (J. Earle) Neue Welt MV GmbH	3'14
13. **The Will To Love**	4'27
(S. Ewing / D.R. Sampson) Edition Opry-Rose, Neue Welt MV GmbH	
14. **Achy Breaky Heart** (Don't Tell My Heart)	2'46
(Donald L. von Tress) Polygram Songs MV GmbH	

Total Playing Time: 59'53

* Studio-recording

Additional Overdubs + Remix by Charly Soyez Studio – Hamburg for V3-Musik Verlag GmbH Vocals - Vocal
Arrangements Johnny Earle Keyboards Christopher Skornia
Lead Guitar Simon Bishop Rhythm Guitar Barry Marche
Fiddle + Mandolins Tony Collins Bass + Backing Vocals Rick Russell
Credit Photo by Stok Zoll

℗ 1994 sigturl gorl

WZ Tonträger Vertriebs Gn bH
Europark Aachener Kreuz
52146 Würselen - Germany

4 005092 980120

WZ 98012

JOHNNY EARLE

The Singer Man

1. THE SINGER MAN
   Written by J. Earle
2. THE NEXT TIME THAT
   I SEE YOU
   Written by J. Earle
3. THE POWER IN ME
   Written by J. Earle / C. Skornia
4. KNOCKED FOR SIX
   Written by J. Earle
5. SHE WON'T
   Written by J. Earle
6. WHEREVER LOVE CAN
   BE FOUND
   Written by C. Skornia
7. BORN A COUNTRY BOY
   Written by J. Earle
8. NO NO NO NO
   Written by J. Earle
9. LONDON TOWN
   Written by J. Earle
10. DADDY'S LEAVING HOME
    Written by J. Earle
11. ALWAYS FOREVER
    Written by C. Skornia
12. LOVE'S ON FIRE
    Written by J. Earle / D. Hayward
13. WHEN HEARTS BREAK
    Written by J. Earle
14. RADIO MAN
    Written by J. Earle / D. Hayward

All tracks published by JEM Music/RP Media
Publishing Ltd

Front Cover artwork: Andreas Schröer
Inside cover photo courtesy of Paul Pipe

17 & 18 My first country music CD
'The Singerman' released in 1997

19 Early photo for country music magazine

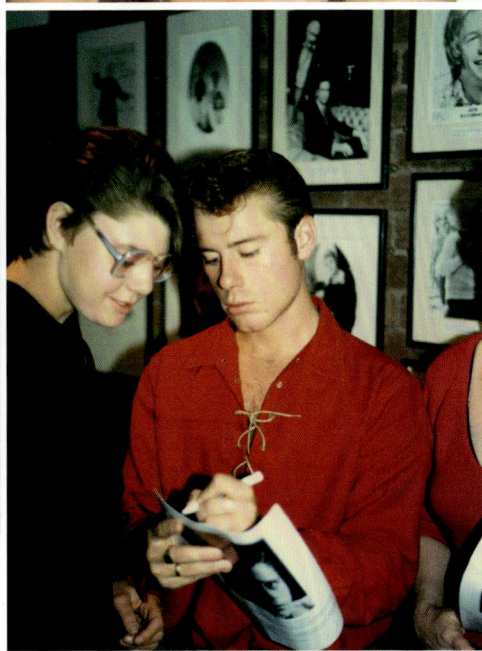

From Holland (clockwise): **20** Nicole's little sister, myself and Nicole; **21** Petra; **22** Lisa
23-25 With fans after a performance.

26 No son could have asked for a lovelier mother

27 (**opposite page**) There has been no prouder moment as this photo portrays, me and my family with the Jordanaires at a performance at home in Devon.

28 Here is another wonderful mum, none other than Billy Fury's mother, Jean Wycherley. With a lovely dedication from Jean to my mum. A very proud moment for me.

29 Me and my darling mummy enjoying our time together admiring the wonderful views from the Spinnaker Tower down in old Pompey.

30 My father Stuart in the centre, taken while he was in the Merchant Navy

31 My sister June enjoying the sunshine

32-33 My brother David in his full glory

sports TV cable network, along with radio and media companies from all over the world, in over 200 different countries. This proved to me how hard Rick Blaskey had worked to make this happen, so to show my gratitude I knew he was a Sheffield Wednesday fan, so I got through to Sheffield Wednesday football club, talked very nicely to a lady receptionist and she worked the oracle and got them to send me most of the first teams signature cards all signed. I put them all in a big presentation frame with a plaque thanking Rick for working so hard and making it happen.

17th June 1994, a day in my life I will never forget. That evening the 1994 FIFA soccer world cup opening ceremony was going to take place in Chicago U.S.A. Attending was the American president Bill Clinton, the Chancellor of Germany Helmut Cole, and Oprah Winfrey MC'd – even Diana Ross performed. These were all sideline things for me as it was the first time I was going to see my song "Gloryland" performed by Daryl Hall and The Sounds of Blackness.

I turned off my phones/fax, all forms of communication with the outside world. Nothing was going to disturb tonight's entertainment, I did not want any distractions of any sort! I got myself ready and prepared with crisps and peanuts on one side of my bed and diet coke on the other, with clothing attire to match: Shorts and a t-shirt with flip flops.

I just wanted that summer feeling as I knew that in just under an hour all was going to happen before my eyes in the very same room the soccer world cup song "Gloryland" was conceived. I watched the TV with great anticipation and the announcer said, 'First off, before the start of the Soccer World Cup ceremony we will enjoy the company of the Brian Conley Show.' I just sat there nervously munching away. When Brian Conley came on he introduced the gameshow, followed by saying the next two contestants (I thought just hurry up and get on with it, I have something much more important waiting to happen) then Brian Conley said, 'From Devon you might not believe it Terry and June', AND I DID NOT BELIEVE IT! IT WAS MY SISTER JUNE AND HER HUSBAND TERRY! OH, MY GOD! I legged it downstairs to Tom and Ros '..you're not going to believe this, my sister June and her husband Terry are contestants on the Brian Conley show!' Tom said - 'I thought you said it was the soccer world cup'. 'Yeah that's on straight after', 'How strange', Ros replied.

As silly as it sounds I ran back upstairs, took up my position back on the bed, and started cheering on my sister and Terry (My moment of glory can wait) and as fate would have it they came first and won quite a few thousand pounds as well, good luck to them. Then the waiting was over, now it was my moment in time, as the announcer cheerily exclaimed 'It's now upon us, the waiting is over. Sit back and enjoy the opening ceremony to the FIFA 1994 Soccer World Cup'.

I was as proud as a peacock. The whole event was entertaining to say the least, even when Diana Ross missed scoring an open goal and Oprah Winfrey fell over when introducing her. Then it was announced '..And here is the official Soccer World Cup song performed by Daryl Hall and The Sounds of Blackness', and they performed '*Gloryland*' like the world professionals they are - JOB DONE.

The 1994 FIFA world cup broke the average world cup attendances which are still held today, as well as the total attendance for the final tournament which is still the largest in world cup history. Brazil won this tournament with Italy runners up. (And my best piece of football trivia ever is, the very first Brazil national football team played its very first game against none other than my beloved Exeter City, 21st July 1914 (honest). The result was disputed, some say 2-0 to Brazil and others say it was 3-3. Even in football there are Blue Suede Dreams).

CO-WRITING THE OFFICIAL SOCCER WORLD CUP SONG

Gloryland

Gloryland, in Gloryland
You're here in Gloryland

It started with a feeling
And a dream was born in you
You hope and pray that come the day
You'll see that dream come true
With every passing moment
You begin to understand
That you're bound for Gloryland

With a hunger in your heart
And with fire in your soul
With passion rising higher
You know that you can reach your goal
Believe in what you do
And you'll go straight to see it through
On the road to Gloryland

(and I say…)
Gloryland in Gloryland
It's in your heart, It's in your hand
In Gloryland in Gloryland
You're here in Gloryland

(This is Gloryland)

As the day gets ever closer
You are reaching for the sky
The flames that burn inside
Are the flames that never die
When you start to believe
It's in your heart it's in your hand
You know this is Gloryland

(And I say)
Gloryland in Gloryland
It's in your heart it's in your hand
Gloryland, hey Gloryland
You're here in Gloryland
Gloryland in Gloryland
It's in your heart it's in your hand
In Gloryland hey Gloryland
You're here in Gloryland
This is Gloryland

Written by: Charles Skarbek, Christopher Skornia, John Earl, Richard Simon Blaskey

Lyrics Universal Music Publishing Group

6

MY ACHY BREAKY HEART

On a beautiful warm summers night in Nashville, Tennessee, Kevin Allen (my manager) and I caught up with Ray Walker (of the Jordanaires) to have dinner and talk about a future tour, and the destination for this meeting was the Gaylord Opryland Resort and Convention Centre. This hotel complex was huge and it's the largest non-casino hotel in the continental United States outside of Las Vegas and is the 29th biggest hotel on planet earth!

A buzzing metropolis, you kind of had the feeling you were somewhere in the Caribbean amidst shops and galleries and all the greenery. Along with some bands performing, the whole place had a calm and relaxed atmosphere. Over dinner Ray mentioned the Jordanaires had just worked with a guy who they strongly believed was going to have a country record hit worldwide, and the song which would elevate him to such levels was called *"Achy Breaky Heart"* - by a new guy named Billy Ray Cyrus. We took in what Ray said and when we returned to the UK it was not long before the airwaves all across Europe were full of *Achy Breaky Heart* – the song was pretty much a smash hit all around the globe.

Kevin and I had not long recorded a new country album and what with the whirlwind sensation that Billy Ray Cyrus had caused, now was the time to release it. Kevin and I had a meeting with Ray Santilli (as we had just finished a very successful project 'Private Elvis' that he was involved with) so he said he would have a listen and get back to us within a week. I was quite confident as the album had new country songs, hits like Garth Brooks *"The Thunder Rolls"* and *"Friends in Low Places"* and the recent US number one

"Heartland" by George Straight. I am glad to say also some originals I had written – *"Losing You"* being one.

I thought the album deal was pretty done and dusted until Ray had a conversation with Kevin and said he wanted to pass on the project. I was quite taken aback, a little rejected but hey, I was used to that by now. We both forgot about it for the time being and prepared ourselves for a new country rock tour with a 7-piece band. It was a big sound with a new direction and we were both eager to get on with it.

A couple of weeks passed and I got a phone call from my German friend Andy Schroer.. 'Hey Johnny, Michael (a friend of ours) he has just bought a Billy Ray Cyrus album called 'Billy Ray Cyrus Live' and although there is a photo of Billy Ray Cyrus on the front cover he thinks the whole album is you'. 'It can't be' I explained, that project never happened, so I asked Andy 'Tell me the track listing', Andy replies 'It starts with George Straits' song *"Heartland"* and finishes with a song I think you wrote *"Losing You"*.

The heaviest penny dropped, my blood pressure came to the boil, 'Andy I got some cleaning house to do...' It is always best in these situations to gather ones thoughts in working out how best to proceed. First on the hit list (which was normally the case unfortunately) Kevin my manager. I took one deep breath in order to exhale both barrels 'Kevin I'll come straight to the point, it just shows you how much respect you command as a manager, that country album we took to Ray ******g W**k**, ****ocks of a waste of space San ******gtilli, yes that's right, the album we gave him and he passed on, well it is now selling like hot cakes all over Europe'.

Up to now Billy Ray Cyrus had not released an album to our knowledge especially not a live performance, so his new-found fandom of millions of European fans (and keep in mind these were the days CDs were all the rage) were very eager to get their hands on this brand-new release. I finished my conversation with Kevin 'I'm not having any more to say on the subject. I'm going down to Sony records Monday morning and demanding to see the representative of the Billy Ray Cyrus campaign for Europe and ask why they have stuck Billy Ray Cyrus's face on the front cover of my new country album GOOD BYE'! As the phone was being put down I heard the fading tones of 'wait, wait, don't put the...' CLUNK.

It was late on a Friday afternoon, I said all I had to say on the matter. I went up the road to the cafe in Ruislip Manor to pull myself together, sat at the back out the way, as the feeling of knowing without a shadow of a doubt my new country album is selling like hot cakes, in all the biggest outlets in Europe and what could have been my first million seller – only to be told they did not want it – and then they have put someone else's picture on the front! ************ Forever!

I tried my best to stay calm and on returning to my room in Victoria Road I looked at my answerphone on my bedside table (in red - 8 messages). The messages were all Kevin and all had the same sentiment.. 'John please, please, just pick up the phone, we can sort this out'. I was not picking up for anything – all I had on my mind was battering down the doors to Sony records first thing Monday morning. About ten minutes had passed and the phone went again. 'After the tone please leave your message', Good old Kev back for more but this time with a different string to his bow 'John I have had a good one to one talk with Ray Santilli, he has told me there has been a big cock up, his German partner had released it without telling him, now if we do this properly I reckon we can get a few thousand out of it'. I paused for a second, so did he. 'If you are not in, call me as soon as you come back'.

Eventually I calmed down enough to ring Kevin and explained I did not care about the money, it was more the manner in which I had been treated and he should feel the same, but looking at it from Kevin's point of view, always trying to find finances to keep the business going was very difficult so I stopped shouting at him, but I did however tell him I am not changing my mind, Monday morning I'm in my car to visit Sony records (Clunk).

Five minutes later the phones going again (doesn't he ever give up?) except for this time it was Ray Santilli, 'Johnny I understand how you feel, I am as shaken by the release as you are, I honestly knew nothing about it, there is no need to go to Sony records Monday, come into the office and Harry will pay you what you asked, please get in touch, here is my personal number', down went the phone. Call it the biggest mistake of my life, call it the country nature side of me that got the better, but I looked at it from all angles and being a performer/singer songwriter rather than an aggressive, lying, cheating, record company scoundrel who can't sleep straight in their beds at night and would sell their own family for a profit, I thought the only way forward was to sleep on the whole episode.

The following morning after a lot of soul searching I rang Kevin, gave him an amount of money I thought was fair. There wasn't going to be any bartering. I also had to factor into the equation that Ray had just released the project *Private Elvis*, which had a lot of my original songs on, and Gary Shoefield taught me one thing in this business: Keep your enemies to a minimum and your friends abundant. I have always respected his opinion; he has a very good showbiz ethic of having an American business approach while having a European attitude. I had Andy send me by special delivery the Billy Ray Cyrus Live album to have in my armoury, ready for Sony records, but it never saw the light of day. Ray agreed my terms and it all became quiet on the western front. The album was sold with different covers and in different formats. One very successful format was called 'In the Can', a very apt title.

Looking back the irony to this whole caper was that Ray Walker – who first mentioned the whole Billy Ray Cyrus, Achy Breaky Heart project to Kevin and me – on the last track of the Billy Ray Cyrus Live album Ray Walker himself exclaims 'Good Johnny, you sound good Johnny'.

So there you have it, my first million seller where only a few people knew it was me performing. The cherry on this achy breaky cake was when I toured Europe and a fan mentioned this album to me and said 'That album Billy Ray Cyrus Live you want to get a copy, he's never sounded so good!'

New Lyrics

But don't break my heart my achy breaky heart
I just don't think he'd understand
Cause if you break my heart, I'll get you' from the start
You might end up being 'In the Can'

7

THE ALIENS HAVE LANDED
(NOW WE CAN ALL RETIRE!)

As ridiculous as this statement might sound, it has meaning! I was asked by music mogul Ray Santilli to put together a Christmas album which I recorded with all original songs, the title song being *"Shiny Balls"*. When I finished the recordings, I made my way to his office in Euston. On entering the office, I was met with Ray slumped backwards in his chair, hands behind his head and a gleeful expression written all over his face. This was unusual I can tell you! He slapped his hand on the desk 'Johnny I now have a project that's so massive, now we can all retire'.

'Tell me more Ray', I exclaimed. 'I can't go into detail, but this really is top secret, and I can tell you, we've all made it'. I did not want Ray to stray from our meeting concerning the Christmas album, so I let him have his moment of excitement with mixed feelings as I was becoming a little lost regarding whatever he was going on about.

The story to this life-changing statement was explained to me by my dear friend Andy Schroer from Germany, so I got him to put it all in writing, so for the first time ever you readers can read for yourselves the truth behind the Alien Autopsy that unbelievably took the world by storm...

By Andreas Schroer:

"While I was writing my first book I met up with Ray Santilli, who at the time was running a company called Merlin Group, along with his associate Gary Shoefield. I was at Ray's office and we discussed the fact I was in contact with Bill Randle, a Cleveland ex-Disc Jockey and media personality, who was connected to Elvis during the early stage of his career in 1955. Randle produced an Elvis movie titled "The Pied Piper of Cleveland" that was filmed in colour. The Four Tops, Bill Haley and the Comets, Pat Boone and Elvis did show appearances in the movie with the under title "A Day in The Life of a Famous DJ".

After the movie was shown in a local theatre and a school it disappeared because Colonel Parker took over Elvis's management in November 1955 and he worked on a movie contract for Elvis with the big studios in Hollywood.

In 1991 I was still working as a private detective and it was me who came up with the first colour images of the movie showing Elvis, Scotty and Bill on stage.

I talked to Bill Randle who told me that a copy of that movie should be in the archives of a movie company in Salt Lake City and Bill agreed to meet up with Ray Santilli himself. Ray told me after his trip to Cleveland that he could not locate any glimpse of the movie, but he met the cameraman who was filming for Randle in 1955. Believe it or not Ray phoned me and told me that this guy was working in the 40's on an American airbase and actually filmed the autopsy of an alien that was taken from a wreck of a UFO that crashed in the restricted area 51.

The moment he told me this I knew it was nonsense. I even phoned Johnny and told him about this "fantastic, amazing and unbelievable" story (Ray Santilli's words). Ray found a guy who had built a plastic alien and then got a butcher who delivered blood and organs and the UFO aliens were fooled. When I saw that on T.V. for the first time I just could not stop laughing."

Thank you Andy for I had not a clue what Ray was going on about. Which brings me to say yes, if you think about, if it was not for Elvis the Alien Autopsy would never have happened.

Back to Ray regarding the Christmas album. As we were in conversation a man walked through the door called Brian Sheridan who I had never met before. Ray explained the Christmas album to him and said, 'Do you want in Brian?' Brian listened to a couple of songs and said, 'I like it, I will think it over by tonight and let you know', Brian looked at me and said, 'Johnny you could be number one at Christmas!' I looked at Harry who was Ray's right-hand man and he gave me the thumbs up. I thought finally there was light at the end of the tunnel ..and I've thrown enough mud at these office walls to create a football pitch.

This brings me on nicely to what happened next at this meeting. Brian's phone rang, a shocked but bright look adorned his face 'Are you serious?' he said. He then gave me a look, paused and said, 'Did you say £250,000?' paused again 'Go for it, I'll do it, yes definitely I'll take it'. He put down his phone, turned and said to Ray 'I have just bought myself a box at Tottenham for the season'. 'Good for you', Ray replied. Brian full of glee got up 'Brilliant', he exclaimed 'that's made my day'. He shook Harry's hand, followed by Ray's and as he shook mine, looked me straight in the eyes 'Well Johnny I'm afraid the album will have to wait, got to go'. When he left, Ray looked at me and said, 'Nearly Johnny, I suppose I will have to release it'. Before I left the meeting, I told Ray I hoped Arsenal would thrash Tottenham both home and away.

I made my way back to the underground thinking to myself, a phone call can change your life, but sadly not always for the better. *"Shiny Balls"* the single was released but with no solid campaign behind it, so it became another collector's item in the catalogue of Johnny Earl.

I bet the aliens liked it!

8

WOMEN AND RELATIONSHIPS

If I must be perfectly honest the music and entertainment world is not the best industry to be in for a long and lasting relationship. I can say this not only from personal experiences but from the many people I have met in the industry that are also sailing in the same boat ..and this boat is no dinghy – an ocean liner comes to mind.

There are the lucky ones who have managed to find a way to put the music and entertainment business second, whilst remembering there is someone else in their life, willing to stay with you bells and all. I've had two long term (10 year) relationships so I can speak a little for the ones who have lasted the course. My most recent one a lovely English lady believe it or not called Lisa Marie. For ten long years, she put up with me and my showbiz way of life. Very early on in our togetherness during dinner one night, we were talking about the music business and she looked me straight in the eyes and said, 'Do you know what John, the one thing I realise with the music business, is that women only seem to get in the way'. At first, I thought how forward thinking and very understanding of her, but a few years down the line I got the dreaded phone call from her, 'John you are a lovely guy but...' enough said.

Lisa did not need to go into detail, and to be honest I am a useless boyfriend and as for being a husband - I never got that far. Depending on how you look at it, I have always loved meeting people and never found it difficult to get on with them, especially women. The difficulties seem to appear when I start going steady, but who knows, one day it could all change overnight.

My other long relationship was with a Dutch girl called Petra. Now any man who has had a Dutch girlfriend will know you can't help but love them to pieces. Dutch women seem to come in two categories, those from the north of Holland who in general tend to be quite reserved, but lovely all the same. I once had the pleasure of dating a lady from the Northern hemisphere of Holland, lovely Nicole. We were steady for about a year and I have a lot of good and fond memories of our time together. However, I soon found out ladies from the south of Holland can be a bit more colourful in their attitude towards life and living a party lifestyle. Petra was the ultimate lady from the south, and I think a lot to do with why we were together for ten years was I only got to see her roughly about once a month, so we were always pleased to see each other, and we made up for any lost time.

It seemed like we would cram four weeks of fun and music into one. Petra is very happily married now, and we still talk occasionally at Christmas, birthdays etc. I really believe marriage is a wonderful way to live if you feel it's for you. I have friends who have been married for 20 years and more and they have never been happier. Just the other day I did a performance and anyone who has been to one of my shows will know I like to entertain and have fun with my audiences as well as sing. I was a little bit cheeky to a lady and when the show was over she gave me one of those women punches which was not too hard but normally means what you said was funny but very cheeky. I then shook her husband's hand and told him his wife has just given me a little bit of a punch and he said 'I get that a lot, but I look at it a lot differently than you do. To me I think at least she is still touching me!'

Today I have a partner, a lovely lady called Sue who I am very happy with. We have lots of fun and laughter together and I can honestly say I was blessed to meet such a beautiful woman.

"Love is a many-splendoured thing"

9

THE JORDANAIRES

The Jordanaires are inducted into The Country Music Hall of Fame, The Gospel Music Hall of Fame, The Rockabilly Hall of Fame, The Vocal Group Hall of Fame. It is astonishing and astounding to be able to put into musical terms all the achievements made by The Jordanaires, which will probably never be equalled by any other music vocal group ever again.

In one U.S. singles chart of 1958 The Jordanaires were featured on no less than 18 of the top 20. If you try to accumulate the records these guys were on, it is just mind blowing.

Let us start by just mentioning some of the legendary artists the Jordanaires have backed.... Elvis Presley, Ricky Nelson, Patsy Cline, Johnny Cash, Glenn Campbell, The Imperials, Connie Francis, Eddie Cochran, Johnny Horton, Ferlin Husky, George Jones, Ringo Starr, Dolly Parton, Tammy Wynette, Don McLean, Jim Reeves and that is just the tip of the iceberg. You can throw in Cliff Richards, Billy Ray Cyrus and Kenny Rogers. The Jordanaires even sang *'It's the Real Thing'* the Coca Cola song.

It had been calculated that on actual sold recordings The Jordanaires have been on EIGHT BILLION and still counting. I'm very proud (and very humbled) to say even I add a little to that tally.

I could start from the beginning of the Jordanaires who were formed way back in 1949, but let me transport you to 1955, six years later, when a quite well established Jordanaires (I mean quite well established in the southern states of America) were performing one Sunday afternoon in Memphis Tennessee with Eddie Arnold. *"Peace in The Valley"* was among the numbers

The Jordanaires performed that day, but what then took place was rock 'n' roll history, which Gordon Stoker had told reporters and the like a thousand times over. Even when I was being interviewed with the Jordanaires, Gordon was always crystal clear on that historic event.

After this performance, a young Rockabilly with blonde hair and a good demeanour ambled his way backstage solely to greet The Jordanaires; this was none other than Elvis Aaron Presley.

Now Elvis Presley was getting some small media attention from being on Sun Records and Gordon says they exchanged polite conversation whereupon Gordon always remembered Elvis saying to all the Jordanaires 'If ever I get a major recording contract, I want you guys on my records'. Gordon wished this cool looking rockabilly the very best, and never really expected to hear from him again.

In January 1956 Gordon got a phone call from Chet Atkins to come and do a session with what was said to be a young greasy haired guy who RCA Victor had just signed and not only that, he wears a pink shirt with black pegs (trousers)! At this session accompanying Gordon on backing vocals would be two members of the Speer family, Ben and Brock, who themselves were signed by RCA Victor. The Speer Family were one of the country's leading Gospel groups. *"I'm Counting on You"* and *"I Was the One"* were the very first Elvis songs recorded to have vocal harmony backing. Incidentally *"I Was the One"* was the original A side and *"Heartbreak Hotel"* was the B side, but the instant and positive response DJ's were getting from the playing of *"Heartbreak Hotel"* was very quickly reported back to RCA who immediately sprang into action. *"Heartbreak Hotel"* became the new A side. Either way Gordon was on Elvis's first number one record. Elvis flew to Nashville in April of 1956 where the classic *"I Want You, I Need You, I Love You"* was recorded and it was on this session Elvis pulled Gordon aside and being true to his word asked him if the Jordanaires could be on all his future recordings.

PAUSE RIGHT THERE.... Now I got to know Gordon very well through my years of touring and recording with him. Gordon was a fabulous representative and manager for The Jordanaires in so many ways, and one thing I can assure you of is that one of his finest assets was procuring the best outcome out of any business situation and as he was always the man in charge with The Jordanaires, he was the main decision maker of the quartet from what I personally experienced. I would on many occasions use Neal

Matthews or Ray Walker to hopefully see my way of thinking, so by the time my idea reached Gordon it had been pretty much decided. To be fair to Gordon, as the Jordanaires manager, on many occasions other members of the group had their point of view. These views were taken seriously, and Gordon would change his mind if it favoured and was in the best interests of the Jordanaires.

On some occasions, even I drew the line on how much to push Gordon and Kevin (my manager at the time) knew that once you crossed the mark with Gordon you were on a slippery slope.

BACK TO THE KING!

Yes, once Elvis gave Gordon the green light, for the next 14 years, number l smash hit records worldwide were the result of the Kings' association with The Jordanaires. Back in the 1950's very few backing musicians were given any fame or glory or any recognition whatsoever, but Elvis made it known that he wanted The Jordanaires on the 'labels' of his records. Through that recognition alone 'Group of The Year' came for The Jordanaires and this was to carry on right through into the mid 1960's.

The very first Jordanaires quartet line up was Bill and Monty Matthews, Bob Hubbard and Culley Holt. Gordon Stoker (lead tenor) joined The Jordanaires in 1953. Also, in 1953 Hoyt Hawkins joined as (baritone) and Neal Matthews (second tenor) both becoming Jordanaires. 1954 saw the departing of Culley Holt (who never gave his reasons why). He was replaced by Hugh Jarrett.

A lot of times in the music business I find it's much better to leave situations with nothing said, one reason being the press and the media can always fuel a situation that was never there in the first place, but as long as it sells and makes money that is the bottom line to them; they do not care about ruining people's lives that's for sure. June 1st, 1958 saw the arrival of Mr. Ray Walker (bass) and this line up of Gordon Stoker, Neal Matthews, and Hoyt Hawkins with Ray Walker, remained for the next 24 years. Hoyt Hawkins passed away in 1982 and Duane West took on the part of baritone. Louis Nunley came to the fold when Duane West became ill in 1999. In April of 2000 Neal Matthews passed away and Curtis Young stepped in.

My friendship with the Jordanaires was always a good one, mainly because I knew a lot about their recording past and I never tried to be Elvis Presley or anyone else but Johnny Earl. Many a time on tour Gordon Stoker would be asked by the press and media 'Why did you choose to tour with this British guy Johnny Earl?' Gordon would always reply 'It is very refreshing to work with a guy who has his own identity, and although he sings Elvis and other artists songs, he writes a lot of his own material and also some with the Jordanaires (meaning Neal Matthews as we wrote songs together), and this stands high in our opinion'.

And what came to pass with my friendship with the Jordanaires was that I got to know each member personally very well. I realized how different their characters and attitudes were and yet they all bonded so well as a group. The group worked right up until 2013 until the passing of Gordon whereupon at his request the Jordanaires were formally disbanded.

WHEN I FIRST MET THE JORDANAIRES

Not many times in my life have I felt nervous about meeting someone famous, but the day had come where call it fate, call it destiny, I was about to meet the guys who lived and toured and recorded with the King – Elvis Presley. Myself and manager Kevin Allen had already spoken to Gordon Stoker (the manager and band leader of the Jordanaires) on many occasions on the phone, but now the tour was set in stone and they were arriving at Heathrow airport tonight.

In my diary were little notes written for everyday events and to me important happenings, for example band rehearsal Monday, writing songs Tuesday and Wednesday and so on, but a different note was written in capital letters this time, written on this page was - today MEETING WITH THE JORDANAIRES.

Kevin and I waited at the arrivals at Heathrow airport, telling one another what to say or not to say and advising one another to try our best not to upset them before we have even started touring. When the Jordanaires walked through the arrivals section, we were first greeted by Gordon, then Ray, Neal and then Duane and straight away, although tired after a long flight, they all were vibrant and great to meet. We had hired a mini bus for the tour so took the Jordanaires straight to their hotel. We did have a social drink with them but they pretty much retired to their rooms as we all knew the following day was the start of a very busy schedule.

First thing to arrange, a 4.30am wakeup call in order to be ready to perform on the BBC Gloria Hunniford Radio 2 show which was going out live at 6am. This was how it was going to be from now on, everyone from the national press was calling Kevin; the Sun, The Daily Mirror and the Guardian were just a few and once it became firm and concrete news that the King's band were now in town with a UK tour, (especially on the Reuters What's Happening network) a media stampede of magazines, radio shows, and national TV cavalry charged their way to our doorstep.

It became a frenzy, just what we had hoped for; everybody chasing us for a change. That night Kevin and I were as proud as punch. We had done it. We had pulled off what in our minds was going to be the biggest Elvis rock 'n' roll tour with the guys that created the music we loved. The blue suede dream becomes a reality.

GORDON STOKER

Being British and a big rock 'n' roll fan I always knew upon meeting American people there was a lot of camaraderie, as well as a common bond of not only language but a good bonding historically. Brits and Americans share a good sense of humour, especially in the music and entertainment world. On my very first telephone conversation with Gordon Stoker back in 1988, Kevin Allen my manager at the time passed me the phone (whispering to me that it is very expensive to talk to the U.S.A.) so with my hands sweating I took a deep breath and said 'Hi Gordon this is Johnny', he replied 'Very nice to meet you old chap', I laughed, and cast any nervousness aside and Gordon and I had a good laugh chatting with one another for about 20 minutes at Kevin's expense. Gordon and I had started a friendship that would last until his unfortunate passing in 2013. Gordon typified to me all that I thought a southern gentleman would be... always polite, cheerful and of good character.

Gordon was the manager of the Jordanaires and this put him in the prime position to have a one-to-one conversation with most of the biggest rock 'n' roll and country music stars of the 1950's and 1960's. I found him to be a dictionary on the who's who of this colourful world, and in conversation I would mention to Gordon a person who I would think of as a music legend and he would know where they lived and even where they hung out or dined, but he always made sure his answers were never in a gloating fashion, only ever in good conversation.

Gordon's pedigree and talent was second to none. When he was eight he played the organ at The Tumbling Creek Baptist Church, Gleason, Tennessee; at the age of thirteen he became the pianist for The John Daniel Quartet. When he left school he actually got to play piano at the Grand Ole Opry. You would think things were going good for the young Mr. Stoker except mankind decided to have another world war. When returning from the Second World War he re-joined The John Daniel Quartet until in 1953 he joined The Jordanaires as their pianist, and this led to him becoming the lead tenor. I think Gordon would have been amazed if the crystal ball had informed him he would now be the lead tenor for The Jordanaires for the next 60 years.

On many of the conversations that I had with Gordon, naturally Elvis was a common subject and I had over the years gained a bit of experience in the recording studio and I always imagined how brilliant it must have been being a Jordanaire and standing in the same room as the King, singing backing vocals along with him and watching him perform. So, I took the opportunity on one of my first recording sessions with The Jordanaires and I asked Gordon what it was like recording in the studio with Elvis and what was he like to be around, was he easy to work with? Gordon replied 'Man he would rule the microphone. He knew how to belt out a rockin' tune and when it came to cuttin' a ballad he loved to set the scene. He would turn down the lights or even turn them off, then he would get up real close to that microphone'. I was spellbound at what I was hearing and my subconscious mind started running wild and I imagined how it must have felt being in the same room as the King when he recorded *"Anyway You Want Me"*, *"Are You Lonesome Tonight"* or the brilliant *"Don't"*. I remember thinking at the time if only I had the power of Spock from Star Trek I would have placed my Vulcan hand on his temple and looked through Gordon's eyes at the magnificence before him. Can you imagine the amount of music legends that would be stood before you – it is just too incredible to think of, especially for a mere mortal like me!

Like any professional musician, Gordon did tell me of the times when recording with Elvis he felt very frustrated, because when any vocalist is in good voice and on form you need to capture as much of that good vibe as possible and you can achieve a lot more progressively throughout the recording session. However, when too much fooling around keeps on occurring it can be very frustrating and the whole recording session can be unproductive. Gordon explained 'Johnny there were times when Elvis just could not stop fooling around. I remember I was lucky enough to duet with him on two songs *"All Shook Up"* and *"Good Luck Charm"* but on *"All Shook Up"* Elvis asked me to stand pretty close so we could both be as close as possible to the microphone in order to get the right sound for a good harmony' (I was listening with intent, after all this was going to be the King's first UK number one). Gordon carried on 'And when I got to my harmony part, especially the yeah yeah yeah line, he would distract me by waving his finger close to the mic until I almost swallowed it! ... but what can I say... you listen to the record and we stuck a fork in that one'.

'Stuck a fork in that one.' I only ever heard that saying from Gordon, so to me that became a Gordon Stoker saying which meant the definitive version. Just like when he told me 'Anyone who has ever tried to do a version of *"The American Trilogy"* well it just does not work', I laughed when he concluded 'Elvis stuck a fork in that one'.

The volume of musical stars that Gordon had associated with was phenomenal; so I asked him if over the years at any time he felt a little star struck. 'Johnny yu' know, working with so many great stars if I have to be honest not really, but it was always kinda special when Elvis was on the phone'. I had a good friendship with Gordon and we spoke quite regularly when not recording or on tour, and one very special time for me was when he invited me to his house when I was staying in Nashville. He came to pick me up from my hotel and I was in my element. Here was I being driven through Nashville, Tennessee with Gordon Stoker as my chauffeur. When we arrived at his beautiful home, which I can only say the thought running through my mind, was his house looked quite like that house from the film *"Gone with The Wind"*. As we walked through the front door his lovely wife Jean greeted us. She was an angel and made me feel very welcome, and pretty much straight away she said, 'I hope you guys are hungry?' I could smell the fried chicken and the gorgeous aroma of corn on the cob which was ready to be served so we sat down to a fabulous Tennessean spread.

After dinner Gordon said to me 'Johnny let me take you to the music wing of the house'. We walked up this beautiful staircase and at the top of the landing stood an upright piano. Gordon stopped, turned to me and said 'See this piano Johnny, this was the piano that was used on the record *"Can't Help Falling in Love"*. I just stood and looked at the piano and replied 'Wow', Gordon chuckled at seeing my reaction with a look of amazement on my face (like a kid in a candy store) he knew this was just an appetizer, the best was yet to come. Gordon led me along a staircase to a door where out of his pocket he pulled out a key and said, 'This is my personal room'. On entering the room all the excitement and emotions you could think of were filling my mind.

I had a feeling like I was the only person in the world with a Willy Wonka gold ticket and this was my prize... I'm about to enter the chocolate factory world of country and rock 'n' roll. We walked into Gordon's music kingdom and I was stunned. Before my very eyes there were framed letters from all the biggest names in the music business, photos of Gordon with every star you could think of from the rock 'n' roll and country music fraternity. In one corner of this majestic room stood a tailor's dummy displaying a 1950's white with black flecked jacket with a black velvet collar. I was so drawn to it I just casually walked over to it 'Oh yeah', Gordon said 'That was Elvis's'... Now if it had been anyone else but him telling me this, I would have had my doubts, but here I was, standing in the personal realm of Gordon Stoker, gold records adorning all four walls.

In my mind, I was thinking this is a dream come true – am I really standing here? I stood silent looking at this 1950's iconic jacket worn by the King then Gordon said, 'Hey Johnny do you remember that white jacket Elvis wore back in the 50's with the black slacks?' (I knew exactly the jacket he was talking about, as there were so many photos of the King wearing this jacket with those black trousers and white shoes). 'Yeah I know the one', I replied 'Well we had finished a show with Elvis and he was sweating like he had a fever, and as he left the auditorium he took the jacket off and threw it in the garbage can. I gotta be honest with you Johnny, the thought had crossed my mind to retrieve it, but we were so close to him I did not want to look like a fool, so I just left it there. Whatever became of the jacket I do not know', Gordon let out another chuckle. 'Come with me I got something that might amuse you'. I started to follow Gordon out of the room, but not before having a final look around the room to soak in the magnificence of the history of this musical Fort Knox of the country and rock 'n' roll world.

We made our way to the garage whereupon he showed me a 1953 Green Plymouth. 'What do you think Johnny?' 'Lovely Gordon, it looks like it has just come off the production line, I mean it is in mint condition'. Gordon smiled on hearing my appraisal saying, 'This just ain't any old Plymouth, Elvis took some driving lessons in this car before passing his test. Next on the agenda of course I got taken for a little joy ride in the Plymouth with Gordon at the helm and I will never forget that smell of real old leather seats along with that interior musk, a bouquet of beautiful 1950's original car aroma. While being taken for a spin he pointed out Hank Williams Juniors house. Gordon said, 'I mustn't forget he's comin' round tomorrow metal detecting in my garden' (WHICH WAS HUGE). I asked Gordon jokingly what treasures he was likely to find. 'Not treasures Johnny, just shot, and odd buttons and maybe even buckles from the American Civil War'. I thought what a way to spend a Sunday afternoon... I would love to try and find some confederate ammo. This was becoming one of the best days of my life. Gordon then pointed out to me a female country music stars' house - Pam Tillis.

I thought to myself the phrase 'I am in music heaven' which would pretty much sum up how I was feeling at that moment, so do not beam me up Scotty and I do not want to go home either. I was considering informing Gordon if he did not have a resident hobo in the area then he has one now!

I treasured this time with Gordon because I knew that being who he was he had to be very careful with what he said at all times. People especially the press and media, soaked in every word he gave them but with me he felt at ease and knew he was with a friend.

While on tour, on more than a couple of occasions Ray Walker or Neal Matthews would start telling me some rock 'n' roll truths of the music legends the Jordanaires had worked with, and Gordon would stop them in their tracks, just to make sure that if there was going to be any dirty washing to be talked about, then leave it at home. The Jordanaires reputation of being some of the best guys in the business to work with was very hard earned, and Gordon guarded their honesty and decency to the hilt, and I can honestly say very rarely was there a disgruntled word to say about anybody by any member of the Jordanaires, not in all the time I was with them that's for sure.

The closest I ever heard were minor disputes like when reflecting their times with Ricky Nelson. They always said for them Ricky was one of the greatest of the 1950's legends they had worked with.

In the 90's when I was touring in Holland with the Jordanaires I was writing a new song with Neal Matthews *"Until Then"*. We both decided to have a break so met up with the other guys in the hotel lounge and Neal turned to Gordon and said 'Hey Gordon, do you remember when Ricky Nelson came running into our dressing room excitedly shouting 'Guy's listen to this song I just wrote, I'm going to record it', and he started to play the song with his guitar. When he finished playing he said to us 'Well what do you think guys', I told Ricky 'I know that song, that's the one I played to you the other day', 'Oh no', replied Ricky 'You got the wrong song Neal, this is a new one'. Gordon quickly interjected 'I've told you before Neal, back off on that one'. I saw Neal become a little taken aback, then he put his hands in the air saying, 'Hell it was a great tune though'. Which Ricky Nelson hit they were talking about, I never found out and I certainly did not want to rattle Gordon's cage over a Jordanaires minor dispute. However, I did feel for Neal a little because in the music business this kind of thing happens all the time, especially when all parties involved think they are all in the right.

On tour, I often sat with Gordon for a one to one chat. We were on the road and a treasured moment was when I asked him why on earth he or the Jordanaires had not written a book on all their experiences along with their magical moments (and sometimes not so magical) in the music business.

Gordon laughed 'Johnny we have worked with so many fabulous stars, who do we leave out?' I thought about it and replied 'Gordon you are right, you guys could fill a library on Elvis alone and seeing how busy you all are, when would you find the time to write it'. Gordon gazed out of the window thinking of the enormous task I had contemplated him taking on, and as the countryside passed us by, I obviously jolted his memory on something that he definitely would of put into his biography. He turned to me and said 'Johnny do you know I once had a phone call from Buddy Holly. Buddy told me that after his tour he wanted to use us guys on the background of his next recordings, because he was into production as well' (I was astonished that on my mere suggestion of Gordon writing his memoirs, he casually mentioned a phone conversation with none other than Buddy Holly). I laughed exclaiming 'See what I mean, my god Gordon, just having a phone call from Buddy

Holly is rock 'n' roll history alone'. He thought for a second then paused and said, 'Yeah man, and he never came back from that tour'. I said 'Gordon can you imagine it... we are talking about one of the greatest rock 'n' roll albums never recorded. Buddy Holly with the Jordanaires!'

Any vinyl record collector knows what a treasure this would have been. It would have definitely been a multi, multi-million seller just slotting in nicely in the Buddy Holly and the Chirping Crickets section.

One thing Gordon was always very amused by was my association with my manager Kevin Allen, as the Jordanaires on more than one occasion said if Elvis was just a little tougher with the Colonel he probably would be here with us now. I think they were advising me not to put up with too much management crap which I took on board as good advice (to Kevin's horror) and it was not unusual that if Gordon had a problem he could not sort out with Kevin he pretty much knew a word in my ear and I would try and re-solve the issue one way or another in their favour.

The strangest thing happened to me one day. I had not spoken to any member of the Jordanaires for quite a while... in fact it was roughly a year, so a courtesy call beckoned, and I decided I would call Gordon. As there was a five-hour time difference between London and Nashville I would aim to call him around 9pm UK time as 4pm is normally a good time to catch people in the music world I find. I rang and not to my surprise Gordon's line was busy so I kept trying a few more times until eventually getting through.

'Hey Gordon, it's me Johnny how are you doing?' 'Johnny my man, I have been trying hard for the last ten minutes to get through to you ... all us guys are missin' you'.

We both though it very strange that we are half the world apart and a year later we both pick up the phone at the very same minute. Whoever said telepathy was not real?

Somehow because of the strange way we caught up, it led onto a conversa-tion that came right out of the blue for me, especially coming from Gordon. He told me 'Johnny I don't really talk about this much, but shortly after Elvis died I received a letter. Now as strange as it sounds I'm convinced it was from Elvis'. I paused for a moment soaking in what he actually said. 'Gordon, are you telling me that not long after Elvis passed away you received a letter from him?' He replied 'Johnny, Elvis and I had our own personal code that was unknown to anyone else, and this code was written in the letter'.

Crossing my mind was the scene from the film Ghost, where Demi Moore (Molly) is speaking to Whoopie Goldberg (Oda Mae Brown) who is a medium that passes on messages to the living from departed loved ones from beyond the grave. Oda explains to Molly she has a message from Sam (Patrick Swayze) Molly's husband from beyond the grave. Molly never believes a word until Oda says 'Ditto... Sam says ditto', and it's this code, just that word that shook Molly to the core.

Gordon carried on 'I don't know Johnny, sometimes in this business strange things happen that even I cannot explain'. I moved the conversation on because I could tell Gordon was uncomfortable reflecting about this letter. I never told anyone at the time of our conversation, but it did play a lot on my mind, and soon I was back on tour with the Jordanaires again, this time in Holland and the situation arose in a hotel lounge where there were two nice comfortable armchairs. Duane West and I had a chair each. Duane was a guy whom I trusted a lot and was very close to Gordon, so I thought this was a convenient moment to discuss with him the conversation that I had recently with Gordon concerning the Elvis letter.

Duane was quite taken back, he paused and said, 'Gordon told you about the letter huh, well Johnny I'm surprised he told you'. Quite a shiver came over me because if somebody claims they have seen Elvis after his death, or even more amazingly received a letter from the King, more often than not no one would listen, unless you have photographic or film evidence. Even then you would be scrutinized by the world's media. But if you are one of Elvis's inner circle, and you have received a letter after his death, with a code only known to you and him, well I will let you come to your own conclusions. If I was to give you my honest opinion, if I was Elvis and I faked my own death, and I was to send a letter at all, who would I send a letter to? Well Gordon Stoker would definitely be worthy of a stamp!

With all the fun and experiences that I shared with the Jordanaires I can see why they were together for so long – over 60 years – especially with Gordon as captain of the ship guiding their every step. Gordon told me once 'Johnny, I had a meeting back in the 50's with the head of Capitol records, he said 'If you guys always stay as a group and do not try to pursue solo careers you will go on recording way into the future', Gordon said 'Boy was he right'.

Today I realize how fortunate I was, as a young budding rock 'n' roller/ rockabilly, to have met the Jordanaires. I had no father to guide me at the time but the Jordanaires kind of took me under their wing. I'm no cry baby but I was deeply moved on hearing the passing of my friend Gordon. All I can say is heaven has been blessed with rock 'n' roll's greatest tenor.

Gordon Stoker sadly passed away at his home in Brentwood, Tennessee, March 27th, 2013. On his passing Gordon's wishes were upheld and The Jordanaires were dissolved.

'Gee were gonna' miss you, everybody sends their love'.

RAY WALKER

Before I met the Jordanaires, they were my vinyl heroes because every time I collected an Elvis record it would always say the words 'With vocal accompaniment by The Jordanaires'. Now mention the name Ray Walker - then as if by remote control, I sing as low as I can "Now and Then There's a Fool Such As I" or when I am warming up to do a bass vocal in the recording studio I normally perform Ray Walkers 'oohs' on the intro of *"Fame and Fortune"*.

I do not think in my 30 years of experience in the music business I have met a more charismatic and likeable person on and off-stage than Ray Walker. As well as being a prominent member of the Jordanaires he was the song director for *'The Amazing Grace'* bible programme, produced by the Maddison Church of Christ in the Nashville suburb. It has been reported Ray Walker has recorded over 200,000 songs (which includes repeats for different services and classes) through the church, along with recording with the Jordanaires. With his 66 years of recording and performing, this accumulation means he is probably the most recorded voice in the history of music. Today Ray is one of the ministers of the Waverly Church of Christ in Waverly, Tennessee.

I remember on many an occasion while performing on stage with the Jordanaires, as the lead singer I would look over to them and would be drawn in on hearing those wonderful harmonies fusing with that mesmerizing sound only they could perform, (I imagine they even snored in harmony). I would walk across the stage towards them and be amazed at how on each of their faces one eye would be on the dots (their musical arrangements written before them) and the other on me. Ray was the one member who really enjoyed the whole stage euphoria of everything that was going on. We would finish performing a song such as *"It's Now or Never"* or *"How Great Though Art"* to rapturous applause from the audience (and may I add the applause was mostly because the audience could not believe the Jordanaires were before their very eyes), I would be on my knees or a similar posture and nine times out of ten a bass voice would exude the words 'Great Johnny, wow that was great Johnny, well done'.

No seal of approval was more reassuring than that of Mr. Walker.

At every performance I had with the Jordanaires all would speak in turn about working with the artistes from their past; music legends like Patsy Cline, Elvis, Ricky Nelson and many others. This left the audiences spellbound. I would say that out of all the Jordanaires no one was better than Ray at getting the crowds hanging on to every word and this made sure they were with you from the very start to the end of the show. Ray was also a good man to have on your side in the studio. Elvis found this out when trying to get that big note at the end of *"Surrender"* (too-ooo-night). Getting frustrated Elvis took a break and went outside the studio for some fresh air, Ray followed him out and told the King to take the deepest breath he ever did take and mix a number two with the word night and perform it as if it was the last breath he was ever going to take. Ray said to me 'As you hear it on the record Elvis went straight back in on the mic and the rest is history'.

Ray told me Elvis would often sing his bass parts of a song and loved trying to get that low bass tone. Once on stage even I had to be careful when singing the song *"Don't"* – I nearly performed Ray's notes as well as mine. He laughed it off, but I kept a mental note not to do it again.

On tour in Germany the Jordanaires and I were travelling by train, I sat next to Ray and asked him what was one of the most haunting experiences, if any, he could recall with the Jordanaires. He replied 'Well' pausing for a few seconds 'I'd have to say one of our last recording sessions with Patsy Cline. I'll never forget it, Patsy came to the studio not long after she had been involved in a bad car accident, and after the recording session she put on a big black fur coat and whipped up the collar and said, 'Boys if I ever have another one it'll be the last', I replied 'now don't you worry Patsy you'll be fine'. I noticed Rays tone lowered and he became a bit subdued. I could tell he was reliving that sad moment in his mind as if he was back at that very recording session then he softly said, 'Do you know Johnny we never saw Patsy again'.

I put myself in Ray's position and couldn't help but have the songs *"Crazy"* and *"I Fall to Pieces"* playing through my mind, which incidentally, were just two of the Patsy Cline classics that the Jordanaires recorded with her.

Patsy Cline was involved in a fatal plane accident just outside Camden Tennessee on March 5th, 1963.

It was always a pleasure to meet up with Ray and his lovely wife Marilyn (who was a joy to be around) especially under the Nashville night sky dining al fresco and these occasions would be a lot of fun and laughter.

Ray loved history and over dinner one night he mentioned to me 'Johnny I found out my family descendants were of English origin, and my grand-mother often spoke of one of our family members being related to one of the Americans who signed The United States Declaration of Independence'. Ray also told me 'She was a strong and true lady who wouldn't make a thing like that up but I can't say for definite, we better hold fire on that one'.

I can honestly say with my 30 years experience in the music world, meet-ing people from both the business and performing side, the one attribute Ray has is he can bring out the best in any person that he is working with. He is blessed to have the ability to reassure any singer/performer (whether in the studio or live on stage) to believe in themselves so to give their very best performance. I could write a book alone on the times I spent with Ray, but then I would spend too much of my life repeatedly singing 'Now and Then There's a Fool Such as I'.

So, I take my hat off to the guy commonly known as the greatest ever bass rock 'n' roll singer, it's an honour and a pleasure to be associated with Mr. Ray Walker.

NEAL MATTHEWS, JR.

Behold the man who was pretty much responsible for most of the doo wah's and the bop bops everybody heard over the airwaves throughout the 1950's and early 60's. Yes, it was Neal Matthews, Jr. who wrote most of the Jordanaires vocal arrangements.

I was present and witnessed Neal endlessly writing these music parts, whether it was for a live performance or in the recording studio and I can say it was an amazing sight to behold for a novice like me.

On many recording sessions, I would be at the mixing desk or in the control room and Neal would call me into their recording booth and say 'On this bridge or chorus Johnny, do you want doo wah or doo wop? And here - do you want wah wah ooh or just ooh's?' One thing for sure, everybody in the music business knows that recording time is very expensive and if I was going to be indecisive every time asked by Neal for my expert advice (or shall I say novice opinion), especially with a new song that I had written with Neal, and to hear every example the Jordanaires had on offer, it would have taken a year a song to record – and Kevin Allen's and my finances only stretched so far.

Whatever backing vocal parts were eventually decided upon, by the time they were finished and recorded I was always on cloud nine, whether the Jordanaires performed in unison or in harmony. For me to have made an input and be able to choose a finished Jordanaires part was worth more than any amount of money. Neal instinctively knew not only what I would love to hear but also the best direction for the composition and he would say 'let's arrange it this way Johnny, then Ray can put a 9th on the major chord etc. etc.' I rarely disagreed with Neal because as far as I was concerned I was not only in the presence, but also being tutored by, one of the best in the world whilst co-writing with this genius at the same time.

One song which became an Earl/Matthews composition was a rock 'n' roll tune called *"Everybody but Me"* and while on tour in Holland we wrote a country song called *"Run Boy Run"*. Both compositions have been released and praised by country and rock 'n' roll critics alike.

Whilst on this tour in Holland the Jordanaires and the show entourage were relaxing at a hotel one afternoon in the hospitality room, equipped with a pool table and darts board and it was then that Neal told me how prior to joining the Jordanaires he was in the U.S. army during the Korean war, where he was a part of a vocal singing group and so when he was discharged a natural step forward was joining the Jordanaires and this was in the year 1953.

As we had some rare free time that afternoon in Holland I asked Neal if he would like a game of darts and he obliged. Now I had played the odd game before and explained to Neal the basics of the game 501 where you accumulate as high a score as possible throwing 3 darts each at a time until one of you end up on an even score of 40 or less so you finish on having to throw a double. Neal told me he pretty much understood the game, I threw first, got my average score of about 40 and as I watched Neal amble up to the oche, placing his foot exactly where he was comfortable, he raised his arm, aimed for the triple 20 and threw his first dart which landed just below the triple 20 wire, second dart landed bang straight in the triple 20 and with his third dart he then finished off with another single 20. Neal's score of 100 was beginners luck or so I thought, until it became came apparent I just could not beat him. Game after game I suffered seconditus (not a real word I know but I associate it with when I or something keeps on coming second, especially when there are only two participating). Neal told me 'Johnny, before I joined the Jordanaires I was going to be a professional pitcher for a baseball team (I think he said for The Nashville Vols) so I have always had pretty good aim'. I took my thrashing gracefully and it showed me how some people just have endless talents in life. To choose the right destiny like Neal did with The Jordanaires was a blessing for the music world, and just think, if the dart playing was anything to judge by, Neal could have been a very successful baseball player. Either way he was born to please the general public.

Neal and I became good friends and I would play a little singing game now and again when we toured. I would sing a note and he would guess the key and he never got it wrong. After this ritual, Gordon Stoker informed me of how Neal had invented the numbering system for chords, which is basically a shorthand version for chords - so if you changed the key it did not matter. This system is now used by musicians all over the world. Neal was a modest and unassuming guy and even when we talked about his army service he never brought it to my attention that he had been awarded the Bronze Star.

During my stay in Nashville, Neal collected me one day and took me to where he went to school, Hume Fogg High School, and what a beautiful building it was, not dissimilar to Hogwarts in the Harry Potter movies. We walked the corridors of this fabulous place and Neal gave me a history of the school and showed me all the rooms he was educated in. It really was a wonderful experience, and what better way to end the day when Neal said, 'Would you like to come home and meet my wife Charlsie?' 'Of course, I would Neal' was my reply 'Well that settles it', he said 'and we will stop off at one of Nashville's best cake shops, and why don't you choose the cake Johnny'. I remember it like it was yesterday, it was one of the hardest decisions I have ever had to make. For once chocolate came second and I chose a big coffee sponge cake with a mouth¬watering coffee cream in the middle and a light sponge either side and oodles of melt-in-the-mouth soft coffee icing on the top - DELICIOUS!

Arriving at Neal's house (a lovely single storied wooden Southern American styled house on wooden stilts), I could have happily moved in straight away. I envisaged myself sitting in a wooden chair playing an acoustic guitar on the porch, drinking cool southern iced lemonade, not forgetting a piece of cake of course. Once inside I met Charlsie who gave me a lovely smile and with a lovely Southern Nashville accent said, 'Welcome Johnny, I've heard a lot about you and it's all pretty good let me tell you', she chuckled 'I see you came past the cake shop'. Neal said, 'Hey Johnny would you like to come and see some of my personal items I've collected through the years?' 'That would be wonderful', I replied. I remembered what a delight it was to see Gordon's personal hall of fame, and now I was just about to embark on another.

Neal asked Charlsie to fetch him the key, and then he led the way to a room which when opened was another treasure trove of pop music, awards, gold discs and pop memorabilia. Here I was, standing in Neal Matthews' 'Mini Museum'. I pointed at a metal plate that had a written letter indented into it. Neal came over and said, 'That is a letter I received from Elvis while he was in the army in Germany, so I had an indentation made of it'. It was marvellous reading about Elvis telling Neal how eager he was to get back to the U.S. and couldn't wait to be back with all the guys in the studio, and how he had missed all the laughs they always had together. I couldn't help but notice Neal reading this letter along with me, most probably re-living the memory from that very day when it was first delivered. I said 'Neal it's not every day someone receives a letter from Elvis', he laughed and said 'That's for sure', paused and said 'I keep the letter locked away safe'. In reply I said 'Oh boy, I don't blame you Neal, because if someone stole your plaque that's one thing, but if the actual letter went missing how you could ever live with that'. I wondered how many other treasure troves Neal held the keys to.

Some of his prize possessions were from Ricky Nelson. He took me to a glass case, opened the lid saying, 'Johnny I would like you to have this', and then slowly reached inside and picked up a cream coloured guitar plectrum which had gold writing in the middle and the name Ricky Nelson printed on it. I was speechless when Neal handed it to me and he could see I was totally overcome with emotion at this once in a lifetime gesture. When I finally got the words together I said, 'This belonged to Ricky Nelson', Neal said 'Yep, a lot of the artistes we performed with had their names put on their pics, and Ricky gave me a couple'. (In later years, I donated this plectrum for a charity auction at a rock 'n' roll event back in the U.K.).

I was in total awe of every item in this musical shrine, even though I had never even heard of some of the artistes. They clearly meant a lot to Neal and he would explain a little about each item and the artiste and how it had come into his possession; the whole experience was just magnificent. I could not thank Neal enough for his hospitality. He very carefully locked the door and we made our way back to Charlsie who greeted us with a plate adorned with that delectable coffee cake. Neal gave Charlsie the key and excused himself. She took this opportunity to say, 'Johnny you might not know it, but you are one lucky guy, Neal has only ever let one other person from the music world into his music room and that was Don McLean, so you must be right up there with the best of them'.

When Neal returned, we delved into the irresistible coffee cake and if ever a cake tasted as good as it looked it was this one. I said my goodbyes to Charlsie and as we left I noticed a stunning red sports car at the side of the house. Neal said, 'That's a present for our daughter Lisa and I hope she is careful with it'. Neal dropped me back to my hotel "Shoney's" on Music Row, and that late afternoon like most days, I called my Mum, thousands of miles away in her little Devonshire house, to tell her of my wonderful experiences that day. She knew I was over the other side of the world, living the dream and she was just so happy knowing that I was safe and would soon be tucked up in bed!

That night in Nashville I remember leaving the curtains open to look out at a beautiful starlit sky, not wanting the day to end. I laid on my bed gazing at the stars with a mixture of feelings. Here was I, on Music Row in Nashville Tennessee, where up the road Elvis recorded, just around the corner Buddy Holly recorded, and in the next road stands the Roy Orbison building. To top it all off, I have been humbled and honoured that on this very day Neal Matthews, Jnr confided enough in me to share his music and personal life. It doesn't come any better than that.

Sadly, Neal passed away on April 21st, 2000. I was blessed to have Neal as a friend and I am sure anyone who befriended him would say the same. He was a true family man with talent in abundance and will always be a music legend in my eyes. I often look into a clear night sky and think back to that warm starlit Nashville evening and think how sad it is that I won't be speaking again with my song-writing buddy, but one thing is for sure – today and every day the Nashville skyline now has another bright star that will shine for all to see – a music legend that will glow for eternity... Neal Matthews, Jr.

DUANE WEST

Duane West was one of the vocalists in a group called The Southern Gentlemen, well known for backing the country music legend Sonny James throughout the 1960's, and Duane performed with the Jordanaires when called upon. He became the Jordanaires official baritone in 1982 following the passing of Hoyt Hawkins.

I always thought Duane was a very likeable guy who took a smile with him everywhere he went as well as having a very positive attitude in most situations. Duane was the one who solved a lot of Jordanaires minor disputes, mainly standard band issues like who stayed in what hotel room and what was a good time for all to rehearse, dine etc., the sort of things that if someone does not take care of, it always results in time wasting and confusion. Duane was always making sure Gordon was eating the right food as he was not allowed too much sugar in his diet. One night at a Chinese restaurant in London's West End Duane went to the men's room and I passed a couple of those small toffee apples that they give you for dessert to Gordon as a little treat. He thought he was in heaven but when Duane returned he gave me a right telling off when he realised Gordon was having a sugar rush caused entirely by my 'kind toffee apple gesture', so I realized in the future my desserts had to stay on my plate.

Back in the U.S. Duane had his own ranch and was always inviting me to come out to visit. Unfortunately, I never got around to it. The guys told me he had quite a few horses, and he loved that way of life as well as being a Jordanaire.

Duane was the guy you always wanted around when on tour, a very helpful character in all situations even when he was performing. As well as singing he had that natural ability of calmness about him that filtered through the group. The Jordanaires had been booked to do a TV special with Freddy Starr and I recall getting a call from Gordon asking if I would come and visit them at their hotel which was very close to Buckingham Palace. I went to the hotel, walked up to the reception desk and noticed Duane sitting in a very plush one-person leather couch with a pot of tea nicely brewing in front of him. He beckoned me over and as I got nearer I noticed he had a very bad skin condition and did not look at all well. We chatted for a couple of minutes before all the other guys appeared.

One by one they told me of their experiences of working with Freddy Starr. They thought Freddie was a lovely guy, just a little bit crazy. But what came over was how much they had missed their buddy Johnny and they were so pleased I took the time to come and visit them, I really did feel humbled, but these were genuine guys. I suggested they come and see where I was living at the time. Duane was the first to say 'I'm there Johnny', and that was it, I brought them back to West London – Victoria Road, Ruislip Manor, Middlesex. Tom and Ros (who I never looked at as landlords but as my London parents who had adopted me whether they liked it or not, and Sue their daughter who had a rock 'n' roll brother whether she wanted one or not), were casually told over the phone 'I'm bringing home my buddies the Jordanaires for tea and biscuits!

Unfortunately, this was to be the last time I saw Duane as Louis Nunley replaced him for the interim. Duane became ill and Gordon did say that Duane would be back when he was better, but sadly this never happened. I missed Duane being around because he had a great spirit and was always positive.

A few years later I got the call to tell me Duane passed away in Shelbyville, Tennessee on June 23rd, 1999. He had worked with the Jordanaires for 17 years and I was proud to be a friend and associate of such a wonderful human being.

10

CARL PERKINS

Nashville beckoned me once more, this time to record with the King of Rockabilly: Mr. Blue Suede shoes himself.... Carl Perkins. Kevin Allen had worked out a one-off recording project with a very well-known man in the record industry called Bill Kimber, who was in the A&R world of the music business and who also had his own label. At the time the Jive Bunny rock 'n' roll medleys were climbing the charts and of course it's hard to tour a cartoon rabbit who was the lead character of the Jive Bunny bandwagon, so it was agreed to get real life rock 'n' rollers onto record in a medley form and Bill Kimber wanted a 7 inch vinyl version with a 3-minute medley, along with a 12 inch vinyl version with a 7-minute medley. This project was aptly named 'Johnny Earl and All the Kings Men' – yes, the bandwagon now had The Jordanaires, Scotty Moore and D.J. Fontana on board and now Carl Perkins was joining the ranks. As any artist who has tasted success will know, having the right producer will make the difference between the record being a hit or not. A lesser production can be disastrous, so on board this vessel was the UK's top-drawer producer Stuart Coleman.

I had to have a meeting with Stuart regarding the project as he could not make the trip to Nashville because not only was he making number one hit records, working with and producing Shaking Stevens, he had at the time been given the job of producing Cliff Richards and The Young Ones charity single, so all the Nashville recordings had to be properly worked out. The drums, keyboards and rhythm guitars were put down in the UK which made up the templates of the back tracks and all the lead guitar and vocals would be laid down in Nashville. Stuart gave me strict instructions that had to be implicitly followed: He looked me straight in the eye to make sure I wouldn't miss a word being said (as if a code was being implemented in my mind) and Stuart said 'I have worked with Carl before and he is fabulous to work with, so this will not be too much of a problem, but when Carl comes to do his guitar solo on Blue Suede Shoes, I want him to play the solo down the neck of the guitar to get a fuller sound', 'I got it Stuart', I replied... next stop Nashville, Tennessee.

I flew to Nashville and knew this time I needed to take a couple of photos for my personal collection. I never really was a big camera person but with all the Kings men in one place I made sure I had my camera at hand.

I arrived at the studio followed shortly by Carl Perkins who walked straight over to Gordon Stoker, embraced him, saying 'How's it going Gordon? It's great to see you'. He then shook hands with Neal, Ray and Duane; Carl let out a laugh and said 'D.J. you still keeping that beat?' he gave D.J. a hug and shook Scotty's hand 'Good to see you again Scotty'. I later found out they were recording an album together at the time, so it was a little like another day at the office for those two Sun recording legends. I thought now is the time to get some good photo shots. I have two Sun Record stars over there (Carl and Scotty), now that seems a good place to start, because the engineer for the recording session had just arrived and I knew that soon we would start recording so I got clicking. I took the photos with one of those disposable Kodak cameras. I just hoped, like most people who used these cameras of the day did, that using such professional photographic equipment meant that I would get at least a couple of good shots. You always collected these photos after being processed with your fingers crossed, and I'm glad to say I ended up with some good ones.

When we started recording it was just myself and the engineer in the control room while D.J., Scotty and the Jordanaires stayed in the large recording room where we had all met. You find in Nashville a lot of studios have quite a few recording rooms. Carl made his way to the guitar booth, while I am in the control room looking through the big window which was about 4 feet top to bottom and 10 feet wide and you could see into the recording room which had all the various booths. I looked over and I could see Carl very clearly in the guitar booth, it was now time for Carl to lay his vocals and guitar work down. In the guitar booth there was also a microphone set up as Carl obviously was not going to put down his vocal on a separate track, he was going to do guitar and vocals at the same time. He put his guitar lead into the amp and you could hear the guitar was pretty much in tune and he started pickin' (Rockabilly at its best) and this was just the warm up.

The engineer at my side was recommended by Scotty so we were in good hands. He pressed the button on the control desk that gave you a direct line to Carl 'Everything okay Carl?' the engineer asked, 'I'm fine, how does it sound out there?' 'It's sounding good out here', said the engineer 'I'll play you the track and let me know how you are for levels'. 'Okay,' Carl replied, 'That's just fine', and about five seconds later Carl said, 'let's cut it'. Carl sang *"Blue Suede Shoes"* then rocked into the solo (talk about spot on, in fact BRILLIANT!) I froze for a few seconds just taking in Carl Perkins playing the solo on my next release and it sounded knock out!

After Carl's first take the engineer turned to me and said, 'This could be a one taker', I said 'You can see why he is crowned the King of Rockabilly', (the trouble with working with someone like Carl Perkins is that every solo, no matter how many different takes, is going to sound brilliant). The engineer spoke to Carl 'Wonderful Carl, I think you might have put it to bed', Carl being the gentleman he was replied 'How was that with you Johnny?' 'Just fabulous Carl, but I have been given strict instructions from Stuart Coleman to tell you to play the solo more down the neck so to get a fuller sound', I saw the engineer fall back in his seat not believing what I had just said. I did understand that reaction, but I had my orders. Carl replied, 'That's fine Johnny, I'll play it a bit more down the neck and let's see how that sounds, cos I want you guys to be happy'. Straight back into the song, take two... and this was the take that can be heard on both the final mixed versions.

Carl took off his headphones, came into the control room and the engineer shook his hand 'That was great Carl', then went next door to grab a coffee and speak to Scotty and the other guys regarding their setting up requirements before recording. 'Are you happy Johnny?' Carl asked, 'More than happy' I replied, 'Thank you, you're very kind, oh and in case I forget, when you get back to the UK would you mind saying hi to my buddy George for me?' I thought to myself who on earth does he mean, so I said 'George?' 'Yeah my good buddy George Harrison'. 'Oh of course I will Carl', then Carl said, 'I haven't been in touch for a while'. I replied 'like you Carl, I am quite busy, but I will pass on your message at my earliest convenience'. I didn't want to let him know that I had never met George Harrison let alone been in the position to relay messages to him. Carl and I sat down and chatted for about 20 minutes and I asked him about his Sun years and what was it like to work with the likes of Carl Mann, Sonny Burgess, Johnny Cash and of course the King - Elvis. Oh, how I wished we recorded this conversation, but I remember a fair bit.

I told Carl when I started out in London I was in a band called The Louisiana Hayride and as soon as I told him he smiled and said, 'Boy I remember that place', and I then informed him 'The band mostly played the entire Sun record repertoire'. His eyes lit up and he said, 'Tell me Johnny, I'm intrigued, what was your set list?' I pretty much remembered most of it because it was not that long ago that I had performed it, so I started reeling off the set list *"Love My Baby"* by Little Juniors Blue Flames, *"Fairlane Rock"* by Hayden Thompson, *"Do What I Do"* by Slim Rhodes, *"Ooby Dooby"* by Roy Orbison and *"I Got Love If You Want It"* by Warren Smith and of course, I laughed 'Not forgetting one of my Sun record favourites, *"Matchbox"* by you!'

As I was reeling off the set list he would stop me after each song and tell me about the times he spent with each and every individual and informed me of what they were doing today, and of the memories and laughs he had touring and recording with most of the artistes' I was mentioning. All those earlier days of Carl's career seemed to be streaming back to him. I was just gobsmacked. I was talking straight up rockabilly with Carl Perkins and one thing for sure, he was loving The Louisiana Hayride's set list.

After about 20 minutes of Sun Records conversation, time was rolling on and more work had to be done, but it was a blast. Carl gave me a hug and said it was pleasure working with me and I told him that the whole session for me was a dream come true! He then went and got his guitar amp, and we both walked into the other studio where Carl said his goodbyes. The Jordanaires, Scotty and D.J. had all done a wonderful job so when I returned to the UK I was immediately back in the studio with Stuart Coleman, so he could listen to all that was put down in Nashville. He was very pleased and started to mix both the 7 inch, and 12 inch versions and when we came to a coffee break he told me the story of when Carl had toured the UK and it was his birthday, where he was presented with a large birthday cake in the shape of a blue suede shoe. Carl started to cry, and Stuart heard him say 'I've never been given a birthday cake so beautiful'.

Personally I have to say, sometimes you can meet someone and have a pretty good idea how genuine they are, and Carl Perkins for me was one of the most genuine guys I have come across in the music business. I often remember sitting with Carl in that Nashville studio reminiscing about my Louisiana Hayride days, and what came to life was all that slogging and gigging with The Hayriders – even though it was great fun at the time – who would have ever thought it would be one day rubber-stamped by none other than the King of rockabilly, Carl Perkins.

11

SCOTTY MOORE

Born on a farm in Tennessee, Winfield Scott Moore the 3rd who was the youngest of four brothers started that Tennessee guitar pickin' at the early age of 8. By the time he was 16 he joined the navy and like Neal Matthews of the Jordanaires, served through the Korean War. In 1954 Scotty formed a band called The Starlight Wranglers and one other member of this group was bass player Bill Black. Scotty Moore and Bill Black then later became two members of a trio who worked with Sam Philips the owner of Sun records, and the new trio were now called The Blue Moon Boys ..oh and by the way, the third member was a new lead singer called Elvis Presley. This trio changed popular music forever!

It was time once more for Kevin Allen and me to reach up to the stars. The music and touring were going very well with the first tours of the Jordanaires, and now Kevin Allen and I wanted to add to the show, so the next logical step was to go all the way and try to procure the one and only Scotty Moore and then why not try and get Elvis's drummer D.J. Fontana as well. We knew that in March 1961, a couple of days after Elvis finished his recording sessions in Hollywood for the film *'Blue Hawaii'* he performed a benefit show for the Pacific War Memorial Commission which was for the Arizona memorial fund, (the ship that was tragically sunk at Pearl Harbour December 7th, 1941) and this show was for the 20th anniversary.

On the billing for this charity event, alongside Elvis were The Jordanaires, Scotty Moore and D.J. Fontana and that was the last Elvis tour that they all performed on together and to bring that line up back together to tour with little ol' me in the UK it would be the ultimate Blue Suede Dream. We had a few discussions with Gordon Stoker who obviously knew Scotty and D.J. very well. It was agreed Kevin and I were both going to fly to Nashville, Tennessee to see if we could meet and get on board the one and only Scotty Moore (Elvis Presley's original guitarist and first manager). Scotty Moore had never toured the UK before and was very busy with his recording business in Nashville. (I have resided in Nashville and it does make you feel 'this is definitely music city so why bother leaving for anything?'). I also knew with Scotty (or so I was informed by a famous rock 'n' roll DJ), history had shown that he was not treated the best through those successful early Elvis years when Colonel Tom Parker took the reins. Maybe past memories had taken their toll, because it was said Elvis was a very generous person and he promised Scotty 1% of all earnings for his help in getting Elvis to the top. As soon as RCA Victor came on the scene though, taking care of business is exactly what Colonel Tom Parker did regarding all finances, and the Colonel personally made sure even the 1% that was promised, was much too high a price to pay.

I was thinking if we could get this tour to actually happen it would mean all the guys that backed Elvis throughout the 1950's would now be on our show. Kevin and I arrived in Nashville with no guarantee Scotty Moore or D.J. Fontana would even join the show let alone tour the UK.

It was an exciting flight to Nashville knowing what we were trying to achieve, and as we flew into Nashville itself as usual I got that excited feeling come over me, because it really is music city and it makes one feel you actually belong to the larger picture of this industry. This time we were aiming very high, in our most ambitious project to date to stage a collaboration that had not taken place since 1961 – the re-appearance of "All The Kings Men".

After settling into Shoney's Hotel on Music Row we were both very tired and the following days important meeting was to be held at Scotty's business quarters, a cassette pressing plant (the modern format of the day), so a good night's sleep was needed. The following day dawned, we had a hearty breakfast after which Kevin collected a big bundle of paperwork and off to Scotty Moore's business premises we went. As we walked into what looked like a small board room with a long table which filled most of the room, Gordon Stoker came over to us and calmed the nerves a bit and introduced us to D.J. Fontana and then Scotty Moore, who both came over as very nice and approachable.

We all then took our seats. I sat silent as I wanted to soak in what to me was an historic moment. I know it seems strange even if Kevin and I created it, but here we were sitting around this table with the Jordanaires, Gordon, Neal, Duane, Ray along with D.J. Fontana and of course with all the presence of the board room director - Scotty Moore. I thought to myself straight away I was now in the domain of the man who was to me the greatest rock 'n' roll guitar legend there has ever been, (besides Eddie Cochran) here right in front of me was the man who played *"King Creole"*, the legendary *"Mystery Train"*, (oh my god this was the man himself), *"Good Rocking Tonight"* and *"That's Alright Mama"* ...here he was in the flesh, but there was business to be done and straight away I could see that although to me he was an r 'n' r guitar legend, this man was no fool!

Scotty leant forward 'Okay guys tell me what it's all about'. Kevin reached for his 12-inch high bundle of paperwork and started his sales pitch showing Scotty and D.J. all the posters and flyers regarding previous Johnny Earl and Jordanaires tours and telling how very positive all the reviews from the shows were.

Scotty and D.J. listened intently and politely The Jordanaires never said a word, but I could tell Gordon had already sown the seeds and had pretty much put this meeting together, and although Scotty and D.J. worked independently you could read through the lines that if Gordon had already boarded and sailed in the ship, they would pretty much sail in her as well, as long as the finances could be agreed on.

Credit where it's due, Kevin sold himself very well (although what was said in twenty minutes could have been said in ten). Kevin finished 'Well guys, that is what we would like to do, and I'll be happy to answer any questions that you may have'. D.J. looked at Scotty and said, 'You go first silver fox', (I found out later this name was administered to Scotty due to his shrewd way of doing business and having silver coloured hair) Scotty just said, 'It all sounds pretty good to me, so I will speak with you later Kevin regarding monies, for now that's it for me'. D.J. then interjected 'Right Kevin, have you finished all that you wanted to say?' 'I think so', replied Kevin 'Okay then, D.J. leant forward in his seat looked Kevin straight in the eyes 'You see all that paperwork you have before you, put all that crap aside, all I want to know is what I'm getting, so like Scotty we'll talk over the phone a little later and take it from there'. 'That's fine', replied Kevin, D.J. then remarked 'Kevin you'll find with me, money talks, bull**** walks, I don't care what the other guys are getting, I'll just let you know if I'm coming along', to which Scotty got up and said 'Okay, I think that's pretty much it'. We all chatted for about five minutes or so, but I made sure I went over to personally thank Gordon for making it happen. I had one worry on my mind, I knew as soon as it got out that Scotty Moore and D.J. Fontana were ready to tour Europe with the Jordanaires, every established agent and promoter (and there were hundreds in our style of music) would want a piece of the cake and that meant all hell was going to break loose unless we wrapped it all up signed sealed and delivered and quick...

Myself and Kevin went straight back to our hotel because we needed to know how we were going to tackle this. I said to Kevin 'Gordon has worked his butt off on our behalf; let's make sure we don't let him down'. Kevin was obviously worried that Scotty might charge tens of thousands of dollars and then there was also D.J. Fontana to deal with. I agreed with Kevin a price that we both thought was fair for Scotty, which I knew there was no way we could pay beyond, as for the flights and accommodation for the tour, that was not a concern as sponsors like Hilton hotels and British Airways with all the promotion they would receive from the press and being on all the tour posters would take care of all that.

Our biggest worry was although Gordon had put together the plan, if we now messed it up at our end, he could take this package to any promoter (and they had many of them in their accumulated years in the business especially in Las Vegas), in fact the more Kevin and I spoke about the tour the more we realised they could tour the whole U.S. why even bother with Europe, this was it! We got one bite of the cherry and we gotta' make it sweet!

With the sum Kevin and myself now agreed for Scotty, later that day Kevin called him and we both said, let Scotty do the talking and let him lay his cards on the table. After all we would like a good working relationship with him, like we already had with the Jordanaires. Kevin did exactly that; he let Scotty have his say but then interjected 'Scotty could you give us a price for five shows?' Well Scotty did exactly that and Kevin gave me a look as if he was just about to be pushed off the edge of a cliff. Kevin said to Scotty 'I was hoping to add D.J. to the tour this time around, so would you agree to this?' It wasn't enough! I felt the whole project slipping away but Kevin could only do so much and finished by saying 'Can I call you a little later?' Scotty agreed so Kevin and I made our way to the bar across the road. The problem with having a few drinks at a time like this is, it might ease your problems a little but somehow it manages to paint a much brighter picture of the whole situation and in our case, print up a lot of imaginary dollars we didn't have, yes you got it! A couple of hours and a few drinks later, back to the hotel we trundled, no messing about now! Straight on the phone to Scotty ....The tour is on, followed in quick succession by a phone call to D.J. Fontana; a quick bit of money talk and would you believe it - he's coming as well!

Sobering up we realized from that moment on, all monies that we had saved and all that were now to be earned were going to be needed for this project!

The euphoria of knowing the tour was on and the star line-up of who we were going to bring to the UK, to us it was just rock 'n' roll heaven. The very next day there was no better way to celebrate than to jump into a hired car, and head off to Graceland, the home of the King. Yes off to Memphis we jolly well went along with a visit to the legendary Sun recording studios. Now with Scotty Moore on-board Kevin and I just could not stop talking about the promoting that was needed. We agreed to start the campaign with the heading – using the title of Scotty's first solo album – "The Guitar That Changed the World" (no one would disagree with that). We were feeling on top of the world; we had travelled to Nashville and aimed for the stars and bought back two with us.

On returning to the UK we phoned a few friends in Germany and Holland and already seats were being booked for what was going to be the biggest rock 'n' roll show on earth!

It was amazing the amount of press and media that were wanting interviews with what Kevin and I now had coined the never before used phrase 'Johnny Earl and All the Kings Men'. It was a busy time and I had to return to Nashville pretty much straight away to rehearse with all the guys. This was held in a rehearsal studio just outside Nashville. I managed to take a few personal photographs at this rehearsal session and had good chats with all involved and Scotty was no exception. We mainly talked about how the music business was changing and Scotty asked me what some of my favourite tunes were so he could see my tastes in music, to which I replied 'To be honest with you Scotty, most of the songs we are about to rehearse including *"Milk Cow Blues"* and *"Baby Let's Play House",* he laughed 'At least you're doing what you love'.

The rehearsal was great, Neal Matthews played rhythm guitar while I, Scotty and D.J. rehearsed the Sun Elvis recording years. This was the first time I saw up close how Scotty played. He was sitting to the left of me, about five feet away, and it was as if he had three pairs of hands plucking those strings and making that guitar come to life, his amp stood on a small table and that sang to me with all those Sun studios haunting licks. Then we got started, I performed *"Mystery Train"*, *"Good Rocking Tonight"*, *"I Don't Care If the Sun Don't Shine"*, *"Milk Cow Blues"* and when we got to *"That's Alright Mama"*, I took a deep breath, (was this really happening) and I took the first take of *"That's All Right Mama"* with Scotty Moore playing lead. Neal Matthews started playing rhythm guitar, then in I came 'Well That's Alright with Mama', and Scotty replied with that famous lick, and just before the solo I yelled 'Hit it', knowing we were just about to go into the guitar solo of what some people say is the song that changed pop music history and when Scotty belted out the solo. I froze, amazed at what I was witnessing and got so spellbound by Scotty's playing I did not go straight back in to the song where I should have, so I ad-libbed singing a loud 'We-ll', for about five seconds as the other guys stayed playing the riff in the key of A and don't ask me why, I went straight into A 'well I said Blue Moon Of Kentucky a keep on shining', which is also in the key A and roughly the same tempo.

Scotty, D.J. and Neal Matthews all just carried on playing as if it was always meant to be that way, so then into the solo of *"Blue Moon of Kentucky"* we went, and thereafter we finished the medley by going back into *"That's Alright Mama"* and this was now in the set as a new medley. After the now newly rehearsed medley Scotty remarked 'That worked pretty well', D.J. remarked 'I'm happy with it', and I felt let off the hook, but as proud as a peacock, and especially as I needed to see if certain songs were still going to have that authentic sound or not. Well I can tell you it surpassed all my dreams, and also the guys did not mind me recording most of the session on a cassette so I could check out if any songs were not working out so well. (The sad thing was I got so carried away with the rehearsal that I forgot to turn the cassette over, so I missed recording some of the songs).

The next songs we rehearsed were *"Bigga Hunk of Love"*, *"Hound Dog"*, *"Don't Be Cruel"* and *"A Fool Such As I"* which of course introduced the Jordanaires, UNBELIEVABLE!! The whole rehearsal was a success and when it had all finished Scotty informed me he had just finished recording an album with Carl Perkins called *706 Reunion* (I think he recorded it where we were rehearsing). He explained on one of the tracks, he needed to record background crowd ambiance with people just having general conversation. He asked us all if we wouldn't mind doing that for him, so an overhead microphone was placed above us all. Scotty explained what he would like us all to do, the thumbs up sign was given from the engineer in the control room and then all went silent.

Scotty looked at us all and said, 'All you gotta do guys is just chat, you all know how to do that don't you?' we all looked puzzled 'What do you want us to say?' D.J. exclaimed. 'Anything', Scotty shouted, I just laughed, and Gordon turned to me and said in a posh English accent 'I think that was a jolly good rehearsal old chap'. Everyone fell about laughing including Scotty and I think he eventually got the ambiance he was looking for. I could not wait to get to a phone (mobiles and the internet were just things of the future at that time – you only saw gadgets like that on Star Trek) so I could tell Kevin how well it had all gone, and I told him, it did not matter how big he wanted to promote the show because after the rehearsal I had just had, the sky was the limit, and I now had a cassette to prove it.

I was so excited, I think I spent most of the money I had on me (which was intended for food and drink for my Nashville stay) on something much more important, phoning my mum and telling her to get ready. I remember excitedly saying 'I'm now bringing all of Elvis's band to Devon, not only the Jordanaires but Scotty Moore, and D.J. Fontana as well.... Mum get the kettle on!'

It saddens me to say it, Scotty Moore passed away in Nashville, Tennessee, June 28th, 2016.

Scotty Moore the man with the guitar sound that changed the music world forever…..!

12

D.J. FONTANA

Born in Shreveport, Louisiana, D.J. Fontana worked his way to be the in-house drummer on The Louisiana Hayride with its Saturday night radio broadcasts. In October of 1954 he was hired to drum for a new up and coming singer who was causing a sensation everywhere he played, and this was to be D.J's first encounter backing up "The Hillbilly Cat" Elvis Presley.

After that night, D.J. would play and record with Elvis for the next 15 years and it would lead to what I think was one of the best musical TV broadcasts in history, the NBC spectacular Elvis's "1968 Comeback Special."

I find drummers come in many guises, always colourful characters with personality in abundance. One thing you generally find, they say what they mean and take very few prisoners. My advice to any front man or woman singer – whenever you see there is discontent among the ranks, pull the drummer aside and he or she will normally inform you what's going on and if need be, tell you exactly where you stand.

On the very first meeting I had with D.J. Fontana, as far as drummers go all the above applied; I knew we would get along just fine. That first meeting with D.J. was at Scotty Moore's business premises to discuss bringing them both to the UK to tour. Once the tour was agreed and D.J. was on board he was great to be around. After this meeting, Kevin and I had a lot to get on with, so it was not until I returned to Nashville a few weeks later to rehearse for the UK tour that I got to meet D.J. personally. This time I was in Nashville on my own and all the guys were very kind as they all wanted individually to take me out for a meal, even though they all had very busy schedules.

D.J. came around to "Shoney's" on Music Row where I was staying, and we had a hearty breakfast. He spoke very fondly of Elvis and told me how shrewd Colonel Tom Parker was and how nobody commanded more respect than the Colonel.

D.J. told me the early years on the road with Elvis were pretty demanding and even Elvis could not believe back in 1956 that the whole world was going to hear about him and of course how his rise to stardom happened so rapidly. D.J. said 'Johnny, I remember even back then after an Elvis performance there was a problem with getting all the monies owed, so the Colonel had me and Ray Walker driving around collecting monies from various clubs and venues until all was paid'. At this little get together with D.J. we both on the spot agreed to never hold anything back. I laughed when he said, 'Johnny you got something to say, say it and we'll sort it'.

No better example of that was when a couple of years later, in the mid 1990's, Kevin asked D.J. (as D.J. knew a lot of important people in the music world, especially in Nashville) 'D.J. do you think Johnny could become a new country music star?' and D.J. replied 'Definitely, and I can put you in touch with the top producers and get you all the A list musicians' (these were the best and busiest musicians in Nashville and were always on a lot of the top ten hit records throughout the 1990's of the country music billboard charts). Kevin shouted in glee 'At last we can have major success', until D.J. reminded him money talks and bull**** walks and he will need $250,000 in order to get the right people involved and make it happen.

By 1994 Kevin was realising if you want to be in the big time you need big bucks and even then, a lot of luck. Money just brings a bit more luck, the more money you pay the more luck you buy.

I liked the chats I had with D.J., straight to the point and more often than not hilarious. He performed brilliantly on the tours, a great rockin' and hard-hitting player with a swing style that filled most solos, (You'll know exactly what I mean when you listen to the intro of *"My Baby Left Me"*). For rock 'n' roll D.J. was one of the most prominent drummers known, like when he performed that constant drum roll on *"Hound Dog"* which was a signature theme of his.

When on tour with D.J. I loved to perform *"I Need Your Love Tonight"* mainly because of the way he would swing that solo and just fill the song. I found D.J. good in the way he conducted his business affairs. He could procure all that he needed when sorting out his various tours, and the bottom line for me was that D.J. was a good guy, hard-working, always positive as well as being a character – just the man you need on board when touring. While D.J. is still around you can be assured somewhere in the world echoing throughout a venue 'You ain't never caught a rabbit, then you ain't no friend of mine'!

Four years it has taken me from writing the very first words for this book and today Saturday 16th June 2018 I thought the very last addition I had to make would be the very last page. Ray Walker of the Jordanaires is eagerly awaiting his copy of Blue Suede Dreams and so was D.J. Fontana however just as this book goes to print, sadly I am informed D.J. Fontana has passed away in Nashville on Wednesday 13th June 2018 aged 87.

He not only performed on more than 450 Elvis Presley records, he joined forces and was the back-beat for Paul McCartney, Ringo Starr, Gene Vincent, Dolly Parton and the great Johnny Cash and he was inducted into the Rock 'n' Roll and Rockabilly Hall of Fame.

D.J. Fontana R.I.P.

13

ON TOUR WITH JERRY LEE LEWIS

(Sorry Rockers he's doing Country tonight)

He is not called the Killer for nothing. The Johnny Earl roadshow was in full swing and we were told by manager Kevin Allen he had now got us booked for a 20 date UK tour with the Killer, yes Jerry Lee Lewis. At the time a little grey cloud hung over Mr. Lewis, which happens with many a musical pop legend and that was the U.S. taxman. It was publicized to the world in all the major press just before the tour started about his problems, which left everyone wondering whether the tour was going to happen at all. When you have a promoter like Mervyn Conn at the helm though (probably amongst the best tour promoters Britain has conjured up), things did get sorted out eventually.

Unfortunately, one of the earliest dates of the tour was at the B.I.C. in Bournemouth and it was sold out. The biggest problem for the B.I.C. was Jerry Lee was not attending, so at the very last minute my manager had a meeting with the venue owners and said the show could go on. This would mean with my band, so we would perform both halves, making sure we put as many Jerry Lee rock 'n' roll classics in as possible. We actually pulled it off. Of course it was not a full house; around 500-600 stayed and they really enjoyed the show. A standing ovation for the band and I rounded off the night, but what was important for me, is I had heard Jerry Lee fans had flown from various European destinations – only to be disappointed at the last minute – so I wanted to give them the best show possible. It was not long after the

B.I.C. show that all problems surrounding Jerry Lee had been sorted out, Uncle Sam was smiling once again, and the tour proceeded.

My next date with the Killer was at the Leisure Centre, Gloucester where I performed the first hour and Jerry Lee the second. I learned a few things at this concert: Firstly, I took a good look at the merchandise that was on offer, excellent quality t-shirts and tour jackets, lovely glossy brochures etc... One thing for sure is quality sells (that was as far as the Jerry Lee merchandise was concerned). Mine and Kevin's humble two merchandise tables came compliments of B&Q – I may stand corrected but I recollect a couple of thin wallpapering tables (Little acorns - stay little acorns, until big financial backers jump aboard).

Another thing that hit home with me was that for Jerry Lee Lewis fans, as far as they were concerned, Jerry Lee is the undisputed King of rock 'n' roll. Elvis, Buddy Holly, Bill Hayley etc., came way down the ladder of legends. I myself was under no grand illusions – I knew my place at this concert (would you like your brothel creepers shined sir?).

From Teddy Boys to the general public, they were all here to see their idol and do not get me wrong, I was a big Jerry Lee fan as well. It's just that I always looked at Elvis being the King, but I kept that to myself especially when performing my show. The band and I were well appreciated, and we certainly did not let the Killer or Mervyn Conn down, and as soon as I finished my performance I made my way to where I was to get changed. I was upstairs changing in an area with big windows all down one side overlooking the concert area which held about 2,000 seats. I heard a loud knocking on the door at the other end of the area where I was getting changed. I walked to the door, and on opening it I was confronted by Andrew Lloyd Webber and a group of other celebrities asking me how to get to Jerry Lee's dressing room. I pointed the way, smiled and directed them to the Killers room.

They did compliment me on the bands and my first half performance and wished me luck for the future; I knew security had obviously pointed the way for them, so I had no problems allowing them through to the Killer. I thought to myself should I follow them and see the man himself? I had second thoughts, as I did not know how much any of the negative press had affected him. I got changed and when I noticed the lights in the main hall start to dim, my anticipation was over, it was time. The announcer exclaimed 'Jerry Lee Lewis' and although it was 2,000 people in the audience it sounded like 20,000 roaring as loud as they could. I am sure most of the audience were just glad that he was actually there, me included, but what a lot of the audience was not prepared for (especially the rockers and myself), was Jerry Lee making his way to his piano stool, calming the audience down then announcing (something along the lines of) 'I no longer perform rock 'n' roll,.. tonight I'm performing country music!'

The rock 'n' roll gods were banished, and the legendary rock 'n' roll classics *"High School Confidential"*, *"Great Balls of Fire"* would have to wait until the Killer decided to perform them once again. Tonight, we were going to have the softer side of the Killer *"Your Cheatin' Heart"* meets *"Crazy Arms"*. When he finished his performance, of course a long-standing ovation ensued.

That evening reminded me a little of when I went to see James Brown (the King of Soul) in Hammersmith, in his last year of touring before he sadly passed away. If I have to be honest, the main reason for me attending the James Brown concert was to know that in my life time I had actually seen him with my very own eyes. I suppose to a lot of the audience attending that night in Gloucester they could say they had actually seen good old Jerry Lee. A few years later I performed alongside his sister Linda Gale Lewis, and she is as good as her brother in holding an audience, and a really good person to work with. Still going strong today in the rock 'n' roll scene, she is a music legend herself.

A notable lesson I learned that night in Gloucester with the Killer, was in the music and entertainment business, when you reach the status of legend, in most situations you only have to turn up, then as far as a lot of the public are concerned it's money well spent.

'GOODNESS GRACIOUS GREAT BALLS OF FIRE'!

14

ON TOUR

Touring is a way of life; you either love it or hate it. When I first moved to London I was used to performing the occasional weekend show but as time went on lots more shows started coming my way.

When you start in the entertainment business I don't think anyone says "that's it, I'm going to spend my life on the road." I have found it is more a case of as you go along you kind of take what comes your way. It also all depends on how successful and in demand you are, but when you get used to touring and spending a lot of time on the road, the question of do you want to live your life out of a suitcase starts to play on one's mind.

Touring can be great fun and a pleasure to experience, but it can also be laborious and very time wasting. For instance, at times you will be in never ending traffic jams and that can be in any country you are touring, along with hours and hours spent at airports, and when you are performing the same show night after night, week after week, this can also take its toll. I do get a lot of members of the public that say surely living the life of rock 'n' roll with all that touring must be brilliant. I find it hard to tell them anything but what they want to hear, because it is definitely fun at times and anyway the general public are not that interested in the boring bits of the music business; they love the live performance and all the naughty bits that go with it. Yes, it is that ten percent, the enjoyment part of touring that keeps all the artistes forever on the road, not forgetting of course, if you are famous or have created a large following, then the money has 95% to do with it.

For some who have never been in the music business they can look at their lives as being a little bit humdrum and to be able to just spend a week touring would be like winning the lottery – that I very much understand, touring from the outside looks very glamorous. My touring through the years has been at all levels. In my first band the touring was really only ever small gigs that were very sporadic and nothing long term as we did not really know from one week to the next if we were performing at all.

My very first gigging footprint on the London scene was imprinted at the Eastcote Arms public house (which was a rockabilly pub) and this was in west London in 1982. Paul Maitland, my friend who had come to Devon and was quite impressed with my early Elvis sounding voice was waiting to get me onto a London stage of any kind, and now the day had come.

He was the double bass player for a trio he had put together performing rockabilly music. Paul wanted me to perform with them and it was to be here where I performed two songs *"My Happiness"* and *"Your Cheating Heart"*. All the audience roared, and that was it, no turning back, my two-song hit parade was my first mini gig, first rung of the touring ladder.

Of course, when my career changed, and I was in a musical the reality of touring hit home. A brilliant time (with more than my fair share of romances) as well as meeting many nice people and getting to see places I would never have been in a position to do so had I not have toured. When I joined the country music band Southern Star, it was all about being on tour at a level of nearly 200 performances a year. As you read this book, the life of touring will become apparent and for me, having experienced touring at all levels, I must say I'm looking forward to the next one!

FREEDOM OF THE SHIP
"AMERICAN AIRCRAFT CARRIER
USS DWIGHT D. EISENHOWER"

(CVN - 69)

In 1991 operation Desert Storm was put into effect with coalition forces after Iraq had invaded Kuwait. I flew to Dubai in 1992 to perform for the Allied troops and it was a bit scary as it was rumoured Saddam Hussain was going to gas everybody who was in the Emirates as they were supporting the allies. Silly as it might sound, when you are actually in what might become a warzone you don't know what to believe. All I knew was that I was there to do my bit for the troops and if that helped them ease their minds a little, it would be a job well done.

In January 1992, the Officer Commanding (OC) of the Multi-National forces invited me to entertain both British and American troops. Over 6,000 soldiers attended the concert and to show their appreciation I was invited to spend the day aboard the flagship of the American Navy, the Aircraft Carrier USS Dwight D. Eisenhower.

The venue I performed in was called "The Seaman's Club" and the American and British troops used it as a club to drink and enjoy themselves. I performed a rock 'n' roll show in front of what ended up being over 6,000 troops and my songs were well received. The resident DJ was a lovely guy named Pete, from Manchester, who I got to know well as a friend. He had a hard job musically, trying to keep all the troops happy. During the day in about 100 degrees of Dubai glorious sunshine he played all the songs that were requested and this was when I noticed how much the American troops loved their music, but the selection was so diverse - the younger crowd were heavily into Metallica and rap and then the other half were requesting Sam Cooke through to the Beatles, and of course a lot of guys were from the southern states and were asking for the new country music stars of the day. Credit where it was due, Pete did his best and kept everyone happy.

When I performed in the evening they were ready to rock 'n' roll and as a result they all rocked the house. I gave them belting versions of *"Lucille"*, *"Summertime Blues"* and even *"Shaking All Over"*. The show went down well, and the soldiers were very appreciative and more than a little surprised that I was a Brit, (Yes, we can rock 'n' roll with the best of them) and then a happy-looking chap came up, shook my hand and thanked me for entertaining the troops.

He asked if I would like to come on board the American aircraft carrier USS Dwight D. Eisenhower as a guest and have the freedom of the ship. This was as a thank you for entertaining the troops. I said I would be honoured. This man was the chaplain of the Dwight D. Eisenhower which is a nuclear-powered aircraft carrier in the United States Navy.

The very next day the chaplain and I were on the boat that ferried the troops to and from the carrier to the shore. Chatting on the way over I found out he loved music and was a big Elvis fan too, so we got on great. As we were heading towards the aircraft carrier it was just an amazing sight to behold. When we started out from the shore looking at the Dwight D. Eisenhower from a distance it just did not look so big, in fact it looked about three inches long on the horizon, but as we got closer to this floating kingdom it was awesome.

I remember that as a child my family would go every year to the "Plymouth Navy Days" exhibition and that itself was a great experience, but this was just unreal. I was wearing a thin cream cotton two-piece suit and a t-shirt, so when we boarded the carrier. All on board could tell I was a civilian, but they did not know who I was. I noticed some looked as if they were wondering was I some sort of dignitary? One thing for sure, I certainly was not dressed for duty.

The chaplain said he had to see to something important and would I mind if I met him back at the boarding area in an hour. We shook hands and off I went. I started to walk through corridors and somehow made my way to the middle of the carrier where I saw missiles positioned up high against the wall and then I asked someone who informed me they were nuclear warheads. I never thought I would ever see one of those up close.

The whole area was buzzing with combat soldiers in camouflage, sailors in blue jeans and guys in cream shirts and trousers and a couple of these guys in cream had green combat jackets on; I guessed some of those fellas must have been fighter pilots. I then made my way through some more corridors realising this was starting to look like a labyrinth of thick metal doors and walls.

You had to get used to walking through these oval-shaped doors; trip up and you would certainly get an injury. I tried to be as careful as possible, but the excitement of the occasion was overpowering me a little until I came to yet another oval door. To the right of me was a hatch where you queued for your food which led to the canteen and one of the guys who looked like a cook said, 'Who's that fella?' then another guy who I think was another cook said 'Ain't you the guy that did that show last night?' 'Yep that's me', I said. They both shook my hand. 'You were good, buddy', said the second guy then I carried on with my unguided tour to wherever I was going to end up next, which happened to be an amusement arcade.

I could not believe it, this place was brilliant. I took a little tour around this mini Las Vegas, which then led onto a small shopping mall. I realised this was a floating America, a home from home for the crew. I carried on walking through more corridors and I could not stop laughing because I was saying 'Hi' to one and all that passed me, not even asking for directions. I was just a lost rock 'n' roll singer from the UK roaming through a maze of corridors aboard a U.S. aircraft carrier – and I was loving it.

The next place I ended up in, all the guys were dressed in cream uniforms and sitting in a room where it looked like a meeting was going to take place. They all smiled, and one said, 'Are you lost', I replied 'Not really, I was told to look around the carrier by the chaplain and I'm now trying to find my way on deck'. He got up then showed me a door saying, 'Through there and just keep going up and you'll get there'. I thanked him and said good luck to all the other guys in the room, followed the man's instructions and somehow made it onto the deck.

Now for some reason what always fascinated me about aircraft carriers was how the deck at the front dipped down and I always wanted to look down it. So as you do, I started walking towards the front of the carrier and just kept going until I came to the bit which started to dip; it was about 30 feet to the edge. I stood there motionless and looked out over the sea into the Persian Gulf, soaking in exactly where I was. What became apparent to me, although I was fulfilling a dream come true, was I wasn't going to take another step forward. Knowing my luck I might trip up and roll off the end. Anyway, I had lived an experience which no one in their wildest dreams could ever believe they would really do.

As I turned to walk back, a tall broad man stood before me dressed in cream uniform, with a cream baseball cap. 'Oh, hello sir', I said, then in a low voice he replied, 'Are you the guy that entertained my boys?' 'Yes, I am sir', (oh dear I thought, this is the ruddy captain! He probably looked out of the control tower that overlooks the deck, thinking who the hell is that guy in the white suit who looks like he is just about to walk off the edge of my carrier?). He held out his hand and I shook it then he said, 'That was very kind of you, entertaining the troops. Enjoy your look around the carrier', 'Thank you sir', I replied and off he went, and as fairy tale as this might sound - it really happened! Me, Johnny Earl, meeting the Captain!

I then went about my business with my throw-away Kodak camera and took photos on deck with some of the crew. I especially enjoyed hanging out of the helicopters... well, it's rock 'n' roll isn't it!

I then made my way back to my embarking place where the chaplain was waiting with a big smile on his face (I think he had most probably been informed that I had met with the captain). 'How did you like your tour Johnny?' I said, 'I couldn't have enjoyed it more or met a better bunch of guys. It was like Star Trek for real, and I can't thank you enough.' He shook my hand and then I boarded the transport boat that took me back to shore.

I sat and just watched all the way back to shore the magnificence of the Dwight D. Eisenhower as the sun silhouetted this enchanting vessel on the skyline until I arrived back at shore where once again it became only three inches long on the horizon.

After it was all over and I had returned home to Ruislip Manor in West London, I was in the kitchen making a cup of tea and I knew Tom (Me London Daddy) had served in the Green Jackets and was very proud of his army years. So as I was making the tea I started explaining my personal tour of the USS Dwight D. Eisenhower and how I was left unaccompanied and allowed to personally tour the vessel, and to top it all off I even met the captain on the edge of the deck. I said, 'You know Tom, the bit that dips down at the end of the flight deck?' Tom just laughed and said, 'Two sugars please John'.

I suppose it is a bit hard to believe especially by someone who has been in the forces, so I said no more about my aircraft carrier experience for a minute or two and when we finished our cup of tea I reached into my coat pocket, held out my hand.... 'Oh, and by the way Tom here's the photos'. He could not believe his eyes. 'Unbelievable', he said 'You might not know it John but even dignitaries and politicians will not get the freedom of the ship, let alone a ruddy aircraft carrier. You got to give it to the Americans for their kindness, the British would never have treated you so well!' but then again Tom wasn't to know - I was living the blue suede dream!

SRI LANKA

May 1994 and I had a four-week tour of Sri Lanka which my manager at the time, Kevin Allen, had negotiated with a long-time friend and musician/promoter, Peter Tobit. Peter was taking a lot of UK acts to Dubai as well as Sri Lanka and Abu Dhabi. I had already toured and had a bit of success in Dubai, so it was a lot easier for Peter to promote me in Sri Lanka with all the positive press I had acquired. To be honest, being a manager was taking its toll with Kevin and any thoughts of it being a colourful life had started fading. As we both now had a few years entertainment experience under our belts one thing became very apparent: It is not easy being a manager. On many occasions now Kevin was under a lot of stress – it was not unusual for him to have one cigarette in the ashtray while having another one on the go in his hand, he needed a well deserved break and if it didn't happen soon the strains were seriously going to take their toll.

Let's not forget that Kevin, as well as taking on the mantle of being a manager, was also a long established disc jockey. He pressed Peter to try and get him on a little tour to Sri Lanka and he would charge very little wages as he knew Peter could get sponsors for the flights and hotels. He kept on so much that in the end Peter gave in and Kevin Allen the DJ was now going to spin the vinyl wax on the shores of Sri Lanka. Although I was there for four weeks my first show was not until 8 days into my stay, so my first week's stay was going to be rehearsing with a local band who were all from Sri Lanka. Peter informed me they were renowned for being the best in town, so I just sent them a cassette of 20 songs that they had to learn parrot fashion. If the rehearsals went smoothly this meant I too could take a bit of a break.

All three of us packed our bags and were off to spread the DJ and singing gospel of rock 'n' roll. On arriving in Sri Lanka man it was hot! ..and I mean very hot! I had not felt heat like this since I was last in Dubai where it was 38 degrees. As we walked across the runway it was like sucking in the warm air out of a hair dryer. Coca Cola was my sponsor, which meant the biggest show on this tour was the Coca Cola private party which was going to be open air and was to be held in the capital city, Colombo. Peter, Kevin and myself travelled by taxi from the airport to Colombo and Kevin was now starting to relax for the first time in months – and why not. A lovely free holiday, not too much work for him to do, so happiness was all that was crossing his mind – although I knew some big performances lay ahead of me.

The taxi drove right to the Centre of Colombo and I do not think I have ever seen so much congestion in my life, this was worse than Piccadilly Circus before congestion charges were introduced. In rush hour we came to a huge roundabout that had massive banners displayed all the way around it with the words in big bold block capitals 'KEVIN ALLEN BIG, LONDON'S TOP WEST END DJ APPEARING LIVE'. I looked at Pete and thought uh oh, is that who I think it is? Kevin said, 'Who the hell is that?' Pete replied, 'It's you', Kevin said 'I told you Pete I am here on a small holiday, what's going on?' Pete quite loudly said 'You kept on and on at me for a holiday and I sorted it for you so stop moaning'.

We drove on through the city passing more and more 'Kevin Allen Big,' banners and posters. I did not know whether to laugh or cry for poor old Kevin as one thing became very apparent, as far as Sri Lanka was concerned the top DJ in the world had just arrived - the one and only 'Kevin Allen Big' oh yes, he was in it now right up to his DJ deck! We got to the hotel and the staff had come out to greet us and stood in two lines creating an aisle, then Pete turned and said to me 'That's for you Johnny', I was quite shocked, having never been greeted like this before and as I passed through, the ladies on either side stepped forward one at a time to put lots of leis of flowers over my head. By the time I reached the front doors I could not really see properly, but the gesture was lovely –and this was just a taster of how lovely the Sri Lankan people are.

We each had our own double room and were now very tired so after checking in we all agreed to meet in the restaurant for a bite to eat before a much-needed good night's sleep. I got to the restaurant first then Peter joined me a couple of minutes later. All of a sudden like a bowling ball being thrown down an alley, Kevin came hurtling through the restaurant doors out of breath and came to the table exclaiming 'I have just had a death threat and I am not joking'. Kevin looked like he had just put his fingers into a plug socket and got a severe shock. 'Calm down, calm down', Peter told him and plied Kevin with a couple of scotch and cokes which did bring Kevin's blood pressure down a bit. 'Kevin relax and slowly tell me what happened', I said to him. Kevin took a deep breath, 'The phone rang, and I thought it must be one of you guys and a man said 'Is this Kevin Allen Big? I realized he meant me, so I said yes, he carried on 'so you are London's biggest DJ, well I'm telling you now my friend you are not even going to perform your first show, I'm speaking to a dead man'. He then slammed down the phone and he did not sound like he was joking'.

Peter interjected 'Look Kevin, it is just like back in London, we are all new kids on the block and we are on their turf; they just think we are muscling in'. I tried to calm Kevin and told him 'I'm glad I'm a singer and not a DJ'.

This was maybe not the best time to bring that to his attention as back in the UK we were hearing a lot about the Sri Lankan troubles involving the Tamil Tigers, with bombings and shootings. Us coming to this foreign land during these turbulent times, well we did not know what to think, so we just kept our wits about us. Kevin calmed down after another couple of drinks, put his hands behind his head 'Oh well at least tomorrow I can spend the day around the pool'. 'I'm afraid that's not possible', said Peter 'You have got a press call in the morning; nothing mad just a couple of reporters, and then you can take the rest of the day off'. I told Kevin I would come along for moral support more than anything else and then we all retired for a good night's sleep.

The next morning around the breakfast table laid before us was one of the biggest tabloids in Sri Lanka with Kevin's face on the front advertising his press meeting, saying should anybody want to meet and greet him he would be at such and such rooms and to be there at 11am (Not To Be Missed). I reassured Kevin, 'Now that you are on the front page and everybody knows where you are going to be at 11am today, this is where you will most probably get bumped off'. Pete said to me 'That's enough John', I apologized but I just couldn't help myself. Kevin went back to his room to collect his box of vinyl records for his first and hopefully not last press call. We all made our way to the designated hotel to meet the press. Arriving, Kevin was a little nervous as he has never had a couple of people interviewing him regarding his DJ career, so it was a first for him.

We came to two big double doors which was the entrance to the function room, Peter opened one side and I the other - BAM * SOCK * POW * Holy mackerel! The room was jam packed solid, wall-to-wall reporters, photographers, even a TV crew had turned up and as Kevin walked through the doors with his box of vinyl in hand everyone gave him a round of applause – "Kevin Allen Big" was now in the house! Then a guy made his way to Peter who was obviously the man who had booked and set everything up for the 'Kevin Allen Big show'. He gave Peter a big man hug and then Kevin got one as well. This guy was gleaming with happiness especially with the impressive turn out for this momentous occasion. Kevin then got ushered up to the DJ booth which in 1994 was a typical disco glass case surround, so in walked Kevin (a cloak of silence enveloped the room, you could feel the anticipation). All photographers had cameras at the ready for the perfect shot, even the film crew were rolling. Standing at Kevin's side was the hotels personal in-house DJ who was watching Kevin's every move and he had the biggest smile I ever saw on a person. You could tell he was just blown away to be standing next to the man himself – the hottest news in Sri Lanka for years!

The room was now so quiet that all you could hear was Kevin's every move. He pulled out an album, swivelled it in his fingers and raised it to his mouth. The in-house DJ gasped, thinking something special was going to happen but realized Kevin was only blowing away any unwanted dust, then like everyone else watched as Kevin placed the album slowly on to the deck. Kevin then leaned forward and said into the microphone 'The first song I would like to play everyone is Bill Haley's *Rock around the Clock'*, he slowly but very precisely lifted the needle onto the record and then stood there motionless looking at all before him. 'One two three o'clock four o'clock rock' blasted from the speakers. Peter's Sri Lankan partner who put all this together looked at Pete and said, 'Very funny, now get on with the real show'. Pete replied, 'What do you mean the real show?' Peter's partner said, 'You know what we have all come to see - London's West End, Number One DJ Rapper - anyone can do what he's just done!' Don't ask me why but I could swear at that very moment - Peter and I were in suspended animation where time had just stood still, and all I could hear was that stabbing piercing noise from the film *"Psycho"*. I now realised what the hysteria was all about.

Rap was the latest worldwide music phenomenon and if you were not from New York you could get away with being a rap DJ from London. The lead balloon had landed, all present gazed at each other, then like watching a silent movie, not a sound. The press did not hang around, they started leaving in their droves along with the photographers to the sound of 'When the clock strikes twelve we'll do our dance, gonna rock around the clock again'.

A lot of disgruntled hotel and club owners who had booked 'The Kevin Allen Big show' started making their way to Peter and his Sri Lankan partner 'What's going on?' was shouted by all and by the time the tones of *'Rock around the Clock'* had finished so nearly was Kevin! There was a bit of pushing and shoving, not a good start to the Sri Lankan campaign. Kevin had now rescued his records, left the DJ booth (and at this point I noticed the in house DJ hastily locking the booth door behind Kevin as he left), he made his way to Peter and the promoter saying 'Is there a problem?' to which one angry club owner said 'I have sold out for two nights and they are expecting the best rapping DJ in the world', Kevin not totally understanding what has just gone on said to the guy 'Oh you were expecting a rap DJ - I don't do that'. 'I can see that', he shouted 'My 9 year old son can do what you have just done', a bit more scuffling ensued.

The outcome to this total cock up was Kevin (who did not have an MC Hammer tune to his name) was now to appear at all his bookings only to introduce the songs and use his talking skills to their fullest and let the in-house rapping DJ use all his skills to rap away to his heart's content. Luckily Kevin managed to blag the whole 'Kevin Allen Big Roadshow' and the good news was - the hit man never turned up. The bad news was not many newspaper reviews but at least Kevin lived to tell the tale.

A week passed, and Kevin's tour was over and now the day had come for my press and media call... It was my turn to walk through the double doors. Peter did the introduction 'Ladies and gentlemen and members of the press, Mr. Johnny Earl'. Like Kevin I now had rapturous applause along with cheers and I am sure a few of them were thinking isn't that the guy we saw last week following 'Kevin Allen Big' into the room at his press call, except this time it does what it says on the tin, with all the major press you could think of in attendance. Peter, Kevin and myself sat at the head of the room behind a twelve-foot table, with bottles of water and bowls of fresh fruit before us and no sooner had we got settled, I realized I was a bit luckier than Kevin as everyone was given all the Johnny Earl information in a full press kit that had everything about my career, so they were all clued up.

The first question was arrowed straight at me by a lady reporter, I'm so and so from the whatever newspaper she represented and twenty or, so photographers just started clicking away at the same time as she stood up 'Mr. Earl what is your opinion on plastic surgery?' I did not have a clue how to answer at first, and then she said, 'Like Michael Jackson, the King of Pop, do you think it's morally right and okay?' I replied, 'Luckily I have not had any yet', the audience laughed, 'What Michael Jackson decides to do with himself is entirely up to him'. 'Thank you', she replied. Oh well I thought, get ready for anything here and the next question 'Mr. Earl, will you be performing the Elvis song *Judy*?' Luckily the day before I had noticed in the paper Elvis was number one in the Sri Lankan charts with this song and although it was not in my set list before it was now. 'Of course, I will be performing *Judy*, it would be silly not to perform the countries number one hit record', and I got rapturous applause and a little bit of shrieking thrown in as well which was unusual from members of the press.

I turned to Kevin and Peter and softly said 'That's another one for the band to learn'. Talk about a stroke of luck, Elvis was number one in the charts and they have the guy performing who is working and touring Europe with Elvis's real backing band, and it was all there in their press kit. When a situation works in your favour like this everything happens at a feverish rate. All the radio stations start going berserk plugging you, shouting from the rooftops that you are in town, and a press and media frenzy is exactly what followed. The next day at the breakfast table Kevin, Peter and I could not believe it, I was in every tabloid, I mean full pages and the other piece of good news, all the shows were now sold out.

I laughed and told them both 'I bet there has not been a music story as big as this since Kevin Allen Big'. Now it was Kevin's last day here, so around the hotel pool Kevin and I went as Peter was sorting things out regarding my tour and also, he had other UK acts that would be soon flying over, so he was having a few meetings with his Sri Lankan partner. I knew this whole 'Kevin Allen Big' charade was a bridge too far for Kevin, but I actually noticed that in a space of a week, his hair had turned grey. I thought to myself I can remember when we arrived roughly a week ago, it was jet black. The worrying thing about this was I knew he was not using hair dye. Little did I know Kevin was on the brink of a nervous breakdown and suddenly sitting there in front of me he started to cry. I had never seen him as bad as this before, so I knew something was seriously wrong. I said, 'Come on mate, let's forget the manager/singer relationship, what's up?' I was thinking to myself 'The Kevin Allen Big Tour' had finally hit home or is it something bigger that was about to surface. Kevin looked at me 'You will not understand, I'm in big trouble'.

"Johnny Earle and All The Kings Men"

Top Row Left to Right: Scotty Moore, Gordon Stoker, Neal Matthews Jnr., Duane West, Ray Walker & Carl Perkins.
Bottom Row Left to Right: Johnny Earle & D. J. Fontana.

Johnny Earle Information c/o Kevin Allen
14 Margaret Cassidy House, 485 Bath Road, Longford, Middlesex UB7 OET.   Telephone / Fax No: 081-759 3816

34 With All the King's Men – an original autographed publicity photo for the 1991 tour

35 Publicity photo of Jordanaires

36 Elvis with the Jordanaires and Millie Kirkham
37 Jordanaires with Ringo Star among others
38 Jordanaires with Ricky Nelson

KEVIN ALLEN & HENRY SELLERS PRESENT

'THE GOOD ROCKIN' TONITE' TOUR

ST★RRING "MR ROCK 'N' ROLL"

JOHNNY EARL

and ELVIS PRESLEY'S LEGENDARY GROUP

The JORDANAIRES

plus from the U.S.A.

JOHNNY PRESTON

(RUNNING BEAR • CRADLE OF LOVE)

PLEASE SEE REVERSE FOR DATES & VENUES

39 Poster from the Good Rockin' Tonite Tour

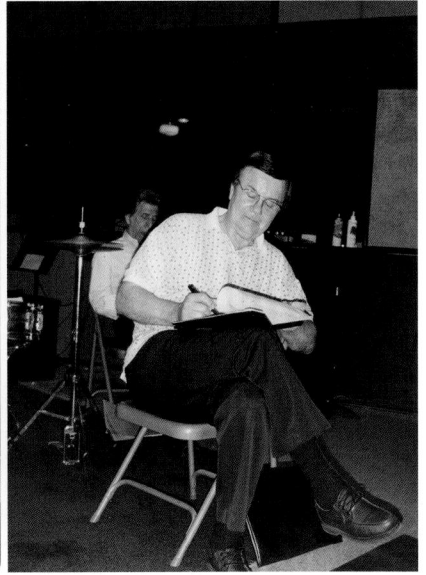

40 With the Jordanaires

41-42 With Neal Mathews Jr in Nashville, working on some song writing

43 Me and Scotty performing live, The Plaza, Exeter, August 26 1992

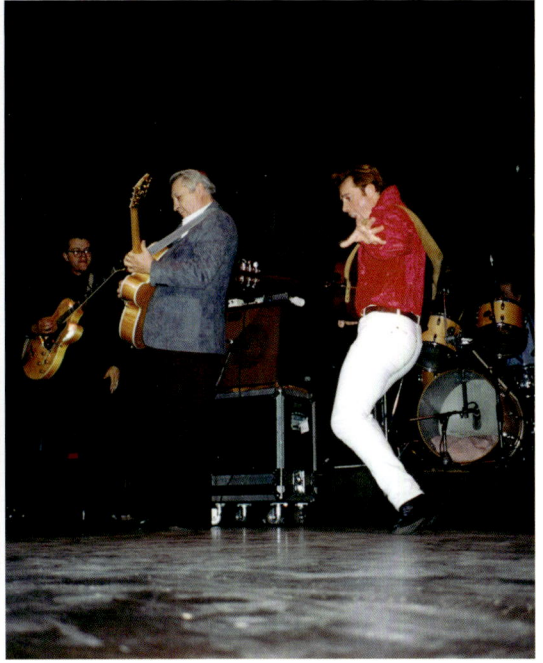

44-47 Performing live, August 1992

48 Myself and D.J. Fontana

49 D.J. Fontana

50 D.J. pointing at Scotty asking me "How come he's having a break?"

51 Scotty, D.J., Neal Mathews Jr and myself having our very own Sun Sessions

52 D.J. with Ray Walker

your Friend
Carl Perkins   Johnny Earl   Scotty Moore

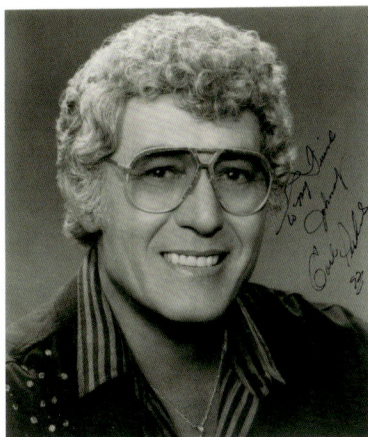

53   Carl Perkins and Scotty Moore signed photo
54   The front and back cover of the Jerry Lee Lewis tour brochure
55   Signed photo, Carl Perkins

56-59 Aircraft carrier USS Dwight D. Eisenhower
60 Me with the Captain on the flight deck

61-66 On board the ship and meeting the crew

63 Myself and the Chaplain who invited me to have freedom of the ship

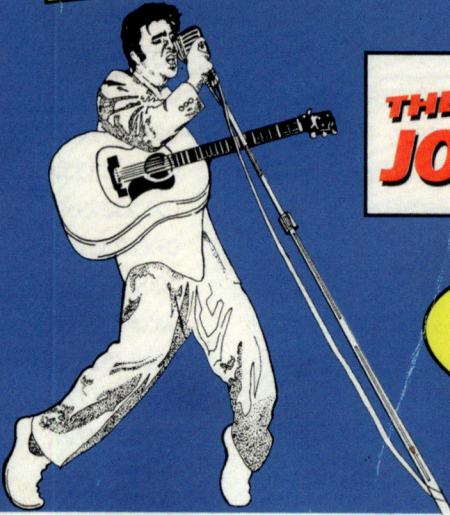

Concert flyer for the Wembley concert

Now I have always been the type of person to sort things out here and now. Especially on big problems, I like to sort them and move on. I said, 'Look Kevin, I do not care how mammoth the problem is, tell me and we will sort it one way or another'. In a tearful voice, he stuttered the words 'Peter has booked the boxing legend Henry Cooper through me, to appear and talk at a big business dinner dance in Dubai. He has given me the deposit and I have spent it', he then broke down. I put my arm around him - one side of me was saying throw him in the pool, the other (which did get the better of me) made me tell him 'Kevin this will be sorted I promise you'. Peter arrived, took one look at Kevin and said, 'Are you alright Kevin?' I interjected and called for an immediate meeting in my room.

At the poolside, Kevin and I quickly dressed and off we all went to my room. Peter sat in a one-person arm chair, I sat on the corner of the bed, and Kevin sat on the other side of the room on a chair next to a writing table. He wanted his own space (or I think not to be too close to Peter when giving him the bad news). Pete could not wait any longer; he said, 'Right what's up?' I looked at Kevin 'You had better tell him'. A grey looking Kevin said, 'The money you gave me Pete for the deposit for Henry Cooper, which has to be in his bank account by tomorrow or he's not coming, I have spent it'. Pete now very straight faced said 'I've paid you Kevin and I'm afraid you'll just have to sort it, I don't care how you do it, but Henry Cooper will be on that plane Tuesday morning'. Kevin just broke down again. No jokes or happy times were to be had here now, Pete looked at me and shrugged his shoulders.

At that point I knew a couple of people I could turn to, but only one man who might be a bit more understanding in the circumstances and that was my long-time friend Tom Keane – who is more famously known today for being the owner of Chiswick Auction House and being on the rostrum. He is a familiar face on such programmes as "Cash in the Attic", "Dickenson's Real Deal", "Flog It" and "Bargain Hunt" and as I was aiming in his direction for financial aid, a little bell rang in my mind, a kind of boxing bell, as I knew very well Tom was also a handy boxer. The silence in the room was deafening. I looked at a worn-down Kevin and realised Pete was in no way going to financially sort out Kevin's situation so I broke the silence 'Kevin I am going to ring Tom and if he does sort this out and you do not pay him back you know he is going to take my car don't you, but there it is, we all have to make sacrifices'. As I was telling Kevin I thought I can't believe it, my lovely recently bought red BMW is about to be pawned, but then again, I have always been a bit of a softy and I know a lot of people would not have helped Kevin in this situation. To be fair though he had done his best as a manager up to date, so the call was made.

As I sat there, phone to my ear, Tom got both barrels of the situation and I recall his words 'John you're a good bloke and we go back a long way, I suppose Kevin's sitting next to you', 'Yes', I replied. Tom carried on 'I'm lending you the money, not him', it was now sorted, and all was understood that when I returned back to London, I was allowed one days jetlag then the day after that I either left the money or my car with good old Tom. Tom being the honourable guy he was, the very next day paid the deposit for Henry Cooper. (I must at this point fast forward four weeks). Driving to Tom's house Kevin had Tom's money in his hand, he paused and thought for a second and said to me 'Do you think Tom will take half now and wait for the other half and I'll pay him in a couple of weeks?' I will not tell you word for word what I said but be assured Tom got all his money. Back to the hotel room... now Tom had saved the day, which enabled Kevin to stop breaking down, Peter ordered a big drink from room service and I carried on getting ready for my tour.

My tour of Sri Lanka consisted of three hotel performances and the main performance – that big outdoor corporate performance for Coca Cola. One of the hotel performances was in a destination called Bentota Beach and the hotel had done a good job with their enthusiasm for promoting my tour and had made twelve life size cardboard cut-outs of me which were placed leading up to the stage that I was to perform on. I quickly noticed that something was not right with these cut-outs, then it hit me right between the eyes, all the heads were on the wrong way, I mean the life size picture of me was taken from a live stage shot, where my body moved to the right, but somehow my head was turned fully around the other way, very odd is all I can say.

It did come back to haunt me about ten years later. I was performing at a show in South Harrow in West London and a lady came back stage for an autograph and while I was signing her album she said, 'Johnny have you ever performed in Sri Lanka?' 'Why do you ask?' I said, 'Well we have just come back from our honeymoon and at the hotel we stayed at they had all these life size cut outs of you with the heads on the wrong way'. 'How strange is that!' I replied.

The other hotels shows were also great fun to perform at. One was in

Kandy, the second largest city after Colombo. The hotel had an interior where all the rooms had their doors facing to the inside, so when anybody left their rooms anyone in the lobby or at the reception desk could look up even while seated or waiting on the ground floor and watch you make your way to floor level. That night the ground floor was where the performance was to be held; in the middle was a spectacular buffet. You would not have eaten better at one of King Henry VIII's banquets, the beautiful displays of peacocks and other exotic birds made from fruit and vegetables, it was amazing.

I had rehearsed in the afternoon with the band and we were due to perform at 9.00pm, so with sound checks finished at 4pm we all had time to rest. All the people coming to the buffet had come for the show and on the posters, it mentioned Sri Lanka's number one song in the charts, *"Judy"*, was going to be performed, so all was set for a good night's show, or so I thought. Most of the audience had arrived for 7pm and all was going good. I was resting on my bed (I never really get dressed ready for a show until 30 minutes or so before the beginning of any performance), and as tonight was mainly an Elvis set the performance started with the Elvis 70's intro *"Also Sprach Zarathustra"* better known as the *2001* theme tune and as any Elvis fan will know this starts with a rumble followed by a timpani drum in between, so I'm lying there with my costume hanging on the wardrobe door, I looked over at the clock, it said 8.00pm, that's good I thought, I have an hour to stage and maybe I'll start me quiff. I sat on the stool in front of the mirror and at first, I thought I was hearing things, but I could have sworn I heard the drum intro theme for *2001*. I thought no more of it and then I heard a guitar join in which to me sounded like the rumble guitar noise that was sounding even more like the *2001* theme. Then I heard a piano sound, I glanced at the clock, 8.04pm, so I got up, put on my robe, checked the clock again, then my watch and went out to the balcony.

I looked over the balcony, down to the buffet and stage area, to see four members of the 7-piece band performing the *2001* intro. I then noticed another musician running down the corridor, guitar in hand and I'm standing there in a bath robe. I ran back inside my room, dressed as quickly as I could, ran back out to the balcony where I noticed the female backing vocalists legging it down the corridor. I composed myself, walked down the corridor to the lift, stepped inside and pressed the button for the ground floor. 'Ping' I arrived at the ground floor, the lift doors opened, and I was confronted with people standing orderly in line ready to enjoy the lovely buffet and all the goodies spread before them, and of course the band are now in full swing blasting away with the 2001 intro. Now was the time for being professional and sorting out why there had been a cock up with the show starting 45 minutes early with no warning? Thankfully the previous week's laborious rehearsals had paid off and the show was brilliant, especially when I told the crowd I had just finished singing and touring with Elvis's band and would now be performing Sri Lanka's number one hit *"Judy"*. That just brought the house down and although everyone was eating as well as standing in a line through most of the show, a standing ovation was the end result.

I asked for a meeting straight after the show with all band members in my room and I was now Mr. Mannering from Dads Army, so for my own amusement I lined them all up including the female vocalists and said, 'Right you horrible lot, can someone tell me what the hell went wrong?' Now they all looked at one another shocked, because up until now I was Mr. Nice Guy who never went anywhere without a smile 'UNTIL NOW'! I listened to all the 'It was nothing to do with me' explanations, I questioned them one by one and finally I got to the bottom of the whole shambolic episode. The drummer who was using electronic drums (which sounded not too bad actually) told me 'Johnny I wanted to be very professional and to make sure my drums were working okay for the upcoming performance. I rehearsed the intro to the show but I did not realize the sound engineer had left the sound fully up and he was nowhere to be seen. I did not want to touch his mixing desk so when I tested my drums by doing the *2001* intro, before I knew it, the bass player ran to the stage and joined in, then the keyboard player came to the stage and he joined in, and I thought they wanted to check their sound as well'. I looked at the bass player and the keyboard player, then they both said to me 'We thought he was starting the show, so to be professional we joined in and before we knew it all the other band members were on stage'. 'Yes', I exclaimed 'and I was in my bath robe watching you all from the balcony up here with a feeling of shall I just jump and end it all now'.

Everybody laughed and so did I, so for the rest of the tour I made everybody promise me after sound checks not to return to the stage until the scheduled start of the show. In any situation like this it is always better to keep everyone happy, there is nothing worse than a discontented band.

One amazing thing that happened after the show which I will never forget: An elderly man walked with his wife to the stage, holding her hand and said 'I am afraid my wife is a little bit star-struck', I replied 'That's okay my friend, you can talk to me anytime, remember we are all here to enjoy ourselves', to which his wife held out her hand, holding an autograph book, looked at me and said 'All my life I have been waiting for this moment and I must tell you, it is an honour and a pleasure to meet you'. She gazed into her husband's eyes, gave the loveliest smile to him – it must be the best I have ever seen a woman give – she looked back at me still smiling and said, 'I never thought I would live to see the day I would actually get to meet Elvis Presley'. I looked at the pair of them and realized they actually thought I was Elvis Presley, so what do I do... sign her autograph book Johnny or Elvis. I kind of squiggled it so you couldn't really tell, but the euphoria and happiness that shone through the pair of them, I certainly wasn't going to shatter their dreams.

My stay in Kandy was wonderful. The very next day there was a wedding taking place and the dancers in their costumes with their fabulous bright colours were a sight to see. I then took a trip on the river followed by a trip to the elephant orphanage at Pinnawala, where I got to sit on one and go for a little ride, a pleasant day's fun. While I was there I noticed a very disturbed looking elephant swaying from side to side. I asked his handler what was up with him and was informed that a couple of days earlier he accidentally walked backwards and trampled his owner to death and basically the elephant was so upset with mourning the loss of his owner he would probably never get over it. A sad situation, but it taught me one thing: Think twice before walking behind an elephant.

My final show in Sri Lanka was to be in the capital city Colombo, a big open-air concert for one of the world's biggest companies Coca Cola, but before the performance I was to appear on a radio show. The phone lines were jammed and after the show, which ended up being around two hours, the stations owner came to the DJ booth really excited, introduced himself, shook my hand and asked me if I would seriously consider having my own show starting the following week. I realised he was serious, but I apologized and told him how busy my career was at the time.

I mean I was in the middle of a worldwide recording and gigging career, no time for staying in one place for a length of time, but boy did I think about that a hundred times over for the rest of my stay. I collected a cassette recording of the show as Kevin and I always made sure as often as possible to record and keep all TV and radio shows for prosperity.

So, the finale of my touring was upon me, the big Coca Cola open air event. The whole stage was made up to look like the front of Elvis's home, Graceland. The show started about 8.30pm, I was back stage at 7pm, the band had all set up and the DJ asked did I have anything to play over his sound system before the show starts as background music, so I suggested using the cassette of the radio show I had been interviewed on that afternoon as it went down so well with all the listeners and it would get the crowd in the right spirit. He loved the idea and put the two hour show straight on.

Hundreds of people flocked to this open-air event. There were massive hot air balloons of coke bottles everywhere as well as giant cardboard cut-outs – Coca Cola were not sparing any expense. Around twenty minutes later I hear a big argument just outside my makeshift dressing room, and then the promoter came running into my room shouting, 'You have done it on purpose', 'What on earth do you mean?' I said, he replied 'look, look at the crowd, you have ruined the show', 'Just slow down', I said, he then drew back a curtain that faced the audience and I could see that everybody was looking very angry and shouting at one another. 'What on earth has caused that?' I asked the promoter. He exclaimed 'The DJ told me you gave him that cassette to play', 'That's right', I said 'Well did you know it's full of Pepsi ads and this is a Coca Cola event and all we are being told through the speakers is that Pepsi is the best drink in the world'. 'Oh sh**' I said, it never crossed my mind that the advertisements were also recorded on my interview, this was a genuine mistake.

I argued my innocence very well and calmed the promoter down. I then asked for a radio mic backstage, so the promoter could talk, and he quietened the audience down handed the mic to me then I publicly apologized and briefly explained the unfortunate mishap. I had a quick thought and exclaimed over the mic 'Anyway I have a confession to make - I can't stand Pepsi but I love Coke'! The biggest uproar, cheering and applause could be heard and the whole situation took a u-turn, and this led to the show being a huge success. The irony of it was that a few years later, I would be the Elvis Presley singing voice for the Pepsi ad campaign throughout the U.S.A.

I loved my Sri Lankan tour. I even got to go to a lot of antique shops which had British Empire artefacts from the late 1800's. Coins, medals, uniforms along with thousands and thousands of photos from those Queen Victoria years. I spent hours looking around these little antique shops that mostly were hidden down back streets. I also noticed a lot of the taxis were original P.A. Cresta's and Ford Consuls and Humber's, good old British rock 'n' roll cars, and because the weather is always mostly dry and sunny in Sri Lanka they were in great condition, a bit like the original American 1950's cars you see in Cuba. But there was another side to Sri Lanka that is hard to put to the back of one's mind and of course it's the poverty - and the scale of it.

I had never before with my own eyes seen old ladies crawling and pushing themselves along the streets, unable to walk, begging for food, and starving children begging. To summarise the unfortunate side of this beautiful country, as I was leaving in a taxi to return to the airport, the taxi went through a bridge in the countryside which took about ten seconds to pass through and I noticed all these eyes looking at me as we passed through. I asked the taxi driver who they were, and he replied, 'They are the bridge people'. He told me 'They live here under the bridge and then go out in the fields to eat and to go to the toilet, and then return to reside back under the bridge'. I thought long and hard about the existence of these bridge people and by the time I boarded the plane I was a changed person. Things of value, money and possessions I had always longed for, were no longer important to me.

My Sri Lankan experience had humbled me and from that day to this I live very simply, take nothing for granted and a lot of the moaning and groaning I hear day in and day out from people I meet, I would love to take them and show them the existence of the bridge people. Maybe then they too would realise what having nothing really means.

I would like to return to this jewel of a country with all its beauty and colours, with all the lovely friendly people in the future. To top it all, in my mind any country having Elvis as their number one artist like Sri Lanka did when I visited, well that was just destiny beyond any blue suede dream.

HOLLAND

Let's put some orange on the Union Jack!

Do not ask me why, but I found with all my visits to this beautiful country, the majority of the Dutch people love us Brits and welcome us with open arms. If you are British and do not like Holland or the Dutch people then your next trip should be a one-way ticket to Mars ..or just stay at home, because I found very little to dislike about the Dutch.

Up until 1989 the record releases in my career were one 45rpm single and one 12-inch album on our own record label "Pride of Devon" along with a few cassettes to sell at the shows. We were very pleased that the Dutch record company "Rockhouse Records" (who were well known throughout Europe and owned by a nice couple, Burt & Frances Rockhuizen), wanted myself and The Jordanaires to be released on their label to coincide with a tour of Holland which they and Kevin my manager had put together.

There were to be two vinyl album releases; the first being *"The Presley Style - Pocketful of Memories"* and the second *"Johnny Earl & The Jordanaires - My Way"*. As with any album release of the day a 45rpm single would also be released from the album. *"Pocketful of Rainbows"* was the single from the first release and *"The Girl of My Best Friend"* from the second. I was informed that *"Pocketful of Rainbows"* reached the number one spot in the Dutch charts. I was to achieve the number one spot twice in my career, this was the first time with me as the performer and the other time was with the soccer world cup song *"Gloryland"* as a writer. Holland was our first European tour with The Jordanaires, so this major tour was really the first experience for Kevin and me at the higher level of the music business and what a start we had.

Like any tour, it had its teething problems: On the very first day all the musicians, the Jordanaires, Kevin and I with all the Rockhouse record company people, were sitting in the dining room of the hotel that we were staying at. Everybody was happy and laughing, but after 15 minutes or so bellies were a rumbling and I noticed Burt Rockhouse looked over to Kevin and said, 'What are you all waiting for, aren't you going to order something to eat?' Kevin replied, 'I don't know how you want us to order, have you sorted out a set meal or can we order anything we want, including drinks?' Burt replied, 'I do not care what you order because I'm not paying for it'. Kevin exclaimed 'Of course you are, you can't let everyone starve can you, and it's you putting on the tour'.

The silence was once again deafening, no one was going to say anything, only spectate ...and this was going to be pistols at dawn between Burt and Kevin. Burt laughed then said, 'You don't think I'm going to supply meals for 20 people for 10 days, do you?' This is where I intervened 'Okay guys, you two go outside and sort it all out then let us know what we are all doing', which they did, while everybody waited with tummy rumbling anticipation to see whether they were going to get fed or not. Thankfully it was sorted out and this was to be one of the many lessons learned on the foreign touring front.

I met my future Dutch girlfriend Nicole on this tour. It very soon came to my attention how pretty and a lot of fun Dutch women can be. The tours of Holland were excellent with the attendances at the shows being mostly a sell-out. There was always a standing ovation after every performance, you could tell the Dutch loved Elvis and their rock 'n' roll. I appeared on Dutch national TV twice and all the national press covered the tour. On a fabulous live radio show in Amsterdam, that was actually held next to the historic replica ship 'The Amsterdam', the Jordanaires and I performed, singing live. It was on this tour to Holland that I met my lifelong friends from Germany, the Schroer family who I still visit in Germany today and it was also on this tour of Holland the friendship between The Jordanaires and me really bonded. I got to know each member really well which led to Neal Matthews and I writing songs together. On my next tour of Holland, I would encounter my next romance with a lovely girl called Petra that was to last for ten years!

Even today when I visit Holland whether on a business or pleasure basis I love every second I'm there. The food's great, and the people are wonderful. I have wonderful memories such as the last big show I performed on: It was with Elvis's army buddy Charlie Hodge, as well as the Jordanaires and Elvis's pianist and Imperials singing man - Shaun 'Sherrill' Nielson. This performance was one of my most memorable stage appearances. The main stage had another piece in the centre that jutted into the audience, about 50 feet. Charlie Hodge and I went right to the end of this stage, we duetted to the song *"I Will Be Home Again"* which was also the first song Charlie performed as a duet with the King. This was released on the 1960 album, *Elvis Is Back*.

I know I have certainly not finished my Dutch excursions or connections as I recently performed a show in Bad Nauheim in Germany, celebrating Elvis's 80th birthday with a Dutch band who were brilliant in backing me, called 'The Explosion Rockets'. We actually performed in the same hall where Elvis celebrated his 25th birthday during his army service. What a brilliant night.

If I have to be very honest, I have yet to see a pair of blue suede clogs, but I would not put anything past the Dutch - ik hou van jullie allemaal - ik kom terug!

SCOTLAND

The musical 'Forever Elvis' first took me to this beautiful part of the United Kingdom, and I loved Scotland and everybody I met, mainly because the one thing everybody had in common was their love of rock 'n' roll and especially Elvis. After all it is well known the King stopped off in Scotland on March 2nd, 1960 at Prestwick airport near Ayr on his way back to the U.S. during his army service.

My first show ever in Scotland was at His Majesty's theatre in Aberdeen with its 1,400 seats. It was awesome. I went to rehearsals in the afternoon and while standing on the stage I took in this amazing view looking out at this Roman Collosseum-styled auditorium, so big and grand, with glorious red velvet cushioned seats and gold embellished balconies and here am I standing on the biggest stage to date in my career. I felt free and excited because I thought, not long ago I was in a rockabilly band, and I had brilliant times, but never thought the day would come where I was going to perform on a stage as grand as this. I walked off the stage, up to the back of the theatre and turned around and gazed at the splendour before me. I thought to myself, this is my first show tonight in this grand surrounding. I looked straight ahead at the awesome size of the stage and to be honest I trembled a little, knowing I would be standing centre stage on my own ...yes just me and my acoustic guitar, performing the song *"My Happiness"*. 'That's it', I thought to myself, absolutely no mucking up, no bum chords, so off to the dressing room I went and rehearsed that song at least thirty times, for there was no room for mistakes, not tonight.

Later, that day I did my very first live radio show with 'North Sound Radio' which was to be a phone-in from the theatre, which worked very well as nobody knew of me, but a lot of people obviously listened to the interview because that night I got a grand welcome when I walked onto that stage. My first lesson learned properly on how important promotion is. That night the nerves worked in my favour. I have always had that 'there's no turning back now attitude' and being a little nervous was my high, and to top it all off at the end of the evening myself and all the cast received a standing ovation (and I can tell you the Scottish people are not the type to hold back on their affections especially when it comes to music). I knew from here on that being in this musical I was turning a new page in my career. 'Forever Elvis' returned, and toured Scotland a couple of times and a very memorable occasion was at the Pavilion Theatre in Glasgow.

One of the London musicians in the musical was a guy called Nick Bunker, who had a gentle persona about him, so he was on the hit list for having fun with. Just before the start of the show I went to his dressing room and I said, 'Nick nearly everybody in the show is predominantly English, I have had a chat with the producer and the director and they thought it would be a nice gesture if some of the band members wore a kilt on stage'. He looked at me a bit puzzled but saw I had a straight face and just as he was about to give me a good reason why he should NOT be chosen to wear a kilt, I said 'Pam's waiting for you in wardrobe so be quick as the show begins in twenty minutes'. Nick very slowly made his way to wardrobe where Pam, a lovely lady who was sort of a tour manager as well, she went along with the set up but did advise me, on my head be it should it all go horribly wrong. A couple of minutes later a quick succession of knocks thundered on my dressing room door. I opened it to see a rather pale faced Nick Bunker wearing the longest blue tartan kilt I had ever seen... from the mid-waist down he had the shape of one of Dr. Who's Daleks but clad in blue tartan and as the kilt was far too long for him! – He started to look like a Dalek that was melting at the bottom.

He looked at me with a rabbit in the headlight gaze and exclaimed 'You've got to be joking'. I reminded him of where we were and if they start throwing bottles and rocks because we have not made the effort then he would be to blame! I closed my door to the haunting sound of the tannoy speaker '10 minutes to stage everyone, 10 minutes to stage'. I waited for about a minute then made my way down the corridor to the stage, and as I passed Nick's dressing room, I quickly knocked while exclaiming 'On stage if you please', Nick came out with a guitar around his neck, shuffled his way down the corridor as best he could, murmuring 'This can't be happening', (as he had not really got the hang of wearing a far too long kilt yet). I turned and looked at him... he was exhibiting the same kind of motion like when wearing a sack doing the egg and spoon race! '5 minutes to stage, 5 minutes to stage', the tannoy exclaimed. We got to the side wing of the stage and Nick ambled his way to his amp, and plugged his guitar in.

Now the producer of the show appeared at the side of the stage where Nick had a fixed eye on him and me, as if to say I'm doing this under instruction with no involvement from myself. The producer, who had heard rumours about the prank that I was going to do, but never thought it would be put into action glared at Nick like a sergeant major who was just about to erupt. He took one look at Nick and in a loud shrieking whisper said, 'What the hell do you think you are doing?' I looked at the producer and said, 'I told him the audience are going to ruddy lynch us if they see him in that kilt'. Nick looked at me, swung his guitar off, grabbed the bottom of his kilt and road runnered it to his dressing room.

The producer looked at me as Nick dashed past and shook his head 'He had better be on stage when the curtain rises for your sake', a few moments later 'One minute to curtain rise', rang around the auditorium and yes, the curtain rose and all were present and correct on stage with not a kilt in sight!

The musical toured Aberdeen, Dundee, Falkirk, Glasgow, Ayr and Edinburgh and on one occasion the cast took the day off and we went to a distillery. It was a good job we did not have a show that evening as we all tried the scotch whisky, and let's put it this way, most of us retired when we merrily got back to the hotel.

Livingstone and Edinburgh were where I returned to in Scotland, this time with the Jordanaires and we flew there from London to Glasgow airport and took two taxis. The driver of our cab was ecstatic when he realized he was taxying the Jordanaires and said how much he loved Elvis and had all the records and just like any taxi driver he was thinking there was a strong possibility of a good tip. I'll never forget when we reached our hotels, we all got out of our taxis and Kevin my manager got out of the second taxi, he came up to our driver introduced himself as the manager of the tour and asked how much the fare was. The driver said £10.50p and Kevin looked at him straight in the eyes and said, 'How come you are 50p more expensive than my taxi?' That was it, I grabbed my bag from the boot of the car and so did Ray Walker and Neal Matthews and we left Kevin to haggle it out. I won't tell you what the taxi driver said to Kevin, especially as the driver came to understand there was definitely going to be no tip, as the extra 50p was becoming a big debate.

The shows with the Jordanaires were well received; all the major tabloids gave us good mentions and praised the shows. The show in Edinburgh was fabulous but that was to be the last time I performed live in Scotland. I made a friend of the Glasgow radio DJ Tom Bell, loved the sea breeze in Ayr, and most importantly I have to say a big thank you to all the Elvis and rock 'n' roll fans of Scotland for supporting the tours and treating us all so well. Who knows hopefully I'll return to enjoy another tour – you can get very used to haddock and poached eggs for breakfast.

IRELAND

Ireland, the land of music and the black stuff in that order. I was booked for two nights to perform with my band in Dublin at a venue called Break for The Border. One lesson I learned on this mini tour is when you are not a household name and people have never really heard of you and you perform mostly original songs that they have obviously never heard of either, it can be an uphill struggle, especially when the audience are a night club crowd looking for a party atmosphere and a good night out.

The first night's performance was met with a lukewarm reception from the audience to say the least, so pretty much straight after the show I had a one to one with the club owner, who agreed a change of set list was needed for the second night's performance. Basically, we were not the right act for his club, but a contract was to be lived up to by both parties so to be fair he did honour the Saturday night booking. For the following night's show, the band and I threw in a lot of standards that we thought the audience would enjoy and this resulted in a better reception than the previous night, but for sure we crossed this venue off the list for future tours.

The hotel we stayed at was a great place for music. The lounge, which was mostly a seated area so people could watch in comfort all the acts that appeared throughout the day, was always pretty full. Music was performed here from midday till midnight with a pub atmosphere and the acts would all perform two or three sets, mostly duos and trios playing country and Irish songs, but what was very obvious to me was the talent of each and every member. This was not just learning as you go musicians, it was in their blood. Every act that performed would say 'Any requests please feel free to come up and ask', and as I had mostly all the daytime free both Friday and Saturday, I watched and enjoyed all the acts that appeared.

As they had different set ups with instrumentation I always asked whichever act was on to perform *"Duelling Banjos"* so even with a Bodhrán drum, Irish flute and fiddles, all the acts did their own musical version. I only wish I could have recorded all the different versions performed. I went to the bar for a drink and got speaking to the barman who asked me why I was visiting Ireland, was it for work or pleasure and of course when he heard I was performing at one of Dublin's biggest night spots we got on to the subject of what was the biggest thing I felt I had done in my career up to date. I said I had recently been recording in Nashville, Tennessee with Carl Perkins along with all of Elvis Presley's original backing group.

'Well that is just amazing, were they good to work with?' the bar man asked, 'Real decent people who are a pleasure to work and be with', I replied, and then I quickly said, 'I'm just off to the toilet'. He gave me directions explaining they were down stairs around to the left, and off I went. When I was in the gentlemen's I realized they had a two-way speaker system in operation, this was obviously as troubles in Ireland were still at a high and should there be a warning announcement for any reason then you would hear it through these speakers, and also should any trouble happen down stairs in the toilets they could hear what was going on from up in the bar area. As I stood there through the speakers I clearly heard a lady bartender say to the guy I was just speaking to 'Who is the new lodger then, what's he like?' The barman replied 'Would you believe it, I only asked him what he's been up to lately, and he has come out with he's been in Nashville, Tennessee working and hanging around with none other than Carl Perkins', the lady started laughing 'Oh that's not it', he replied, 'To top it all off, he then spent time hanging around all of Elvis Presley's original band, the lying B*****D'.

I made my way back upstairs to the bar 'My drinks still here then', I said, 'Of course sir, it'll help the vocal chords for tonight's show'. 'You're very kind', I replied, then I took the opportunity to ask him a question. (Ros, my London mummy, asked me to bring her back a little Leprechaun), 'A lady back home asked me to bring her back a Leprechaun; do you know where I can get one?' the barman looked at me in a strange way and said, 'To be honest it's a bit of a problem at the moment as they are all sleeping', 'Oh I see', then I said 'Give me a shout when they are awake then', 'Of course I will sir'. I thought I would leave him with another party piece should I visit the rest room again. Unfortunately, this was it for my Ireland experience, as after the Saturday night's performance at The Break for The Border club I was on the early flight back to London Sunday morning. I was in my taxi retuning to the airport whereupon I noticed a poster showing that Joe Dolan who I thought was a fabulous artiste, was appearing the very next week and I sang all the way home his hit *"Make Me an Island"*.

A few years later I was back in Ireland on a couple of occasions, this time on another recording project, and I appeared on TV twice. The first occasion live on "The Late Late Show" with Pat Kenny, and the second live on "The Kelly Show" but I must say I would love to return to the Emerald Isle one day and tour, so I can take time to smell the flowers and enjoy all the splendours this beautiful country has to offer.

WALES

My first visit to Wales was again with the musical 'Forever Elvis', appearing at the Coliseum Theatre in Aberdare which is a town in the Cynon valley area of Rhondda Cynon Taf. Aberdare actually dates from the Middle Ages with a lot of history and culture, having a coal and iron industry attached to its making. The Coliseum theatre was actually built using subscriptions from the miners in 1938, a lovely 600 seated auditorium. I noticed as we were driving in, all the little houses (that were obviously built for the mining community). I always felt these people deserved a good show because they worked their fingers to the bone and I for one was not going to let them down. Keith the producer was from Wales, so it meant a lot to him that we gave it our all. This was to come to the fore during rehearsals which took three times as long as usual, but well worth it because the standing ovation on the first night went on for ages - a job well done! Rather than celebrate the night at the hotel, we went to the social club around the corner where we ended up having a very merry evening.

As well as Forever Elvis, one of my best performances (or so I have been told) was with the Jordanaires at a rock 'n' roll weekend in North Wales at a holiday camp where I had my own dressing room back stage. Just before I was going to perform I wanted to catch an act I always admired, Burt Weedon, who was the first British solo guitarist to have a hit in the UK charts with the song *"Guitar Boogie Shuffle"*. I stood in the wings watching his act and he really was a professional, made for the stage. I could not stay long as I had to get ready myself for my performance. While I was getting ready I heard a knock on my dressing room door and a voice said, 'Can I come in Johnny?' It was Terry Dene, one of the original stars of 'The Six Five Special' who was regarded as the British Elvis back in 1958. Terry had some great classic hits *"A White Sports Coat"* along with *"Stairway of Love"* and I had not long ago sat at home (when I lived in Ruislip with Tom) and watched the Terry Dene film 'The Golden Disc'.

Tom informed me he was in the same tent as Mr. Dene when he had to serve his national service in the army, but Terry got picked on so much he was discharged from the army on medical grounds. Unfortunately, the press were very unkind to Mr. Dene which really played a major part in ruining his career. But here he was in the flesh; he wished me well, said how much of an Elvis fan he was and how unbelievable it was to meet the Jordanaires. Terry seemed a really nice guy. I never saw him again, but I do wish him luck with all he does.

This show in Wales was brilliant and the version of *"How Great Though Art"* was I think my best ever live stage performance of this song. I performed in Cardiff a few years later with my band and if I have to sum up Wales, I would say it is a beautiful country and from what I experienced they love their rock 'n' roll.

GERMANY

The Jordanaires and I first toured the Fatherland in the early 1990's and we all loved the country. The Elvis and rock 'n' roll fans turned out in their thousands to attend the shows, among them my best and closest friends, the Schroer family who I still see today. I make sure that every year I try my best to visit Germany either to see my friends or perform shows. I laugh to myself when I think back to when I was younger; naively I really thought that besides the Americans and the Brits, I did not know of anyone else who could love rock 'n' roll as much. Think again Mr. Earl, Peter Kraus was a German rock 'n' roll star way back in the 1950's and he sold over 12 million records, and never forget you can throw in the pot Elvis Presley who during his army service was stationed in Germany for 17 months, and it was there he met his future wife.

The German people absolutely love their music and recently I had a show at a hall in Bad Nauheim to celebrate the Kings birthday (as this was where Elvis was stationed in the army) the very hall he celebrated his 25th birthday in. I performed the show and it was one of the most memorable performances of my life.

My favourite European dish is Sauerbraten, and to my delight when I was performing in Düsseldorf you could actually buy it as a takeaway. Cologne was an amazing city to see, full of history and of course the Cathedral (Der Kölner Dom) as well as Roman sites and lots of museums, a brilliant place to visit.

I perform with various bands when in Germany, one being Danny and the Wonderbras, a good country, rock 'n' roll and blues outfit. Today I work with the German band called the Dukes, with our first album release *(She Wants It All)* to be released this year 2019 and I love the songs that have been produced. To be honest most bands in Germany are quite competent, so it never really bothers me even if I have never performed with them before, and as any U.K. rocker will tell you, it is always a good laugh. I could definitely live there one day and rock away my days until the sun sets over the Rhine. I can only say a brilliant country with fabulous people.

BIS BALD! (See you soon).

DENMARK

Even the Vikings love to rock 'n' roll, and Denmark was the destination for The Hall of Fame Show. We were ready to invade these shores except for the first time I was wearing as many hats as could be worn for the Hall of Fame show – yes with me now as the manager/promoter/agent/performer, was I ready for all these roles as well as starring in the show?

This production was a musical tribute to Roy Orbison, Buddy Holly, Brenda Lee, and Elvis. Not long before this I had held a rock 'n' roll all day event at the venue the Townhouse, in Enfield, North London which had two floors so acts would play upstairs and if preferred the audience could see the act on downstairs. A brilliant venue where I put on all 'The Hall of Fame Show', as well as Mike Berry, Linda Gale Lewis, (Jerry Lee's little sister) and The Rapiers who were one of Britain's top instrumental bands. The whole event was brilliant, and I invited a person I got to know quite well, Mr. Elliot M Cohen, owner of the famous London studio Red Bus. He had an associate in Denmark who put on musicals and shows that were actually from Broadway USA, so I was on tenterhooks most of that day. I was glad Elliot took an interest as I lost around £6,000 putting on the townhouse event.

(If you want to be a promoter sometimes you learn the hard way, and I found if you decide to put on a show, especially on a bank holiday when most people have gone to the coast, well.. once bitten). Oh well it was a great show though. But the light shone at the end of the Viking rainbow: Elliot enjoyed the show so much he asked for a meeting at his offices Tuesday morning, at Red Bus Studios. I loved Red Bus as a studio as previously I had recorded there and was privileged to have been produced by the legendary music producer John Hawkins. I sang a song especially written by Mort Shuman who wrote a lot of Elvis's hits, and this was for the BBC TV production 'Perfect Scoundrels' the song was called *"Blue Kisses"*.

But this time I was a promoter and now it was all agreed 'The Hall of Fame Show' was bound for Denmark, my next mission to find a helmet with cow horns. Denmark itself was beautiful, the people were very friendly and they loved the show, but it was a mini tour and even I could tell the show was not really up to the standards of the Broadway Musical status the promoter was used to. To put it in layman's terms 'The Hall of Fame' was really four people singing the songs of four legends with a great band backing it; no dancers, no acting, no stage props just a big gig really.

I think the Denmark promoter expected a little bit more glitz than that, and when I saw the brochures of the previous shows he had toured 'Riverdance' etc., we were a long way from that level of production.

I learned a big lesson touring Denmark, if you want to be a manager of a touring musical, whether you like it or not you have to listen to all the bickering of the performers, sort out all the travel arrangements for all the members of the show and their wages, and in return hope they all give you a 100% commitment for your hard work. Think again. This is a very selfish business and when you take the helm it takes a certain type of person to become a good show manager, and that person does not care whether people like them or not and is not looking for friends or comrades, just people who can get on with the job who can easily be replaced. So good old Devonshire Johnny decided on the shows return to England that 'The Hall of Fame' was no more.

I would love to return to Denmark in the future and I would certainly see more of the sights of these English invaders and take time to enjoy the country rather than go as a show-manager/promoter/agent SLAVE!

FINLAND

One of the countries the Jordanaires and I toured was Finland. We flew into Helsinki and were met by a mini bus which then drove for five hours and took us to the top end of Finland. We did stop after a couple of hours for a break, and at this stop there was the most beautiful fjord with mountain hills either side with water that was so clear that I stood on a rock and stared right through to the bottom. I thought it looked like it was three or four feet deep, so I dropped a pebble which I thought would take a second to hit the bottom. It took about five seconds to finally hit the bottom which must have been 20-30 feet deep, it was just so clear and beautiful. As I looked down the fjord it reminded me very much of the film set of the 1958 film 'The Vikings' starring Kirk Douglas and Tony Curtis and you could imagine Viking long ships sailing these magnificent waters.

When we reached our destination at the top of Finland I had to share a room with my manager Kevin Allen and to our surprise we found out that at that time of year it does not get dark. It stays light 24/7 and that took a bit of getting used to. The venue we were to perform at was a big sports hall with a makeshift stage. I walked around the venue with Gordon Stoker and we were amazed to see the whole interior was covered with Elvis banners and flags, posters and clothes and record stalls, looking like an Elvis Aladdin's cave. Gordon and I stopped, and he turned to me and said, 'Do you know what Johnny, Elvis would never have believed all this'. I said, 'RCA Victor and the Colonel certainly did their job'. The show was great and just like every country we played, the Finnish people were very nice and kind and loved their rock 'n' roll. Believe it or not nothing went wrong with this tour which leaves me only to say Finland is definitely on my return to tour list.

Nähdään Pian! (See you soon)

MONTE CARLO

Performing at the sports club in Monte Carlo was an experience of a lifetime. At the time I was backed by the Hall of Fame band who I performed a lot of my rock 'n' roll shows with, so no problems with putting on a good well-rehearsed show. Brendon the drummer was a Formula One fanatic, so he was in his element walking through all the tunnels and along the roads (which when the racing is on becomes the track). We all stayed at the Hermitage Hotel, very posh and very luxurious. The show was a legends show with lookalikes of Marilyn Monroe, Elton John, and so on, who mingled and danced with the audience even when I was performing. It was quite odd to see right in front of you Del Boy and Rodney shaking their legs to *Hound Dog*, and Elton John getting *All Shook Up*. It was a great laugh.

On my day off I went down to the harbour and there I sat at a table at a cafe called the Coffee Shop and watched the billionaires in the harbour aboard their yachts, lazing in the sun. It was a beautiful sun-drenched day and I was quite surprised how everybody who passed me smiled and said hello, which shows you, money aside, it costs nothing to be polite. I looked around the harbour, then at all the glorious hotels which were beautiful to look at and I could not help but notice lots and lots of beautiful looking ladies walking everywhere. I wish I could have driven there in my old Datsun Cherry (my car at the time) that would have turned a few heads!

I had only the one appearance in Monte Carlo and would love to return, and who knows play some roulette with the big spenders, but hey, would they spend a little time with me!

AUSTRALIA

The world of touring pointed its finger at Australia and the opportunity arose for me to perform in Perth, a destination I had always wanted to visit strangely enough. When I was growing up in Dawlish in Devon we had a beautiful running stream which flowed through the middle of the town into the sea and there was a bird sanctuary on the bank, but what was most beautiful of all were the black swans that inhabited the brook. There was a big sign that displayed the origins of these black swans which showed that they came from Perth, Australia. As a small child I always vowed to myself that if ever I had the chance I just had to visit Australia, and of course fabulous Perth.

I was booked on Singapore airlines, who I'd never flown with before, 12 hours to Singapore with a 4 hour stop off, then another 5 hours flight to Perth. This was definitely long haul, but one thing that has always been an asset of mine is I am never ever bored, for any spare moments I have is a good time for song writing which will take up every spare second of any day. I boarded the flight, sat in my seat which was very comfortable, and I took one look at the 50 or so movie's I could watch and the "Lord of the Rings" - yes, the whole trilogy was screening. This pleased me as now for the entire journey I could join my best film mates of the day "Sam" and "Frodo" and as far as I was concerned we were all on an adventure to the land of "Mordor" to journey to the inside of the volcano of Mount Doom to finally melt that golden ring! Brilliant, that was the first 12 hours sorted. Luckily the 4 hour stop off in Singapore went pretty quick as I looked at everything I couldn't afford, had a couple of coffees and then I was bound for Perth where song writing took to the fore, so the next 5 hours just flew past.

Anyone who arrives in Australia will know how strict the customs and immigration are and it takes quite a while with custom officers making their dogs have a quick smell of every person in the never-ending queue. Finally, I got through and there to greet me was one of the promoters, Gregg Ross. He had a big Aussie smile, held out his hand 'Great to meet you Johnny', 'It's great to be here', I replied, and we hit it off straight away. I got to meet the other guy who was putting on the event, Keith, who was the owner of Brookhampton Vineyard (the venue for the performance) which was just on the outskirts of Perth. This was no ordinary performance, there was a twenty-piece orchestra performing who were going to back me as well as the band. We all had lunch at the vineyard and then I had to go and be the guest on Perth's biggest radio show where the DJ interviewing me was also the compère of the evenings show.

Off to the radio station I went with Gregg in his lavish brown Rolls Royce, gleaming in the Australian sunshine, while everybody else stayed at the vineyard to listen to the live radio show. I thought it was going to be just a normal chat show about the music business and as I went in and sat down the DJ said 'Gud day Johnny, today's show is all about the Sun Record label', 'Brilliant' I told him 'Not long ago my whole live show with my band was a Sun Records set list, so we're going to have a ball', the DJ said 'Tell me one of your Sun Record favourites so I can play it, then you can talk about the song and give us the reasons for you choosing it'. The sun record catalogue was full of gems so rather than the obvious sun record hits I chose a rather unfamiliar track which was a Barbara Pittman song *"I Need a Man"* which I had also recently picked up at a record fair on a Sun 78rpm.

We all got on great and the DJ had the usual Elvis, Jerry Lee, and Carl Perkins Sun repertoire. By the end of the 2-hour show (which I think I was only supposed to spend twenty or thirty minutes' tops), I talked with them regarding all the other Sun recording artistes that I liked and grew up listening too - Hayden Thompson, Warren Smith, Jack Earls, Rufus Thomas Jr, Junior Parker and the like. The phone lines were now buzzing with people wanting to speak to me. It was a great atmosphere and I think because I had not long ago worked with two Sun Record legends, Carl Perkins and Scotty Moore, that just put the icing on the Sun cake. Luckily, I got the show recorded on CD and who knows, maybe it will be released one day.

When I got back to the vineyard I got a hero's welcome. They told me their phone lines were very busy selling tickets and Keith said to me 'Do you fancy a swim?' 'I'd love one', and I was driven to a man-made big water pool with a square wooden pontoon in the middle, about 10-foot square, the water was quite deep as they used this water for most of the vineyard, but as the sun was so hot the water felt very cold. Although this was the water lifeline to the vineyard, to me it was my own little oasis under the scorching Australian sun and I was like a dolphin in his own aquarium. I swam for a good half hour with not a soul in sight. It was beautiful, and then I swam back to the pontoon and laid there for a good hour with not a care in the world. As I laid there basking in the glorious sun I noticed on the horizon a car drawing nearer, my chariot was arriving... fun time over. I swam to the shore and was then taken to the show area where the orchestra was setting up and pretty soon rehearsals were under way. After sound checks I met up with Keith the owner and he explained how all the vineyards in this part of Australia were all growing the same grapes and nothing but the labels on the bottles differentiated the vineyards, so by using their vineyards for concerts it was a good way of earning extra income.

Recently a neighbouring vineyard had Rod Stewart and Bryan Adams performing and this kind of live music concert in vineyards was getting very popular. The rehearsals went well, and it was getting late in the afternoon and people had started arriving. I went to the tent at the side of the stage and started getting ready for the performance. Then out of the blue in came the DJ who I had met during the day... he came up gave me a hug, did not hang around then got straight on stage, grabbed the mic and exclaimed 'Gud evening yu b*****ds, how yu all doin', the audience roared and cheered, and wolf whistled at his very bright introduction. He said, 'Did you all hear my show this afternoon, bl***y great wasn't it, well here is the guy that you all loved, he's toured and worked Europe and America with the Legends we all love to listen to', and I must say by the time he finished introducing me I was the biggest thing since Fosters and sliced bread.

Just like in any country in the world that I had performed, the Australians were no different; their love of Elvis Presley and his music was unbelievable. It certainly brings home how well Colonel Tom Parker and RCA did their job and proved to me the Colonel was pop music's most influential music manager ever. All through my performance the audience jived and danced, and I looked out from the stage over the crowd to an unforgettable sight. Before me was this Roman Colosseum-styled (not stone but grass) stadium and as the sun sank lower the whole event was breath taking. I finished my show with *"The American Trilogy"* – it was a magical ending to a magical night. (I stuck a fork in that one)

After my performance, I got to meet members of the audience and loved their friendliness, but quite a few thought it strange that a Brit could vocally sound that close to Elvis, to which I would always say 'Yes I get that a lot'. Just one regret of my whole Australian experience was only being there for five days, and then I had to return to the UK for three performances and then fly straight off to Nashville to record. I did however get to visit Perth's biggest old record shop which had an original Australian Gene Vincent LP from the 1950's and it made me think that even in Australia it's amazing how my beloved rock 'n' roll music was loved the world over. I did not get a chance to meet any aborigines or get to swim where great white sharks roamed though.

I truly loved Australia and hope one day to return and rock 'n' roll with these lovely people, and once again be able to share another glorious sunset as that's what blue suede dreams are made of...

15

MY TOP 20 ROCK 'N' ROLL TUNES

I could give you a top hundred and beyond and they would all stand up as strong as one another, but I cannot wrack my brains any longer. My top twenty rock 'n' roll tunes are as follows with a brief explanation why.

1. Don't Be Cruel *by Elvis Presley*

Put a coin in the jukebox, choose this song and see the instant reaction of the crowd. Tapping of feet, swirling of skirts, euphoria of happiness fills the air. When Elvis exploded onto the music world in 1956 he was asked by a reporter what was his favourite song of that year that he had recorded. Elvis replied *'Don't Be Cruel*, sir'. If that wasn't strong enough as a legendary A side classic, with the flip side being *Hound Dog*, 45rpm singles do not come any better; you just had to play both sides. Ironically a lot of artistes from the 1950's only had one or two big hits and toured forever on the back of them. Now if this was Elvis's sole hit record he would probably still be touring the world over today - but we're talking about the king and there's a list of world-wide smash hit records as long as your arm in this man's discography, enough for him to keep touring until the earth stops turning.

2. Rock Around the Clock *by Bill Haley and His Comets*

It says it all in the title. Fun was needed by the youth of the 1950's not only in America but the world. There had not long been a world war, the time was right, and I reckon most people in the world probably knew the Lord's Prayer off by heart and now the youth had a song they would now start learning off by heart: The rock 'n' roll bible of lyrics was now being written - One, Two, Three O'clock, Four O'clock Rock, Five, Six, Seven O'clock etc. etc. Amen.

3. **Tutti Frutti** *by Little Richard*

Tutti Frutti means all fruits in Italian, especially when it comes to ice cream. Little Richard co-wrote this song with a wailing saxophone fused with a pulsating rhythm. If you can jive and you hear 'A wop bop a lu bop a wop bam boom', need I say more.

4. **Johnny B Goode** *by Chuck Berry*

There lived a country boy named Johnny B Goode; this is the ultimate drive-in American Diner anthem. Any guy doing a duck walk while giving you a first-class rock 'n' roll guitar solo tells me here is a rock 'n' roll legend, a unique one-off with so many rock and roll classics under his belt it is hard to believe Chuck Berry's only UK number one was *"My Ding a Ling"*.

5. **Rave On** *by Buddy Holly*

You are telling me you can hiccup your way into a song, get away with it and then that song becomes a worldwide hit? Of course, you can! Especially when you get the energy this track oozes. I saw Buddy the musical in London's West End four times and absolutely loved it. The full house audiences proved again and again that one of the rock 'n' roll ten commandments is when attending a rock 'n' roll event - thou shalt Rave On and on and on.

6. **Summertime Blues** *by Eddie Cochran*

As soon as I hear the opening beats to Summertime Blues, I have implanted in my memory of when I was sixteen walking along that beautiful bridge from Teignmouth to Shaldon in glorious sunshine in Devon. At the time that bridge seemed a mile long, and back in 1981 there were about thirty rock 'n' rollers, the guy's in drape coats, the girls in circle skirts and stilettos. We were all going to the Shaldon Hotel which was hosting a rock 'n' roll night. It was a beautiful summers evening, all the cars passing were beeping like mad and we kept singing "Well we're gonna raise a fuss and we're gonna raise a holler", as if we were on a G.I. army slog. A fabulous memory which proves there ain't no cure for those summertime blues.

7. Move It *by Cliff Richard*

Yes, it's time for a Brit to make an entrance into my top twenty. Until *"Move It"* came along the Americans didn't know anyone else could even play rock 'n' roll - why should they, as they invented it and had all the legends. *"Move It"* believe it or not was originally going to be the B side and *"Schoolboy Crush"* was the original A side. *"Move It"* was written on the top of a double decker bus by Cliff's Drifter's guitarist Ian "Sammy" Samwell.... Well done mate, you put us Brits on the rock 'n' roll map.

8. Great Balls of Fire *by Jerry Lee Lewis*

'Too much a love drives a man insane'. When rock 'n' roll made an entrance to the world in the 1950's back then all the connotations relating to sex were mainly kept to magazines and said quietly under one's breath or down a dark dingy alley, but when you recited any of the lyrics to Great Balls of Fire you were making a statement. I can imagine back in the day at a dance, a coffee bar, drive in, how often you must have heard - 'Kiss me baby - ooh feels good'. This song gave people the chance to say exactly what they were feeling and how they wanted to express themselves... yes you were ready to rock 'n' roll with all the suggestive meanings you could ever want. With Jerry Lee's pumping piano and unique style of lyrical content this has to go down in history as one of the greatest rockers ever recorded.

9. The Wanderer *by Dion and The Belmonts*

The ultimate stroller, still filling every rock 'n' roll dance floor from the 1950's until today, but more than that, I can honestly say I can relate to the story of this song (except I don't have Rosie tattooed on my chest).

10. At the Hop *by Danny and The Juniors*

Great intro, great song - gets your blood boiling from the very start. If you're into keep fit, dance to *"At the Hop"* from start to finish and you'll have done a twenty-minute workout in three. Doo Wop meets pulsating rock 'n' roll at its very best.

11. The Great Pretender *by The Platters*

Pop Doo Wop at its best. Listening to this song and you just want to embrace someone and get them to slow dance - I normally do, with the nearest lady possible. A wonderful song performed by the most famous ballad group of the mid to late nineteen fifties.

12. **Runaway** *by Del Shannon*

Never really worked out how to dance to this classic so I always save it for cruising in the car, and it's great to hear this loud at fairgrounds. Even in the 1980's we all wondered how that keyboard sound was made. It was actually one of Del Shannon's band members, his keyboard player Mr. Crook, who made a self-built version of a Clavioline - basically an early synthesizer. He modified it with spare parts from television sets and household appliances and with a cocktail of electronic wizardry came up with that haunting riff on this masterpiece of a song which the world will forever know as - *Runaway*.

13. **Blue Suede Shoes** *by Carl Perkins*

When Carl wrote this song, he approached Sam Phillips of Sun Records and told him 'Sam I think I've written something special'. That something special was to become a smash hit for Elvis as well as making blue suede shoes the iconic footwear for rock 'n' rollers and not forgetting this very book. What rock 'n' roll artist has not recorded or covered this song? I would say it is the one rock 'n' roll song that's been covered and recorded more than any other. Carl certainly made a Blue Suede foot print for rock 'n' roll eternity.

14. **Donna** *by Richie Valens*

He wrote it for his girlfriend; velvet and satin laced with all of the sentiments of puppy love straight to a teenager's heart. I don't think there are many occasions where a guy can sing "I had a girl and Donna was her name, since she's been gone I've never been the same", even though his girlfriend might be called something else and get away with it. Well done Richie - a one up for the guys (so we think).

15. **The Shape I'm In** *by Johnny Restivo*

Come to think of it there are quite a lot of Johnny's in the rock 'n' roll world, and here is another. Being a body builder himself the lyrics were quite apt, even though this song was a one hit wonder, in my opinion it will always be one of the greatest rock 'n' roll jive tunes ever recorded.

16. Jungle Rock *by Hank Mizell*

This song sowed the seed for me, with its brilliant rockin' rhythm. Making number 3 in the UK charts in 1976. When the Gator and the Hippo were doin' the bop, so was I.

17. Why Do Fools Fall in Love *by Frankie Lymon & The Teenagers*

Teenagers just love growing up as fast as they can; falling deeply, madly in love with their boyfriend/girlfriend and this piece of poetry with a wailing saxophone solo was the chocolate cake of teenage romance.

18. Reveille Rock *by Johnny and The Hurricanes*

Imagine you are competing at the World Olympics doing the 100 metres. You walk slowly to the starting block, crouch down, then you hear "All right you guy's rise and shine". Off you go like a guided missile going like the clappers except for this time you are either jiving or bopping, and if you reach the end of this song - WELL DONE grab your silver medal, you are a world class athlete. If you're going to go for gold stay on the floor for *At the Hop* - Coffin at the ready, please.

19. Reet Petite *by Jackie Wilson*

Every Disc Jockey needs to have floor fillers in their armoury so play *Reet Petite* and nine times out of ten the jobs done. Not many rock 'n' roll songs in their original format that entered the charts in the 1950's and then in December 1986 re-enters and finally reaches number one, thus becoming chart history for entering the UK charts and taking twenty-nine years to become a chart topper. Jackie Wilson was way ahead of his time as a recording artist, a sensational performer. A regular at Jackie Wilson shows was Elvis himself who admired his talent and persona. Do not be surprised in the near future if Reet Petite tops the charts once again.

20. Shake Rattle and Roll *by Big Joe Turner*
or by Bill Haley and His Comets

Both versions are brilliant. *Shake Rattle and Roll* (Bill Haley's version) was the first rock 'n' roll song to hit the UK charts in 1954. There was no better way to open the ears and eyes of the world to what was to become an explosion of sounds, bringing a style that changed the course of popular music forever. 'My lord's ladies and gentlemen behold ROCK 'N' ROLL will always be, it'll go down in history'!

16

THE COUNTRY MUSIC YEARS

I grew up loving country music without knowing what on earth it was. My parents were rock 'n' rollers and I sort of stumbled onto country music. *"From A Jack to a King"* by Ned Miller was the song that lit the fuse, and from then on, I was open-eared when it came to country music. I had always been a staunch rock 'n' roller but ironically my first release on a 45rpm single the A side was a country classic – the Hank Williams legendary hit *"Your Cheating Heart"*. Country music for me wears more than one Stetson; I have been very lucky in life to visit many times and for a while to reside in Nashville, Tennessee and that broadens anyone's country collection.

A lot of the fusion of rock 'n' roll is country music and in all my years in the entertainment and music business, not a week has not gone by where I have not sung a country song somewhere along the line. In this book, you will read (in the chapter of Johnny Earl and Southern Star) those years certainly bought out most of the country music I had in me. No one will ever be able to persuade me otherwise; you can feel country music, you can live country music, sing and perform country music, but if you want to become a country music star or be taken seriously performing country music - you have to be American or be one of the very rare artists who is not American then try and climb the country music ladder in the U.S.A.

Country music is all-American from the American civil war to the cotton fields back home. Throw in some Polk salad 'n grits, you get what I mean. While on the road with Southern Star I said to an American 'I perform and write British and European country music'. 'Oh, I do not know what that is', was his reply... I rest my case.

A big change in my country music life was when I heard for the first time *"Copperhead Road"* by Steve Earle. It had the same effect as when I became a rock 'n' roller after I first heard *"Rock Around the Clock"*. Both songs hit me right between the ears, but *"Copperhead Road"* was certainly not the traditional country music I was used to listening to.

Soon after hearing *"Copperhead Road"* I was ready to get on board the new era of country music that was coming out of the U.S.A. There was a new wave of country music stars as well who were hitting the airwaves... Alan Jackson, Dwight Yoakam, Mary Chapin Carpenter, Reba McEntire, The Mavericks, and Garth Brooks were just a few that were on this new train to Nashville. The sun was setting on a different stage and from what I was hearing of this new country I was hooked, so a career change was on the horizon. (Every man sees his flaming star and Southern Star was just over my shoulder).

JOHNNY EARL AND SOUTHERN STAR

Lawdy Miss Clawdy was I in for a shock, three forty-five-minute sets, to be timed to military precision so as to not interfere with the raffle, along with endless encores if asked for, four, five, six nights a week. The British boot camp of on-the-road gigging had arrived: Get ready Mr. Earl, you're about to hit the British Country Music scene. Yes, that's the one, the scene that was described to me by touring American country singers as the scene with plenty of smoke but no fire. The Americans are a bit slow in understanding their British cousins have ambitions in country music as well, or so I thought until I actually started touring the British country music scene. How true the saying, play a country song backwards and you get your house back, your car back, and your loved ones back, and if ever there was a music to portray love and heartbreak country music is it.

Routed deep within the American south, and based on family values, *"Stand by Your Man"*, *"Coward of The County"*, *"Blanket on The Ground"*, Patsy Cline put the cherry on the cake with *"Crazy"* as well as *"Walking*

After Midnight". Now that was the traditional country that I knew and had listened to. I was used to performing *"Put Your Cat Clothes On"* and *"Twenty Flight Rock"* which was now Injun territory. The year 1994, I had not long come back from touring Sri Lanka, and it was unfortunate, but I gave Kevin Allen (my manager at the time) his marching orders after ten years of us working together. All good things come to an end, and we left on pretty good terms as I explained to him he was really a much better agent than manager in my eyes.

The word was out that I was looking for a new band. For the first time, I was without a manager, so wisely did not really want to start setting up auditions, getting a musical director, finding new agents, promoters and so on. I was really looking for an already established band that needed a new front man. I got a phone call from Tony Ryan who was the pedal steel player for a country band called Southern Star. Their lead singer had parted ways with them, so both I and Southern Star were on the prowl. A few rock 'n' roll bands were calling me, and I was open to talks, but Tony seemed a plausible fella with a good attitude about him with the added bonus of an immediate gig list as long as your arm, so a meeting was set in a cafe on the A12 motorway.

At the meeting was Tony and also the bass player Mike, they both told me all their tales of woe regarding their previous singer and at first Mike was not too happy about the name Johnny Earl and Southern Star (he preferred it to be just Southern Star). Tony jumped in and said, 'We can sort that out at a later stage'. I did not carry on with that discussion as I wanted to know more about the other band members and what was the format of the show. On drums was Richard Butcher known as Butch, formerly with Dominic Kerwin, a well-known top drawer act on the British/Irish country music scene. I found out at a later date that on one occasion, at one of Dominick Kerwin's performances, Butch was playing soft brushes and not sticks on most of Mr. Kerwin's set – and that was because it was all roughly the same steady beat, which a lot of traditional country music can sound like especially when throwing in some Irish country music songs – and unfortunately on one occasion performing live, Butch kept the beat going until he actually fell asleep right in the middle of a song and was nudged by the bass player to wake up.

Personally, if that had happened to me I would have told the audience to keep quiet and without a sound led the band off stage, sat us all in the audience and taken photos of Butch asleep at the drums with the stage to himself! ..and even paid for the pictures to be front cover on the Southern Country magazine. On guitar Billy Levin... Billy was a fabulous country rock guitarist as well as a great country music songwriter. I am sure if he had been born in Nashville that man would be a star today, I do not say this lightly, but Billy could stand shoulder to shoulder with any of the American pickers I played and recorded with. So, at the end of my meeting with Tony and Mike it was decided 'JOHNNY EARL AND SOUTHERN STAR' were on the road.

The show consisted of country standards old and new from *"Your Cheating Heart"* to *"Chattahoochee"* and because I was well known for my rock 'n' roll a couple of rockers with a few Elvis songs always went down well. We must have played every village hall and social club, be it Conservative, Labour, Lib Dem, or otherwise in England. It also did not take me long to work out the wages or should I say the monies that were involved. Basically, you got paid, then after working out all your expenses you realized it was not uncommon to try and borrow some money until the next show and so on. There are a lot of harder ways of making a pittance let me tell you and anyway you're doing it for the love of the music.

Four years we actually stayed together as a band. It was a lot of laughs but amazingly all we produced recording-wise to sell, was just one cassette titled Johnny Earl and Southern Star (I think we sold 30).

The next country music release for me was my first solo country album titled *"The Singerman"*. One of our last performances was in a country club in Gillingham and after the performance Tony Ryan ushered us all together to let us know he was packing it all in. As Tony was the booker for all the shows, working endlessly to keep our diaries full, he received very little gratitude for his endeavours and anyone who has tried running a band will know there comes a day when the light turns on and echoing through your mind those everlasting words 'What am I doing this for?' Which gets repeated just once too often. I did not blame Tony at all, as I had been in his position many a time and had vast experience of putting not only bands but shows together, and I'm afraid the term 'I do it for the love of the music' might get you to the grave a lot quicker than you had planned. We did however have a lot of laughs – some I would love to share with you.

On one show that we were performing at, all of us were very late arriving.

It was right up on the East Anglian coast, I'm talking Cromer, and we were all travelling individually on a busy Friday night from London. Pulling up at the venues back doors was Butch, so we all rushed to give him a hand with his drum kit. Now anybody who has worked the British Country Club circuit will know punctuality dictates whether you have a future on this scene or not. Butch flipped open his car boot and yelled 'Arghhhhhhh I've left my drums in the other car', he turned and looked at me and went from white to red within seconds. When he went over to tell the other band members they did not believe him and had to come and take a look for themselves. A local country drummer who was happily sitting at home eventually came to our aid and it was very fortunate for us that he had a night off.

We were among the first British country bands to really push the new country style and we actually introduced a Garth Brooks set as he was taking the American Country scene by storm. I'm afraid to say the British scene was not ready for this at the time as we quickly found out, because clubs that had been there since the dawn of time (and some might say were very blinkered, but not to them) and now we were hearing from the established audiences 'KEEP IT COUNTRY'.

Poor old Tony bore the brunt of most of this, word spread like wildfire of our new country set list. Within days Tony was endlessly on the phone with club owners who had booked us having to justify our set lists and not only that, a lot of club members at the end of each of the following performances were a bit unsure of our tact in song selection. It was as simple as this; as soon as word got around that you were not playing traditional country music the phone stopped ringing so finally we had to drop a few numbers and replace Garth Brooks songs with traditional songs like *"Crazy Arms"* by Ray Price.

I was starting to understand the old British well-established country music circuit was going to need a right cowboy boot up the jacksie in order to change their ways, and gradually, very gradually more and more new country artists and songs were GRADUALLY!!! being accepted. New country magazines were coming out now and hitting the shelves sitting alongside the music magazines of the day. I could not believe one day strolling through Ruislip town centre walking into WH Smith's and seeing three different new country magazines on the shelves next to the NME.

Just when the traditional country music fans opened their minds and hearts (only a little bit mind you) for a newer style of country music they had to see whether they could ease it open a tiny bit further because a new craze was about to fall upon them. Yes a craze that was going to make a massive entrance onto their dance floors - and it certainly did - encroaching like a bolt of lightning into their clubs, filling the floors, oh dear oh my, yes the devil went down to Georgia, carried right on through to all the southern states of America, stopped took a bow and bestowed on all the traditional country music lovers... Line Dancing. "KEEP IT COUNTRY" – I'll personally shoot the next person that I hear saying that.

Brilliant!!! To me this was just what the scene needed, and it soon became very evident which side of the fence I wanted to be on. We rolled the dice once again and put together an all new country line dance show and that would mean performing songs from new country artistes like Vince Gill, Mark Chestnut, Brooks and Dunn, The Mavericks - I'll have some of that thank you, unless you were happy keeping the same set list and should we say just stay traditional. NOW AS ONLY THE BRITISH MUSIC INDUSTRY COULD DO, when this whirlwind of fantastic sounds coming straight from the states was hitting the airwaves, the only way forward for Britain was 'Hillbilly Rock, Hillbilly Roll, Stand in a Line and Away We Go', SO AWAY I WENT!

Unfortunately what no one foresaw was you did not need a band to supply the Line Dance fraternity. They were quite content to go to any club, be it a country club, bowling club, social club, sports hall, village hall, even a scouts hut. All you needed was to bring your bottle of water, and there to dictate procedures was a line dance instructor who could have any size sound system, and with a radio mic or a head set, he or she would stand in the middle of the floor and teach one and all to get in line and follow their lead, normally starting with heel toe, then slide to the left etc., (oh dear, oh my, we have just rehearsed for two months a show that nobody wants!). Line Dancing was not just taking off in the UK it thrived all over Europe. I think the most successful pop UK Line Dance hit was by the pop group Steps - *5678*.

To sum up the British country music scene, the bible which nobody strayed from in the south of England was the Southern Country Magazine which was sold on every door of every club you went to. This magazine wrote about all the bands on the circuit, reviewing most shows on a weekly basis and a directory of where all the acts would be performing in the weeks ahead. Most reviews were positive of the acts; thus, Johnny Earl and Southern Star became very popular on the scene I'm glad to say. One country song

I wrote which was put in our set list *"The Next Time That I See You"* always packed the hardwood floor every time we performed it.

I have not been to a country music club for quite a while now, but from what I remember it was a lot of lovely people enjoying the music they loved, and I had the pleasure of seeing and visiting nearly every village hall in England. The British country music scene also gave me the chance in life to take the time to smell the flowers. I had very little pressure while on the country music scene; Tony Ryan took care of most of that.

So, thank you to everyone I met through my country music years; all the musicians, band members, club owners and members, and I hope life is treating you all well. I will leave you with this 'Our Father Who Art in Heaven..' KEEP IT COUNTRY!!!!

My Top Twenty Country Music Tunes:
1. From A Jack to A King - *by Ned Miller*
2. Your Cheatin' Heart - *by Hank Williams*
3. Ring of Fire - *by Johnny Cash*
4. Take and Give - *by Slim Rhodes*
5. Folsom Prison Blues - *by Johnny Cash*
6. It's Only Make Believe - *by Conway Twitty*
7. Alibis - *by Tracy Lawrence*
8. It Sure Is Monday - *by Mark Chestnutt*
9. Look at Us - *by Vince Gill*
10. The Race Is On - *by George Jones*
11. El Paso - *by Marty Robbins*
12. Crazy - *by Patsy Cline*
13. Independence Day - *by Martina McBride*
14. Amazed - *by Lonestar*
15. He Stopped Loving Her Today - *by George Jones*
16. Guitars and Cadillac's - *by Dwight Yoakam*
17. Angel of No Mercy - *by Collin Raye*
18. Before the Next Tear Drop Falls - *by Freddy Fender*
19. Copperhead Road - *by Steve Earle*
20. Heartland - *by George Strait*

17

STYLES OF MUSIC

DOO WOP

A rhythm and blues, vocal harmony style that pre-dates rock 'n' roll by a few years. I would say the first vocal harmonizing group that hit the airwaves and sounded like Doo Wop as we know it today were the Ink Spots way back in 1939 and they were having hit records in the UK as well as the U.S.A. One of these hits was one of my all-time favourite ballads *"My Prayer"* only to be equalled with *"Unchained Melody"*.

Doo Wop music was the people's music, from the car mechanic to the barber to the student. If you had a decent voice you got together with your friends and started a vocal harmony group. Nowhere did this happen more than on the streets of New York. It was common in New York in the late 1950's to see a group of guys ranging from three to six members harmonizing on a street corner or using the echoing effect of a subway using just their voices, which in some instances took the place of instruments, and this vocal harmonizing sound was coined as *a cappella*. It is very surprising but the term "Doo Wop" did not appear in print until 1961 but had been first used on a record by The Turbans on the song *"When You Dance"*. I have put this song in my top twenty doo wop chart because I love to play it when I'm in the doo wop mood.

What is marvellous about doo wop are the names of the groups associated with the songs they perform... in fact they fit like a glove, e.g. The Five Satins *"In the Still of The Night"*, The Monotones *"The Book of Love"*, The

Moonglows *"Sincerely"* – aaah what beautiful music this is. Not only do you hear the heartbreaking beautiful ballads but there are fast doo wop classics as well, like the up tempo *"Gee"* by The Crows, *"Whispering Bells"* by The Del-Vikings. This is the finest chocolate cake of music to me, as I'm writing the titles these fabulous tunes play endlessly through my mind. It really is a world of colourful vocals, and this style was brought to the masses by that sensational vocal group The Platters. I think The Platters career was exceptional and were definitely the most popular of all the vocal groups of the 1950's as it was they who popularized doo wop. When you have a portfolio filled with the likes of *"The Great Pretender"*, *"Only You"*, *"Harbour Lights"*, and *"Smoke Gets in Your Eyes"* you certainly have some of the greatest songs ever recorded.

Two of the most important ingredients of the making of a doo wop group has to be making sure all the group are good harmony singers, then equally important the name of the group which will need to last a lifetime. This can be quite a daunting task with a lot of head scratching but usually the simplest is the best. I can name six top drawer doo wop acts that decided that the way forward when naming their group was to call themselves names of birds... yes, it's as simple as that. The Penguins, The Crows, The Swallows, The Flamingo's, The Orioles, even The Larks, each becoming legendary in the doo wop hall of fame. Other groups decided they wanted to be introduced and to be associated with the space age chariots of the day, those fabulous 1950's cars: The Cadillacs, The Impalas, Little Anthony and the Imperials. Don't you just love it, it rolls so freely off the tongue.

A classic tune I first heard was *"Sh-Boom"* by the Crew-Cuts and thought it sounded pretty good, until I heard the original brilliant doo wop version by The Chords, and of course Elvis's version of *"Crying in The Chapel"* which in my mind was equalled by the Orioles version. What this was telling me was just how much I needed to dig into my music ethos and find out as much as I can about doo wop. Some songs could be very raunchy.. *"Sixty Minute Man"* which was a hit for Billy Ward and his Dominoes. This tune was classed as doo wop - rhythm and blues and considered very raunchy for 1951. This music had no boundaries and once you start appreciating the wonders of doo wop it becomes part of your life. As I started delving I found doo wop had origins with the African American influence of The Ink Spots and The Mills Brothers and as doo wop evolved you had the emergence of the Italian influence which came to the fore.

These Italian groups were also regular churchgoers who ingrained singing together in their pedigree. This was to lead to a doo wop legend emerging from the Italian fraternity, "Dion DiMucci" who joined The Belmonts and in 1958 the fruits of this partnership was an instant success with the classic *"I Wonder Why"*, which becomes engrained on one's mind (much like when Ray Walkers intro on Elvis's *"A Fool Such as I"* was engrained on mine. Once heard never forgotten). Rock 'n' rollers were being given a new language to speak I mean just look at the intro of *"I Wonder Why"* ... Nen Nen Nen Na Nen Nen Na Nen Na Nenna Nen Nen Nen Na Nen Nen a Nen a Nenna.... I Don't Know Why I Love You Like I Do". What a bunch of Nen's, how cool is that? Not many people can talk like an alien and make it into a multi-million seller.

Dion and The Belmonts were being called the sound of the city and we're talking New York. Music history books tell you that Dion and The Belmonts song *"Teenager in Love"* has got to be one of the classic songs of the 1950's and I certainly would not disagree. Let us not forget the other fabulous Italian doo wop groups which included "The Capris" with *"There's A Moon Out Tonight"*– wow what a power ballad, and the brilliant *"You Belong to Me"* by "The Duprees". The Italian doo woppers can be proud of their deserved stardom.

By the time 1961 came along, doo wop had hit its peak with the song *"Blue Moon"* by The Marcels, what a curtain call. Little did The Marcels know but their masterpiece in the future will mostly be remembered by the metamorphism of someone changing into a werewolf. Today in the UK one of the leading doo wop vocal groups are called "The Roommates" (not to be confused with the U.S. Roommates). They are still touring Europe and I am very glad to say that in my early years I performed a lot of shows with these guys. They did good renditions of The Jordanaires as well as their own material, and in my opinion if you put the UK Roommates in Dr. Who's Tardis, transported them back to 1957 and let them perform down New York subways they would have top twenty hits under their belts.

It's funny recalling how I got into doo wop music. Like a lot of other people did, by listening to rock 'n' roll, doo wop quietly slipped into the record collection. One 45rpm single I played to death was *"I'm Sorry"* by The Impalas when I was just twelve years of age, along with a few of The Platters classics and this to me was just the slower side of rock 'n' roll. A couple of years later I was at school in Teignmouth, Devon and one of the teachers was a teddy boy. I'll never forget him because he looked the double of Abraham Lincoln without the hat. His other job was the barman and handyman at the Dawlish Inn Hotel in Dawlish, Devon where rock 'n' roll nights were held at the weekend, and what with my newly acquired box jacket suit, the two were destined to meet.

At these events at the Dawlish Inn, along with your admission ticket you would get chicken in a basket and compared to school dinners, I was at the Savoy Hotel, London. Even though I was only in my early teens I was earning quite good money down on the fish quay in Teignmouth helping unload the trawlers, and now I could even afford a couple of beers which my teddy boy teacher, bless him, turned a blind eye to. At this event, you had Devon's finest Disc Jockey, Eddie Falcon, and during the evening there was going to be the screening of the Alan Freed film *'Rock, Rock, Rock'*.

His film had me mesmerized as I had not seen or heard of any of the artistes before. The Moonglows with *"I Knew from The Start"* ...well hello, this was my introduction to Doo wop. Johnny Burnette and The Rock 'n Roll Trio *"Lonesome Train"* ...well hello rockabilly. From that night on there was a new horizon, a rainbow appeared and at the end my pot of gold... two new fabulous styles of music equally as good as my beloved rock 'n' roll. Thank you, Mr. Alan Freed, for not only coining the phrase Rock 'n' Roll but introducing me to the wonderful vocal world of doo wop.

My Doo Wop Top Twenty:

1. These Golden Rings - *by The Jive Five*
2. Come Back My Love - *by The Wrens*
3. I Knew from The Start - *by The Moonglows*
4. I Wonder Why - *by Dion and The Belmonts*
5. Whispering Bells - *by The Del-Vikings*
6. My Prayer - *by The Platters*
7. Speedo - *by The Cadillacs*
8. When You Dance - *by The Turbans*
9. Gee - *by The Crows*
10. Earth Angel - *by The Penguins*
11. Sorry - *by The Impalas*
12. There's A Moon Out Tonight - *by The Capris*
13. Trickle Trickle - *by The Videos*
14. Duke of Earl - *by Gene Chandler*
15. Remember Then - *by The Earls*
16. Church Bells May Ring - *by The Willows*
17. Oh Rose Marie - *by The Fascinators*
18. Sh-Boom - *by The Chords*
19. In the Still of The Night - *by The Five Satins*
20. Wow Wow Baby - *by The Roommates (The UK ones)*

ROCKABILLY

I'm a rockabilly rebel from head to toe, anyone remembering that quote will recall the group Matchbox having success in 1980 with the song *Rockabilly Rebel*. In the 1980's Matchbox were a good, bang up to date rockabilly band with a good lead singer (Graham Fenton) who I know quite well and hold in great regard, especially when he performs his Gene Vincent classics, but to many stalwart hardened rockabilly's, Matchbox were for the general public. Similar were the thoughts of ardent teddy boys whose views on Shaking Stevens and Showaddywaddy were they did not regard them as real rockers, just up to date pop artistes.

Rockabilly is a cult, the music and clothes both make statements. The dress style for the guys varies; one is a code of being rough and tough - Marlon Brando and James Dean styled t-shirts, jeans and motor cycle boots. Another is western style or Hawaiian shirts with moccasins, loafers or suede styled ankle boots with crepe souls called chucker boots, and for the smarter styled rockabilly, box jackets with half-moon pockets, parading brogues for shoes. At the other end of the spectrum plain old donkey jackets with steel toecap boots are acceptable within the rockabilly fashion.

The guys' hairstyles are commonly a quiff with optional D.A's. Another hair style is called a Mac Curtis (also known as a flat top) which has shaven sides with a spikey top ...today in many cases just a polish and shine! Yes, there are no-hair rockabillies as well, shall we say baldy Billies.

The female rockabilly can wear dungarees or pedal pushers, Marilyn Monroe styled 1950's dresses and many styles of shoes - saddle shoes, wedges, stilettos, heel pumps, loafers, moccasins and brogues. Women's hairstyles are victory roll along with pony-tails. Both men and women are usually tattoo friendly, on all areas of the body. Rockabilly's have an inbred attitude not to take any abuse from anyone ...'Don't Mess with My Duck Tails, I'll Get So Mad at You'.

Throughout my rockabilly days, rockabillies generally always hung around fellow rockabillies, as did the punks with the punks and skinheads with their own fraternity. Rockabilly dancing is quite a bit different from the Teddy boy rock 'n' rollers; the jiving is more a swing jitterbug fusion and the bopping not having any Teddy boy cartwheel heroics, and even the strolling is different.

Well here is a list of just 30 of my favourite all time rockabilly tunes and all of these are the tracks I used to constantly pester the DJ's with. This now gives me a great opportunity to personally thank a few of those DJs for putting up with my constant request harassment. (I was lucky in those early days there was no such thing as a DJ Asbo).

Devonshire DJ:
Eddie Falcon - The Devonshire legend all through my early years in Devon.

London DJ's:
Fifties Flash - The first London DJ I had the pleasure of bopping to, a legend in the rockin' world.
Rockin' Boogie Dell - It was Dell Richardson who booked the Louisiana Hayride more than any other person on my first gigs down at the Clay Pigeon venue in Eastcote, West London. Still today he spins the rock 'n' roll discs on Radio Caroline. A true ambassador for the music I love and he belongs in the Blue Suede Dreams, Rock 'n' Roll hall of fame.
Wild Cat Pete - Deserves the acknowledgement of being inducted to the Rockabilly Hall of Fame (See what happens if you put up with pests who keep coming up for requests).
Tom Ingram - A great DJ and a great guy who deserves all the success that has come his way.
Mouse - Always a star, pure rocker through and through. I started gigging when this guy did. (Red Hot & Blue v The Louisiana Hayride was the battle cry with Paul Ansell and The Blue Rhythm Boys rocking the club circuit).

(Recently) **Noel 'Razor' Smith** - London's very own DJ Rocking Legend

There are and were many more great r 'n' r and rockabilly DJ's I have been in the company of including **Geoff Barker**. He and his family are good friends of mine and he is a great guy to work with. Another great guy is **Willie Morgan**. Both are brilliant at their job – "ambassadors of the airwaves" – but all the guys I have mentioned were the ones who bore the brunt of my pestering, so each deserve a mention of gratitude from me personally in writing. If I have not mentioned any deserving DJ's, then I obviously did not pester you enough.

133

My Top Thirty Rockabilly Tunes (including Jivers)
In no particular order as they are all brilliant:

1. The Train Kept a' Rollin' - *by Johnny Burnette & the Rock 'n' Roll Trio*
2. I'm Coming Home - *by Johnny Horton*
3. Go Away Hound Dog - *by Cliff Johnson*
4. Miss Bobby Sox - *by Benny Joy*
5. Good Rockin' Tonight - *by Elvis Presley*
6. Crackerjack - *by Janis Martin*
7. Jitterbop Baby - *by Hal Harris*
8. All The Time - *by Sleepy LaBeef*
9. School of Rock 'n' Roll - *by Gene Summers*
10. You'll Be Mine - *by Howlin' Wolf*
11. I Got Love If You Want It - *by Warren Smith*
12. Matchbox - *by Carl Perkins*
13. Whirlwind - *by Charlie Rich*
14. Shake Your Hips - *by Slim Harpo*
15. Hip Hip Baby - *by Dennis Herrold*
16. Three Alley Cats - *by Roy Hall*
17. Blue Jean Bop - *by Gene Vincent*
18. Barking Up The Wrong Tree - *by Don Woody*
19. Pink Cadillac - *by Sammy Masters*
20. Do What I Do - *by Slim Rhodes*
21. She's The Most - *by The Five Keys*
22. Why - *by The Cues*
23. Bloodshot Eyes - *by Wynonie Harris*
24. Don't Be Angry - *by Nappy Brown*
25. Lucky Lips - *by Ruth Brown*
26. How Low Can You Feel - *by Ray Campi*
27. Red Headed Woman - *by Sonny Burgess*
28. Ducktail - *by Joe Clay*
29. Slip, Slip, Slippin' In - *by Eddie Bond*
30. One Hand Loose - *by Charlie Feathers*

Can't stop to keep rocking kid, yeah. The above are a lot of the tunes I used to pester the DJs with and anyone into rockabilly music knows there are hundreds more fabulous songs where they all came from. What was great about rockabilly was when it hit our shores in the late 1970's and early 1980's all these fabulous tunes came at once. Whereas the disco smoothies of the day were into the charts and each week waiting for the top twenty countdown and eventually finding their number one hit, when you were into rockabilly every song being played was a chart hit number 1 – it was just brilliant.

You are what you eat and I'm always hungry for classic ROCKABILLY.

SKIFFABILLY

Rock 'n' Roll + Skiffle + Country + Rockabilly = Skiffabilly!

Skiffabilly also = singers + songwriters + entertainers + people with good attitudes in the music business + people who have had some sort of success either performing or playing an instrument from the 1950's right up to the present day. This was the pedigree for this band wagon. Even though a few of them were in their own minds musical legends and thought Skiffabilly was lucky to have them, we knew we had to sort out the egos and attitudes which is pretty much 99% of all showbiz people. Once they were told the rules they needed to abide by, only then could they be a member of Skiffabilly.

Who wrote the Skiffabible - Robbie Mac, Annie Freeman, and me. We never left out musicians who played something other than guitar, bass and drums. If you had a talent with a washboard, a stomp stick, or the spoons, you would also be considered to join Skiffabilly.

The band was formed for the sole reason of fusing lots of music styles as well as many types of characters. Skiffabilly played mainly in shopping centres and theme parks and should any member decide to be ill or fed up with performing in the band, then there was no end of replacements (we would have been better calling ourselves the revolving doors!). One way of making sure there was always a band to perform Robbie Mac decided to put together a rehearsal in the Norbiton Social Club, South West London, with the sole intention of having a lot of musicians in attendance; in fact nearly everyone he had in his phone book. The theory behind this was to have an endless list of musicians and singers available at any time and this would also send out a message that nobody was more important than anybody else, and everybody was replaceable.

A sort of King Arthur and the Knights of the Round Table effect or so we thought. I went along with it but thought it a bit strange when at this mega musician rehearsal, we had 4 drummers (Brendon Coleman, Clem Cattini, Tony Donegan, and Mark Main Ellen), five lead guitarists (among them Terry Dunham who was a good club and country styled lead guitarist and Eddie Wheeler who in my opinion is one of the UK's top ten guitarists), three bass players (Terry Peaker, Bernie Hagley, and Pete Oakman), and four keyboard players (two being Steve Oakman and Chris Skornia). Only one stomp stick player though, and that was Johnny Podd, who played this amazing contraption which was a kind of an upright broom handle with a tambourine nailed to it, jingle bells, a furry toy animal, a small dustbin lid and to finish it off, a chamber pot on top!

Also, attending this rehearsal was Mr. Rock Island Line - Lonnie Donegan, the King of Skiffle, as he and Robbie knew each other well and skiffle was a large part of the music repertoire. Lonnie liked the idea of what we were doing, not only because it was a lot of fun, but also thought business wise there was a lot of mileage to be had out of Skiffabilly. As I have mentioned, one of the four drummers of Skiffabilly was Lonnie's son Tony Donegan, who not only looked very much like Lonnie but sang very much like him as well, so he got promoted from being a drummer to drums and vocals. The rehearsal began and was like paratroopers jumping out of a plane. You played a song, just getting into the feel of things and then Robbie would say 'Next' so up would come the next musician, quickly shake the hand of who he was taking over from (kind of like when a footballer is being substituted, but in this case the person leaving was probably thinking 'what was that all about?'). Then it came to half time.

Lovely Annie had prepared sandwiches for everyone, and much welcome liquid refreshments were provided by the bar staff. It was at this moment drummer Clem Cattini from the Tornado's pulled me outside and asked 'Johnny what is this all about, I thought it was a rehearsal, or so I was told, and well it's a sort of mayhem'. 'I know what you are saying Clem, but the idea is to see who would join the ranks and to see if they are going to give it their all'. Clem replied, 'You've got to give it to Robbie, I do not know anyone else who could get so many people together in one place on just an idea, even Lonnie Donegan's turned up!' 'Okay Clem, let's get back inside, finish this massive rehearsal and go from there'.

Once back inside we were all ready for round two. Robbie clearly excited about how everything was going, collected packages from various musicians in one hand and had a large folder in the other. He came charging over to me, then unfortunately fell backwards over a monitor speaker that was on the floor. He landed like someone had just given him a judo throw. Now the whole rehearsal came to a standstill, Robbie now the centre of attention, lying on his back in a starfish shape, not able to move but somehow still clutching the folders and biogs, he was clearly in great pain. An ambulance was called, and the second half of this rehearsal was Robbie being carried out by the ambulance crew. All the musicians realized it was best to call it a day for now, so they started setting down their equipment, packing away everything into their cars. I decided to tell everyone they would be called in the next couple of days as soon as Robbie was fit and able to do so.

I thought it only right before the ambulance left to let Robbie know all was okay with everyone, as he had worked so hard to put the whole venture together. I went to the back of the ambulance, knocked on the door and when it opened I was confronted with Robbie seated with an oxygen mask smothering his face so I asked the ambulance lady 'Is it okay to talk?' she replied 'Be quick' so I said 'You don't have to say anything Robbie, but everyone's okay and I told them we'd call them, just nod if you understood what I just said', Robbie turned to me, breathing slowly like Darth Vader, he nodded that he understood, and although his face mask was all steamed up he gave a little smile, I smiled back, so I took it he understood. I then closed the ambulance door and returned to the rehearsal.

I had a few minutes chat with Lonnie Donegan who wished us well, but I told Lonnie this was all fine but this whole project was going nowhere until we could find a manager, and he agreed. I did not see Lonnie again until Skiffabilly's TV appearance. I think the whole occasion was pretty much a success as everybody who attended was still on-board the idea and Robbie, after a couple of days (and an operation to fix his badly broken wrist) was back in the full swing of things. When Annie, Robbie and myself had the next meeting though it was agreed that finding a manager was our next venture and although we did not know it, he was already amongst the ranks, – Arise Sir Pete Oakman. (See content regarding managers)

The whole project lasted for three years with a TV appearance in Canary Wharf called The Spanish Archer (a talent show which was on cable), but we had to have an original song for this show. Two days previously, Lonnie Donegan gave us a song he had penned called the *"The Respecting Line"*, which was along the lines of his past hit *"Cumberland Gap"*. The TV producer wanted a Skiffabilly original - so starting its life lyrically on the back of a cigarette packet was *"Skiffabilly Line Dance"* written by Robbie, Annie, and myself, and that was the eventual song performed on the TV show.

The band played a few pubs and clubs but the live performances in shopping centres was where the bulk of the work was performed. Skiffabilly did invade foreign shores... In Gelsenkirchen, Germany we played a show for R.E.M.E. (the Royal Engineers and Mechanical Engineers for the British army). What a journey, what a laugh! That was partly because after the show we knew the very next night we had a show back in England at the Royal Oak public house in Surbiton, London, which at the time was owned by Fred Mudd the lead singer of the 1950's group The Mudlarks. (The song *Lollipop* being their biggest hit.)

Fred ran it with his lovely wife Leila who was previously 'Miss Great Britain' and was one of the first female presenters of the iconic Blue Peter TV show. They loved Skiffabilly and let us use their venue for rehearsals.

This was a memorable show for me as before we started I went across the road to the nearest restaurant for an Indian meal. As I looked at the menu the chap sitting opposite me on the next table started talking to the lady he was with. I thought that his voice sounded not only distinct, but familiar for some reason. Then the light switched on in my mind, the previous week I had been writing songs with Brian Connolly from The Sweet and strangely enough he was mentioning a possible tour he had been approached to do with David Essex, and if Mr. Essex was interested, it was game on. Believe it or not, there he was David Essex was sitting right opposite me. I thought maybe if I were to ring Brian he could sort it out right there and then, but I have never been the one for imposing and David Essex was entitled to eat his meal in peace. It was probably a rare chance for him to be left alone from the constant attention of the general public, so I didn't mention anything and sat back to enjoy my meal before Skiffabilly once more hit the stage.

With Skiffabilly, the wages mainly came from the shopping centre themselves. They would pay us a small fee and we collected donations in a bucket which paid for the coffee and sandwiches. The person in charge of that task was sometimes Annie, but on many occasions, it was another member of Skiffabilly, a lovely lady called Babs (who I still see from time to time). She turned up on all those freezing winter mornings at town centres and sold our merchandise, swinging and swaying along to the music while selling, and never without a smile. Babs was a Skiffette through and through.

We started getting quite a following in the shopping centres, and although we mostly performed covers we always got the most audience response from our self-penned *Skiffabilly Line Dance* which became our theme tune. This led to us having a group of dancing girls called the Skiffabilly line dancers. One of them was Jo O'Meara who not long after became one of the lead singers of S Club 7. I wonder if S Club 7 ever considered singing Skiffabilly Line Dance. I wonder if Jo ever told them about her Skiffabilly days!

Peter Oakman who was our one and only proper manager informed us 'You can't manage what can't be managed', and so Skiffabilly gradually faded out in 2002, especially as by then the bulk of the bands line-up were also members of Vanity Fare, who were very busy on their own.

Even today, amongst Vanity Fares many performances, their Solid Silver 60's tours backing all the 1960's legends... Chris Farlowe, P.J. Proby, Dave Berry, Mersey Beats, Wayne Fontana etc. are always a sell-out. With people moving in other directions, like the Roman Empire, Skiffabilly conquered, but disbanded stone by stone to the fading tones of the washboard and the stomp stick.

I'll let you into a little secret. If you ever see a large number of pigeons walking together in a shopping centre, I mean fifty or so, you will notice they all walk in the same direction then quickly all turn just like sequence dancing and then they all walk in the other direction. One day at Braintree shopping centre a crowd of about two hundred people turned up to watch us, but as they crowded around they left a large space in front of us, the usual concrete dance floor. Somebody must have thrown some breadcrumbs down in this area because when we kicked off with *'Skiffabilly Line Dance'* the crowd roared and then to the bands and the public's hilarious amusement all these pigeons flew in from everywhere and hit the floor. It looked like they were all dancing in sequence, all the way through Skiffabilly Line dance, and unbelievably they were in time with the rhythm. You got it; they stole the show (ruddy pigeonbillys).

Yes, we were troubadours of the shopping centres, our moment in time had come and gone and although with Skiffabilly the writing was on the washboard, today on You Tube you can see for yourselves *Skiffabilly Line Dance* has gone Global. Tens of thousands of people around the world love to dance to the song (..they would never have believed the songs origins stemmed from the back of a fag packet). Skiffabilly was all about the music, it may not sound too rock 'n' roll but alcohol and drugs were out..., a hot tea and coffee was our buzz. As crazy as it sounds whether I am in Germany, Holland or the UK when I walk through any shopping centre I smile to myself as I imagine the whole place coming alive and shoppers stopping in their tracks, placing their bags on the floor, cheering and clapping, dancing on the spot with one and all rejoicing in the freezing weather, all bonding together as one, singing that eternal shopping centre anthem...

'Skiffabilly Line Dance Rock Rock, Skiffabilly Line Dance Roll, Roll, Roll'!

Skiffabilly Line Dance

Skiffabilly music is a here to stay
It's a line dance craze and it's comin your way
We know you'll love it so give it a try
C'mon join the dance and you'll see why

Chorus:
Skiffabilly line dancin' rock rock
Skiffabilly line dancin' roll roll
Skiffabilly line dancin' rock rock
Skiffabilly line dancin' roll roll

You hit that floor using heel and toe
Slapping leather is a way to go
It's a sure fine way to make a new friend
C'mon everybody we'll do it again

Repeat Chorus

Two step, four step Cotton Eyed Joe
Hit them hips baby nice and low
Tush push tush push let ya feet glide
Now you're ready for the electric slide

Repeat Chorus

Solo

Repeat Verse One

Repeat Chorus x Two

Discography of Skiffabilly
1998-2002
Released Cassettes x 4
Released CD Albums x 2
CD 3 (in negotiation with Lonnie Donegan but never released)

Skiffabilly Drummers:

Brendon Coleman: A good guy with a great spirit – definitely everybody's friend. He kept a strong beat that worked well in the clubs as well as being a good laugh, always gave it his all. Brendon drove everywhere in his Sweeney styled brown original Ford Granada. Only ever little issue with him was when he drank two tins of red bull one after the other at a social club in Wimbledon right before going on stage and could not help playing every song at a hundred miles per hour, including the ballads.

Clem Cattini: (Read my section on British rock 'n' roll regarding Clem), only performed a couple of shows for Skiffabilly as he was always very busy with The Tornados. Clem saw the potential and was only a phone call away should we need him, but after the Norbiton Club get-together he kept the rehearsals to a minimum.

Mark Main Ellen: Drummer for 60's group 'Vanity Fare'. Still drums today and is resident DJ on the 'Isle of Sheppey' playing Country and

Bluegrass classics. A true Scotsman, a decent and loyal fella who often does a duo performance with Johnny Podd... "No Comebacks". Marks daughter Holly is the drummer of a punk band, 'Less Than Worse' ...she could not have been indoctrinated by a better tutor than her father.

Tony Donegan: Drummed at the beginning when joining Skiffabilly, playing all the shopping centres and theme parks, pubs and clubs but did not please his dad Lonnie too much when he turned up to our TV appearance forgetting his drumsticks (but made up for it with a great TV performance). Tony kept a good beat but really came to the fore when he played rhythm guitar and sang lead vocals, not only because his dad was Lonnie Donegan, but when he did a rendition of *'The Rock Island Line'* or *'The Battle of New Orleans'* or any of his father's million sellers, it was as if Lonnie was back on stage. Tony sounded just like his father and looked very similar as well.

I liked working with Tony; he was a straight up guy and had I the finances and the backing, I would have toured him on his own and would have definitely recorded original material as he was a good song-writer as well. Today you can see Tony at various theatres and venues performing those Skiffle hits, an act well worth seeing, and he deserves his place in the Skiffabilly Hall of Fame.

Skiffabilly Bass Players:

Terry Peaker: A music teacher by day but also a hardened musician, Terry has been around for years and even performed with Emile Ford and the Checkmates on *"What Do You Want to Make Those Eyes at Me For"*, and *"Slow Boat to China"*. Terry also worked with 'The Commitments' and 'The Walker Brothers'. A very dedicated musician - one thing I always said about Terry, you ring him and tell him you have a show tomorrow night 500 miles away; if he agrees to be there he'll be the first to arrive.

Rod Demick: A good guy who has always performed brilliantly and has a good pedigree. He was in 'The David Essex Band', 'The Strawbs' and worked with an old acquaintance of mine, 'Screaming Lord Sutch'. Like most Irishman he was one of the gang with the right attitude and always made the best of any situation, a good guy to be around. I liked working with Rod mainly because on stage he came alive and had a great ambience about him. He fitted well into Skiffabilly.

Peter Oakman: A credit to the British music business. I got on with Pete as soon as I met him, and I told Robbie and Annie that to have Pete on-board was good in any capacity, and he was a terrific bass player. He started in his first band in 1957 in a skiffle group called 'The Spacemen' alongside Joe Brown, which ended up becoming 'Joe Brown and The Bruvvers'. He then backed artists like Marty Wild and Englebert Humperdink. He backed one of my favourite rockers, Gene Vincent.

When Gene first toured the UK, he used Joe Brown and The Bruvvers as his backing group. Peter also co-wrote Joe Browns biggest hit *'Picture of You'* and when very first touring, Pete laughed when he told me often back in the early 1960's standing in the wings was his warm up act who were none other than The Beatles. He also toured with Dion and Del Shannon, and the list of music legends he has worked with is endless - and to think Pete too, walked those concrete pavement slabs and Skiffabillied along with the rest of us. 'Well done mate'!

Bernie Hagley: Bass player for 'Vanity Fare' but a great saxophone player as well and always plays the flute on that famous song *'Hitching A Ride'*, Vanity Fares biggest hit. Bernie never stops working. If he is not filming, he is playing bass or recording or rehearsing, also working the P.A. sound system. When it comes to the all-round music man they do not come any better or hard-working than Bernie. He is never doing nothing, that's why he is not the easiest guy to get hold of. Bernie is a model of consistency, excellent bass player and the big feather in his cap - he too kept rocking through all those freezing shopping centre mornings; never moaned just got on with it.

Skiffabilly Guitarists:

Eddie Wheeler: I have already said in my opinion Eddie Wheeler must be at the top end of the very best of British lead guitarists, a very gifted and talented player. Eddie is best known for being the lead guitarist in 'Vanity Fare' as well as being the lead singer for the group. Eddie played lead guitar for Skiffabilly on and off throughout the group's 4-year life span, always committed, and still today Eddie is knocking them dead throughout the UK and Europe with his show performances. No great surprise with the talent he has.

John Clare: A brilliant lead guitarist, especially in the field of Country and Rock 'n' Roll, John worked alongside Pete Oakman for many years with 'The

Bruvvers' and teamed up with producer and songwriter Roger Greenaway (famous with 'Blue Mink'). John was in the group 'Harley Quinne' and backed many a famous name: Paul McCartney, The Troggs, Brenda Lee, to name just a few. Another strong link in the Skiffabilly chain.

Terry Dunham: Played in a lot of club and pub band line-ups. A good country rock player, usually performed in bands with Brendon the drummer as they both came from north London, Terry was great in the shopping centres and brought his lovely lady partner Kathy to every show. She must have known every song off by heart. At one stage Terry told me he had bad trouble with his eyesight. Of course, when people get on in life this can start to be a huge problem, but Terry had an operation on his eyes and his playing got even better. The band had an in-house joke about how it might change his life when getting his eyesight back. I am very glad to say he is still rocking today. A good songwriter as well, he was a great asset to the band.

Mick Payne (Pedal Steele): Mick was the full package for that sound, a fabulous Nashville feel to his playing and he looked the part as well, cowboy hat and boots at all times. Never seen him in anything else. I would not be surprised if he always went to bed with his hat and boots on! Sadly, Mick is no longer with us. God bless him, he will never be forgotten.

Skiffabilly Keyboards:

Steve Oakman: The son of Pete Oakman, performs in 'The Bruvvers' and tours with the Solid Silver 60's shows, a member of 'Vanity Fare', a music teacher and talented keyboard player. Steve worked a lot with Skiffabilly and recorded on the albums. I still work a lot with Steve today and am very proud to be associated with him. His talents are endless, a bit like Norman Wisdom who could play most instruments, but nobody ever really knew it. Steve is in the same league and will receive his Skiffabilly badge through the post very soon.

Chris Skornia: Chris Skornia is one of the most comical people I have ever met (tailor made for Skiffabilly). He started his humble beginnings in the punk rock band 'The Truth' and is today playing with 'The Overtures' who work with major artists like Elton John, a great musician and songwriter and my anchorman for many years, a good guy to have on your side.

Skiffabilly Lead Singers, Front Men & Women:

Wee Willie Harris: Known as the wild man of rock 'n' roll, the smallness attribute in his name is because he is 5ft 2ins in height, not for any other part of his name! Willie was dying his hair in all sorts of colours 30 years before, (the original punk rocker!), and it was when he was given a golden career chance by TV Producer Jack Good, who at the time had one of the greatest rock 'n' roll shows on television 'The Six Five Special' aired on the BBC. I've got to give it to Willie, a good showman who can whip up a crowd on any occasion. When he performed with Skiffabilly he would always wear a Teddy boy drape coat with drainpipe trousers and brothel creepers and lime green or pink socks. His early career goes as far back as 1957, with his self-penned song *"Rocking at the 2 i's"*. Willie started performing at all the top rock 'n' roll and Skiffle clubs, among them London's 'The Hundred Club' in Oxford Street.

Willie has been performing shows all his life and when in Skiffabilly he fitted in well with his skiffle and r 'n' r show. He would do his bit, and a bit more and then a bit more after that until on some occasions somebody would say 'Fetch me the sheep crook,' because you just could not get him off. He mostly always received a standing ovation and that speaks volumes in the entertainment business. From 'The Six Five Special' to 'The Wheel Tappers and Shunters Club' Wee Willie Harris's suede shoes must have walked across every single stage in Great Britain. If you are into rock 'n' roll check him out at a performance, I guarantee you won't be disappointed.

John Allison: John Allison was one of the two Allison's, the pop duo who came second in the Eurovision Song Contest 1962 with the song *"Are You Sure"*. He was one of the many artists who came to the massive Skiffabilly rehearsal at the Norbiton Club. Like so many artists I have come across that had been mistreated by record companies and dubious managers throughout the 1950', 60's and 70's (because they were the golden years for ripping off artists) John Allison was obviously one of them. He brought it to my attention straight away. He asked me at the Norbiton rehearsal if I wouldn't mind taking a look at his original contract as he knew I had a few litigation matters regarding publishing and managerial differences in the music business. Owning my own record label and music publishing business, he was thinking maybe I could shed some light on what went wrong, so as well as coming to rehearse he made sure he had brought a copy of his original

1960's recording contract with him. We went outside, and I was hoping I'd have enough time as my last contractual agreement was twenty pages of intense music jargon, where you can scrutinize every single line in what it really means in legal terms, not what you think it means. To my amazement, he pulled out an A4 piece of paper out of a folder and started telling me how badly he had been treated. I looked at this one-page contract and after reading it 'What do you think?' John asked me 'Well for a start, it's over thirty years old and in my humble opinion if you try and resolve this, basically you've got no chance. All the monies, accounts and records pertaining to this contract are long gone. If I was you I would just put it behind you and move on, as I do not think today there is anything to get. Like I say, the monies are long gone and basically irretrievable.' He looked at me very disappointedly and never really spoke to me again throughout the rest of the rehearsal.

John Allison did perform well through his short spell with Skiffabilly and his name is etched on the washboard. I say good luck in whatever he does. I often wonder if he still carries around a copy of that contract, you never know he might have caught up with all the guilty parties of his earlier years - if not I hope he has got rid of the ghosts, 'Are you Sure!'

Annie Watts: Today better known as DJ Annie and was the only female singer with Skiffabilly also co-writing *"Skiffabilly Line Dance"* and performing lead vocals on the song *"My Dixie Darling"* which was released on Skiffabilly CD 002 – and she was there from day one till the Skifflin' end. Annie played bongo's, tambourine and was a brilliant asset to the group, always happy, (made all the sandwiches when required for rehearsals etc.), and along with myself and Robbie she made most band decisions including hiring and firing. The trouble for people like Annie, when you are a truly decent person, show business can take its toll on the softer natured person and Skiffabilly had its fair share of egotistic self-indulged stars 'The me, me, me clan.' Annie today DJs at special occasions and is always there when I need sound and proper advice – 'The top end of the Skiffabilly who's who list.'

Lonnie Donegan: I TOLD ROBBIE - 'He did not need an audition' Lonnie loved the whole Skiffabilly ethos and from the very start wanted to get involved at some stage. Although living in Spain, Robbie always kept Lonnie updated, and Lonnie had put pen to paper with songs and ideas that he wanted to put to the project, especially as his son Tony was playing drums and singing in the group. Unfortunately, on the 3rd April 2002 Lonnie passed away, which was quite a blow for Skiffabilly, not only as we loved to be associated with the King of Skiffle, but we were in negotiation with Lonnie regarding Skiffabilly's 3rd CD release featuring him with a couple of newly written songs by him, to coincide with putting a UK tour together. It was all in motion with the Bruvvers as the band to back Lonnie and the posters were being made with Lonnie headlining and also on the billing were The Tornados, John Leyton, and of course Skiffabilly. It was a sad day for all Skiffabillies on hearing the passing of Lonnie. Always in our set list were at least 3 or 4 of Lonnie's classics and every time we performed those classics the audience's response was electric. One thing that came to the fore, while Elvis was hailed 'The King of rock 'n' roll', Lonnie certainly deserved the title 'The King of Skiffle'!

Robbie Mac: Robbie Mac, co-formed a skiffle band in 1958 called 'Skiffle 58' along with another band called 'City Skiffle' in West Yorkshire, so he had this music in his blood from its birth. Co-writer of *Skiffabilly Line Dance* he always gave the project his all, and I mean dedication 24/7. Robbie is no longer with us and was laid to rest back in his beloved Scotland. If ever Skiffle had its most ardent follower, it was the man with the tartan washboard... Robbie Mac.

Eddie Wheeler, Bernie Hagley, Rod Demick, Pete Oakman, Terry Dunham. All played bass and lead guitar but also sang lead vocals through the show.

Session Musicians:

Guitar/Banjo: **Derek Mandell**
Fiddle: **Bob Loveday**
Washboard/Stomp stick: **Johnny Podd**

18

BRITISH ROCK 'N' ROLL

In my opinion, there is no getting away from it; most of the best rock 'n' roll is American. The standards were set very high with Elvis, Buddy Holly, Gene Vincent, Eddie Cochran, Bill Haley, Little Richard and the like. However, I am a Brit and I am very proud of our input, and equally proud to have shared the stage and enjoyed the company with many of the British rock 'n' roll legends that we all have come to love and adore. Everybody has their British favourite and only a few always end up as top of that list. Personally, I loved most of them but the iconic image, the rawness of our very own Billy Fury followed closely by Johnny Kidd and the Pirates are amongst the best for me. Funnily enough Germany, France, Holland and other European countries had their own rockers too, but I think as far as Europe is concerned the British rockers were at the helm.

DAVE SAMPSON

While I was living in Ruislip Manor, West London, a British rock 'n' roll star was residing just up the road in South Harrow. My manager of the time Kevin Allen (who was a big British rock 'n' roll fan) got very excited at the chance to walk his fingers through his record collection and pick out all his British Columbia singles of one of his biggest stars of the early 1960's. The man I'm talking about was a teen rocker of the early 1960's, Dave Sampson. Kevin arranged a meeting at the Breakspear Arms public house on the outskirts of Uxbridge, we arrived early and picked a table out the way so as not to be bothered by anyone, and we waited eagerly. Dave arrived right on time and to our surprise he had brought along some of his original recordings. Amongst them his fabulous EP Dave Sampson & the Hunters, along with some original flyers from the 1960's and he spread them all out on the table - a nice display of memorabilia. I was quite an avid pop memorabilia collector and Dave noticed my eyes were lighting up very brightly, but he was not here to barter with his little treasure trove. He had a look of eagerness on his face, ready to get back into action on stage and you could see he was ready for a comeback.

After the introductions, it became quite evident Dave had been off the road for far too long and was interested in putting a band together, and just like any artiste who had tasted fame, would love to see the stage lights turned back on. Kevin hung on every word Dave had to say and we were both intrigued when he told us of his encounter with legendary agent and promoter entrepreneur Larry Parnes. Larry had arranged a meeting with Dave at his London flat, and Dave being a straight guy, was pre-warned by some friends how affectionate Larry could be.

Dave with a serious look on his face said 'There I was sitting on Larry Parnes couch and all that was going through my mind was remembering a warning from another singer who had said that whatever happens do not let Larry close the electric curtains'. Dave carried on saying that to his horror out comes Larry wearing a bath robe and slippers and starts the electric curtain game. Dave got up and in no uncertain terms told Larry his father was a policeman (I think that was actually true). With a look of relief on Dave's face he happily said, 'The meeting soon came to an end'. You could say that was Dave Sampson's last curtain call, well - as far as Larry Parnes was concerned.

The conversation moved on very quickly to Sir Cliff Richard, who was really the thorn in Dave's side. Dave Sampson sounded very much like Cliff and there was only room for one chap who sounded like that. It is well known Cliff Richard in the beginning was just walking in the shadows of Elvis like most early 1950's rockers and eventually Cliff was told he had to be himself, which left him lost at first, but he did find his own identity and the rest is history. Being an Elvis no 2 meant even back then you could tour the world and make a good living but as a Cliff no 2, living in the same country, well, ..this town ain't big enough for the both of us. Dave seemed as though he suffered a bit from what I call seconditus, no matter how much talent you have, how hard you try, no matter what you do, destiny points the arrow in the favour of someone else. To his credit, Dave still had a good voice and got back on the road performing rock 'n' roll shows country wide, and when interviewed said it was his meeting with myself and Kevin that made him put his rock 'n' roll shoes back on and perform his 1960's classics once more.

Dave Sampson passed away March 2014 aged 73 and as far as I'm concerned, he can be very proud of the winkle picker footprints he left behind as one of the British rock 'n' rollers. A well-deserved place in my British rock 'n' roll Hall of Fame.

TOMMY BRUCE

I've been very proud to have worked with some of the best British rock 'n' roll stars, but nothing hits home more than when you remember playing a 45rpm single to death, which is exactly what I did with Tommy Bruce's hit record of *"Ain't Misbehavin'"*, which was on that fabulous green Columbia label. I was on the stage with Tommy a few times while working with the band Skiffabilly and I am sure not just I, but anyone who ever met Tommy can only say what a lovely guy he was. Tommy, when being interviewed once said 'My voice is a mixture of sandpaper and gravel and you can also throw in a cockney accent, which all together sounds diabolical'. Now tell me that's not honesty.

I drove Tommy home one night after a show that we'd both performed in Sunbury-on-Thames (he lived in Watford) and he talked about a lot of the good times he had experienced, especially working with a few of the original rockers. Tommy also loved listening to stories about the laughs and times I had with the Jordanaires.

I always remember something Michael Caine once said when asked the question 'how do you become a brilliant actor?' His reply was along the lines of 'Choose your best actors and actresses, study them very closely and when you see their best performing moments and all the charisma that makes them brilliant, nick it and make it your own, then you will find you will just get better and better'. I suppose when you think about it, that is pretty much what Elvis did. Well I certainly learnt a little of my stage trade from Tommy Bruce and loved the way he got straight to the point where business was concerned without boring you in the process. Most of all I loved the way he worked the audience, laughing and joking (especially with the ladies), looking sharp in his tailored suits that fitted perfectly, and a tan that never seemed to fade... yes Tommy was tailor made for the stage.

Obviously, his cabaret years bought about professionalism you can only learn from years on the road. It was well known he came from humble beginnings and his parents both died when he was a child, so Tommy was brought up in an orphanage and from there worked in Covent Garden as a van driver, and like so many stars of the day also had to do his national service which he served in Belgium.

Tommy joined forces with a Birmingham based band called the Bruisers and they endlessly toured like so many other rock 'n' roll stars of the day and featured on the bill with some of Britain's biggest stars, among them the fabulous Billy Fury.

Tommy passed away in 2006, and I am sure I speak for the many that saw him perform and who got to meet this lovely fella... Tommy Bruce certainly was one of Britain's best!

CLEM CATTINI

I was approached by Maestro records who after coming to one of my performances liked the idea of me recording a jive album for their dance label. As any record company would do, we struck up a couple of meetings whereupon it was agreed that they gave me total control to record a jive album for their label.

Straight away I put pen to paper and started to write the song *"Jive Time"* which eventually became the title of the album. The mammoth task that I had undertaken meant that I needed the best musicians in the rockabilly and rock 'n' roll world in order to produce a great jive album and there was no better place to begin than with finding the right drummer.

I rang some top producers who gave me their thoughts. Whilst doing so, it hit me that I needed to look no further than Britain's very own legendary rocker Mr. Clem Cattini. Anyone who has drummed on 44 different UK number one singles from *"Shaking All Over"* by Johnny Kidd and The Pirates to *"Telstar"* by the Tornado's as well as *"You Really Got Me"* by The Kinks certainly warrants respect and should be good enough to play on my *Jive Time* album. I already had Clem's phone number as he was part of the Skiffabilly bandwagon, so I called him straight away and in doing so I managed to find a little space in the work diary of one of Britain's most famous and prolific drummers.

I told Clem I needed a drummer to be able to give a rockabilly swing treatment on some tracks as well as a pumping rock 'n' roll style on others. I was looking for nothing but the best so that is why I called him, because to me in the music business people being famous or having egos or a great reputation is one thing, but when I am looking for the best musician for the job in hand I had to be 100% certain of my choice – lucky for me as far as getting Clem Cattini on board (cometh the time cometh the man).

The way Clem controlled that rhythm on *"Swing Me Baby"*, the best rockabilly jiver I have written to date (thanks partly to his performance), was a taster of things to come. How he performed on the song *Jive Time* was knock out! ..and not forgetting how he rocked on the Bill Haley's medley *R.O.C.K Rock* and the Little Richard medley, basically Clem came to the fore resulting in the *Jive Time* album being one of my favourite albums I have ever recorded.

I always usually supply food and beverages for refreshments during recording sessions as I find musicians work a lot better on a sandwich rather than an empty stomach. These are always good times to have a break from hard working sessions and normally are quite interesting, as I found in conversation with Clem, and on most of our breaks all the discussions were great. He told me of how he loved working with Dusty Springfield, T. Rex, along with Johnny Kidd, and of course some funny memories while working with the producer Joe Meek. I really enjoyed my recording with Clem Cattini which showed me he definitely is one of Great Britain's finest rockers and he is another who very deservedly belongs in my treasured memories of British rock 'n' roll greats. Keep the beat Clem!

JOHN LEYTON

Hey there wild wind, blow away my blues... Johnny I remembered you when we were both on the same billing at Bob Potters Venue, the Lakeside Country Club. There was a list of British rock 'n' roll legends appearing at this event including the fabulous Tornados and it was all in aid of the charity "Chain of Hope" at Harefield hospital, founded by renowned heart specialist Professor Magdi Yacoub, to enable children from oversees with serious heart problems and no hope of life saving surgery in their own countries to come to be treated at the hospital; a very worthy cause. I was looking forward to this event because I was going to meet long time British 1960's legend John Leyton. I had brought with me an original 45rpm single of *"Son This Is She"* on the HMV record label for Mr. Leyton to sign. John is not only a singer, he was well known for his legendary film roles, among these classics The Great Escape. I was thinking of bringing a trowel, piece of rope and a candle just for a laugh and was going to ask him which tunnel it was to the stage, but he did not know me at all and that might not of have been such a good introduction.

So, there I was backstage in the dressing room and got to meet the man himself. We started chatting and he gladly signed my record, and then a couple of ladies managed to get backstage and push their way up to John. They were the purest of rock 'n' roll fans, original teddy girls dressed in the full rock 'n' roll attire with the name John Leyton embroidered on to their lovely silk dresses. Both ladies were gazing into their idols eyes and I was not going to stand in the way of these most loyal and dedicated followers of Mr. Leyton. We finished having a quick conversation about music, I shook John's hand, wished him a good show as did he back to me and we both got ready for our performances. I was on a high that night because to me the John Leyton song *"Lonely City"* from the 1962 film, "It's Trad Dad" along with the hit record *"Wild Wind"* makes one feel very proud to be a British rock 'n' roller. And here was I performing on the same stage and billing as John.

68-73 (clockwise) Cast of the theatre production 'Forever Elvis' – (From left to right) Peachy Meade who played Colonel Tom Parker, myself and lead guitarist Nick Bunker; Photo on-tour; Three early publicity shots; Relaxing at home; His Majesty's Theatre Aberdeen

GIGLINE U.K.
Presents at the

Hippodrome
LONDON

Direct from the West End Musical
"FOREVER ELVIS"

Ricky Dean

Nº 005475

(formerly Johnny Dumper)

Wednesday 17th February 1988

Live on stage with his commercial & original Rock 'n Roll Sound
by popular demand

On stage at midnight
Doors open 9 p.m.

MANAGEMENT RESERVE THE RIGHT OF ADMISSION

Admit 1 or 2 at £4 each

GIGLINE SHOWCASE
Party Night/Rock 'n Roll

KEVIN ALLEN
& HENRY SELLERS
PRESENTS
THE TWENTY FIFTH ANNIVERSARY CONCERT TOUR

**STARRING
BRIAN
CONNOLLY
& SWEET**

WITH VERY SPECIAL
GUEST MR ROCK N ROLL

**JOHNNY
Earle**

★ PLUS FULL SUPPORT ★

BRISTOL
HIPPODROME

An Apollo Leisure Theatre

Managing Director Paul Gregg General Manager John Wood

SATURDAY 20th MARCH 1993 AT 8.00 p.m
TICKETS £6.50/£7.50/£8.50

74 (**opposite page**) Hippodrome, London ticket

75 (**opposite page**) The show that never was, so all posters were thrown away besides a handful of copies; 76-79 Posters from around the world, including Holland and Sri Lanka

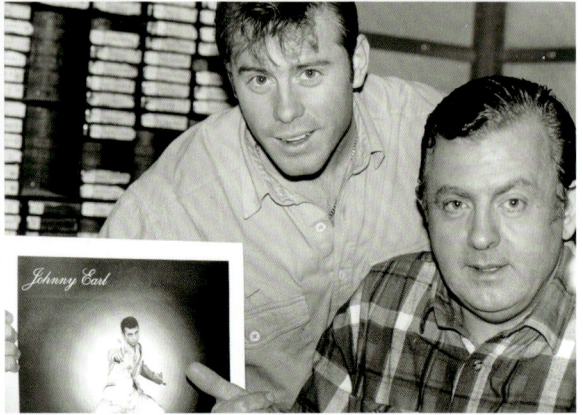

80-86 (clockwise) Myself and Star Wars' very own Darth Vader also known as the 'Green Cross Code man' - Dave Prowse MBE; To the left of me Linda Gail Lewis (Jerry Lees' little sister); On Devon Air radio; Me with Big Jem 'A Legend'; With original member of the Louisiana Hayride, Paul Maitland - 'Great actor, musician and performer - friend for life'; Myself with Kenny G; At the airport

Page Three **FELLA**

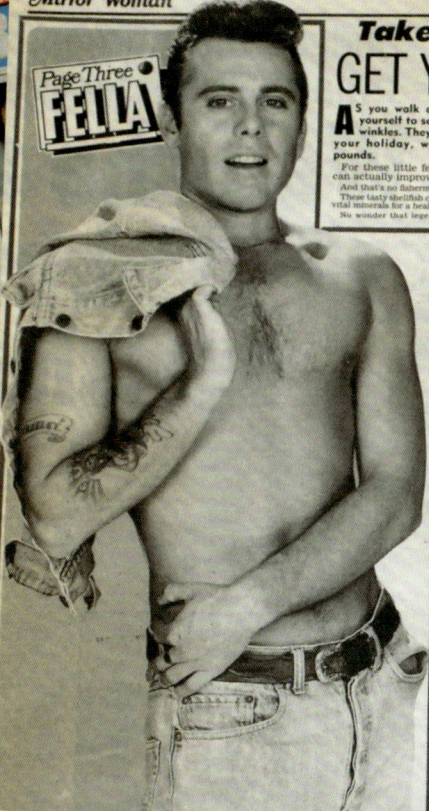

Take some fishy advice . .

GET YOUR HOOKS INTO THIS SEXY DIET SLIMMING

by CHRISTINE GARBUTT

AS you walk along the prom, treat yourself to some cockles, whelks or winkles. They may add extra zing to your holiday, without adding extra pounds.

For these little fellas, along with oysters, can actually improve your sex life.

And that's no fisherman's tale.

These tasty shellfish contain up to eight times more vital minerals for a healthy love-life than fillet steak.

No wonder that legendary Latin lover Casanova downed more than 50 oysters a night to keep up his stamina. Zinc and selenium are the minerals responsible for improving our love life, according to Robyn Wilson the author of a new book on fish.

And fish is one of the healthiest, protein foods you can eat, providing it is not coated in thick greasy batter. It keeps

you slim and wards off heart attacks.

Four ounces of white fish — such as hake, haddock and cod — only contains 85 calories, providing it is steamed, grilled or poached. Dipped in batter and crispy fried, the calories nearly treble.

Eskimos and the Japanese have the lowest incidence of heart disease in the world. Doctors and

nutritionists all agree it is due to the fish they eat — or more precisely, the oil in the fish.

Fish oil has a unique substance called Omega 3, which is known to break down cholesterol.

If that all seems a bit fishy to you, two Danish doctors studying the life-styles of Eskimos in Greenland, found not one single case of heart disease in 10 years.

So which fish will do the trick for you?

● **Improve your love** life: Cockles, whelks, winkles, caviar, oysters.

● **Help keep you** slim: Cod, sole, haddock, hake, halibut, plaice, prawns, lobster, mussels, turbot.

● **Ward off heart disease:** Herring, kippers, mackerel, perch, pilchards, sardines, tuna, trout, whitebait.

*Fish by Robyn Wilson, published by Sphere Books Ltd. Price £3.50.

——BEAUTY SPOT——

PEACHES and cream glamour girl, Suzanne Mizzi, keeps her skin soft and supple by using vitamin E cream all over her body.

Suzanne, who recently lost a stone in weight, says rubbing in vitamin E night and morning stopped her getting stretch marks as she slimmed.

"I never use soap," says Suzanne. "And, however tired I am, I always cleanse and tone my face before going to bed."

VITAMIN E: Suzanne

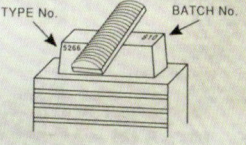
How Johnny makes Elvis live on . .

■ DISHY Johnny Dumper is not just an incredible hunk. The 23-year-old singer has a real talent for imitating Elvis Presley and Eddie Cochran.

■ Johnny hit the big time in the stage production of *Forever Elvis* and he starred in the movie *The Eddie Cochran Story.*

■ Elvis' old backing band The Jordanaires were so convinced by him that they reformed for his tour of Britain this autumn.

■ Johnny will also be taking part in an Elvis Presley memorial show next week, to mark the 11th anniversary of the King's death.

BUER · HORST · WESTERHOLT

SzeneGEflüster MIT SEBASTIAN KONOPKA

Wenig Weihnachtsstimmung in der Szene.
Stattdessen gibt's Funk, Rock und auch mal Roll.

Dienst am Schall

Nachgang frönen dann die alt eingesessenen Recken **Red House** aus Buer-City mit ebenfalls alt hergebrachtem Bluesrock. Ganz nebenbei wird der rote Trommler **Rainer Gollan** noch für seine mittlerweile schon zweijährige Tätigkeit im Dienste des freien Schalls bei der On The Rocks Session geehrt. Veranstaltungsort ist wie gewohnt die Erlenstraße #0.

Hoher Besuch hat sich dann für den kommenden Mittwoch, 12. Dezember, in buerschen Landen angekündigt. **Johnny Earl**, eigentlich derzeit auf Konzertrundreise durch England befindlich, macht Station im **Dorfkrug**. Woher man den kennt? Rock'n'Roll-Insider dürften in den letzten fast 30 Jahren kaum am Johnny vorbei gekommen sein, war der Gitarrist doch kaum bei ausufernden Solo-Eskapaden auch schon mit Carl „Blue Suede Shoes" Perkins und Elvis-Saitenarbeiter Scotty Moore unterwegs. Dementsprechend werden sicherlich auch Klassiker wie „Viva Las Vegas"

Johnny Earl rockt am nächsten Mittwoch mit seiner Band den Dorfkrug in Buer. Der Eintritt zum Konzert ist frei.

WATER GIRL! Drenched Di at the H

BIG C

MoT men rubbish Ron's perfect car

A B

HERO: Private Presley

KITTED OUT: Johnny gets ready to rock in his idol's GI uniform

ATTEN-SHUN! Singer Johnny Earl is set to march into the spotlight — wearing Elvis Presley's GI outfit.

The uniform has been kept in a military museum in West Germany since Private Presley left the American army in 1960.

But now Earl, 44, is to wear it. The 39-year-old British singer based his Wembley concert looka-like anniversary concert marking the 14th anniversary of Elvis's death.

Johnny said: "Elvis was the greatest rock 'n' roll singer ever.

"I am the first person to wear this uniform since he was demobbed."

GEE — I'VE AN ARMY OF ELVIS FANS

'Super union' bid

THE giant engineering union is on a interview vary which was a interesting bid

Vid
for

PATRICK SWAYZE
STEEL DAWN
Steel Dawn (Cert 18)
£5.99

UB40
CCCP
THE VIDEO MIX
£5.99

88 Article, German newspaper.
89 Article, Daily Mirror - in the King's uniform (with Princess Diana at back)

THE BIG BREAKFAST

16/12/94

Dear Johnny,

Just a quick letter from all of us at the Big Breakfast to thank you for coming on to the show today, and making the Elvis feature so special. I think you'll agree if you see the show on 2/1/95, that your outfits look absolutely fantastic.

I have passed your video on to the appropriate department, so hopefully that will be featured as well.

Many thanks again, and good luck with all your projects.

Yours,

Anna Richardson
Researcher: Big Breakfast Christmas shows

NOREX COURT, THAMES QUAY, 195 MARSH WALL, LONDON E14 9SG. TEL: 071 712 9300 FAX: 071 712 9400

---

ka kevin allen
Management & Promotions

14 Margaret Cassidy House
485 Bath Road
Longford
Middlesex UB7 0ET
© 01-897 9302

FAX TRANSMISSION

TO : JESSIE KENT

FROM: KEVIN ALLEN (RAMADA HOTEL DUBAI)

DATE: 01 FEBRUARY 1990

SUBJ: JOHNNY DUMPER

In receipt of your fax ref Jerry Lee Lewis, yes would be interested in the tour.

Currently touring the Middle East to capacity crowds due to support Little Richard in June back in the U.K.

Will be returning to London February 8th. Please call me at above address and phone number to discuss further.

Sincerely

KEVIN ALLEN
Personal Manager to Johnny Dumper

ANY OFFER CONTAINED WITHIN THIS LETTER DOES NOT IN ITSELF CONSTITUE A CONTRACT
VAT Registration Number 494 0167 39

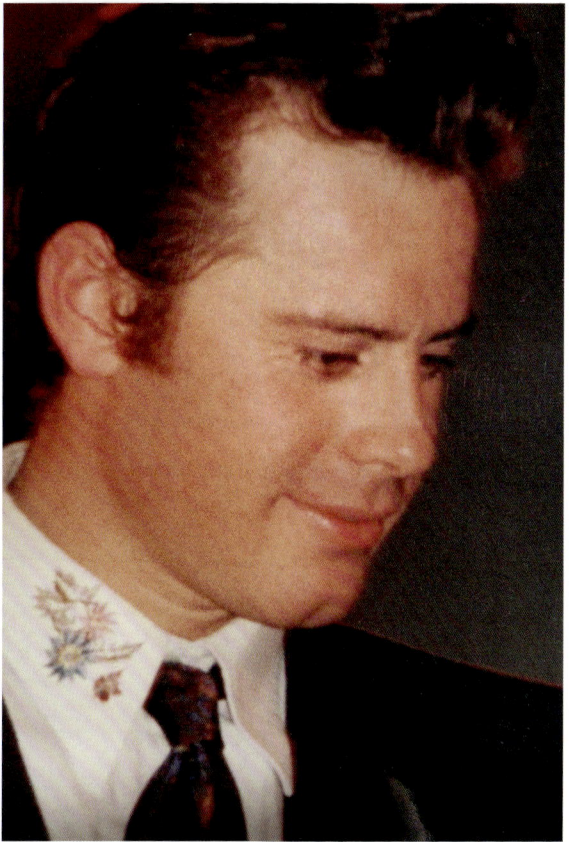

BECK THEATRE, GRANGE ROAD
HAYES, MIDDLESEX   01-561-8371
'ELVIS THE LEGEND'
TUESDAY EVENING 8.00PM
16-AUG-88

MR JOHNNY EARLE
IN CONCERT
Sat, 13 Mar 1993 8:00 PM
Row: D Seat: D23 £ 6.50

90-94 Letter from The Big Breakfast; Photo taken while being interviewed on Devon Air radio; Getting ready for my Jonathan Ross T.V. appearance; Tickets from Beck Theatre shows; Letter regarding Jerry Lee Lewis tour

A ♪ from the desk of . . .   **Gordon Stoker**

Johnny —
We want our special
friends to have a copy —
Pages 22 – 25 .
    We were lucky to get
this write up — since the magazine
is not one to give a write-up.
    Enjoyed being with you
in Holland.

Gordon

95 It was a big surprise when I received this letter from Gordon Stoker

COUNTRY Weekly

YOUR Country Music And Entertainment Magazine

July 29, 1997 | $1.69 Canada $1.99

The Jordinaires article in *Country Weekly* © Photo: The Jordanaires

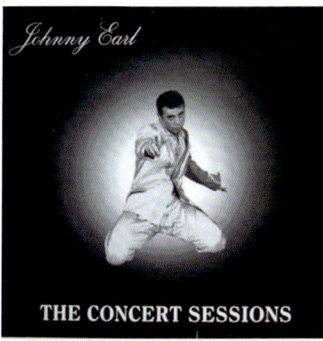

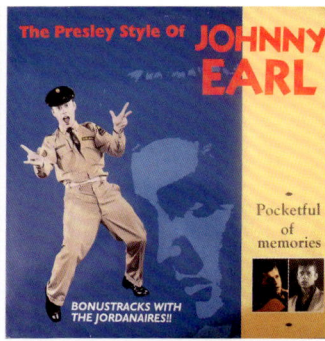

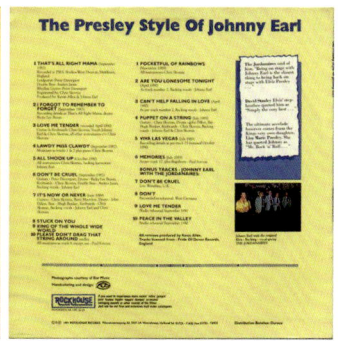

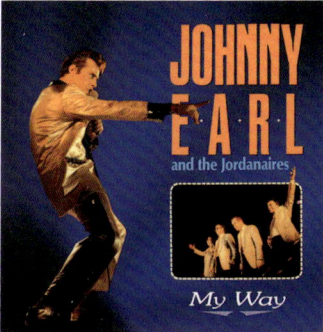

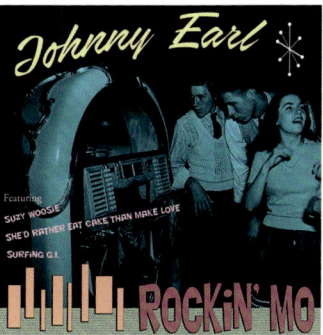

97 My very first 45rpm single release. Only a thousand were pressed - 250 in four different coloured 45rpm sleeves. 98 Let the Boogie Woogie Roll single; 99 Pocketful of Rainbows single; 100 The Girl of My Best Friend single; 101 Cassette covers including Skiffabilly tapes

102 The Concert Sessions LP; 103 The Presley Style of Johnny Earl LP; 104 My Way LP;
105 The American Dream LP; 106 Blue Suede Dreams CD; 107 Swing Me Baby CD;
108 Rockin' Mo CD; 109 Swing Me Baby / Anne-Marie Valentine double-A side

110 Front cover of the German fan club magazine 1991; 111 Before a performance, Germany 2018; 112 I told my friend Andy Schroer if you meet any Elvis royalty on tour take a photo and he only got hold of Priscilla Presley..!

113 With the Comic Crooners from Germany. My good friend Dirk the Elvis guy, one of the best German Elvis tribute acts I have seen. These are a German band I occasionally perform with and in the cowboy hat, good friend and brilliant performer Danny Wuntstell. Laying at my feet(!) my good buddies Andy Schroer and Thorsten.

His performance was superb, and you could tell he was at home while on the stage. Although getting rarer, its brilliant when you come across his original records on the HMV and Top Rank labels and for you ardent vinyl collectors, if like me you were wondering if any of his material was ever released on 78rpm the answer is yes, *"Johnny Remember Me"* but only in South Africa. Still I wouldn't mind finding a copy.

MEETING BILLY FURY'S MUM

Whilst on tour with the theatre production of Forever Elvis, one of our UK ports of call was Liverpool. This may have been home to the Beatles but for any British rocker this was the home to our very own rock 'n' roll great, Billy Fury.

I heard through the grapevine that a very special guest had taken the time to come and visit the cast of the show, and shortly would be coming back stage to greet us. When I was told it was going to be Billy Fury's mum, for me it was like someone saying the Queen was coming to visit. All emotions hit me at once, if it wasn't for this lady there would have been no Billy. 'Quick get me a camera', I shouted, (because if I could get a photo with her I would get it signed to my mother and to me that was just another blue suede dream).

I couldn't help but start to sing tracks from Billy's ten-inch album *"The Sound of Fury"*, *"That's love"* and *"Turn My Back on You"*, being just a couple. I was a little nervous and when the producer of the show knew how lit up I was at knowing Billy's mum was coming to see us, he tapped me on the shoulder and in my ear, he whispered 'This way Johnny, Billy's mum has just arrived'. I couldn't believe it; I was going to have a one to one with Billy's mum. I tried my best to leave the room as inconspicuously as possible then quickly followed the producer as he led me to the mother of Billy Fury, Jean Wycherley.

The producer introduced me as performing the songs of the young Elvis in the musical and Jean said, 'My Billy loved those early songs of Elvis,' I said, 'Jean we are all blessed to enjoy such fabulous songs from Elvis, but equally to me, as a British rocker, I am blessed with listening to the hits from your son Billy'. Jean smiled as she knew how much Billy meant to his fans (which I am certainly one of). She had most probably heard a million times over what I had just said but she still replied, 'You are very kind'. I asked if she would be so kind as to allow us to have a photo together, and if at a later date, she wouldn't mind signing it and dedicating it to my mummy. She was happy to do so, and I told her it would reside on my mother's wall in her little Devonshire home. That later date was actually at a Billy Fury memorial which I attended in Mill Hill, north London where Billy was laid to rest. I left Jean with a promise, I told her 'Jean at my next performance I'm going to dedicate a song to you as well as my mummy'. She looked at me and said, 'Which one would that be Johnny?' I gave a cheeky smile... *"That's Alright Mama"* of course!

19

A HANDFUL OF SONGS FROM THE JOHNNY EARL SONGBOOK

Queen of The Night

Verse One

There she stood with golden hair
The starlight gleaming from her eyes
Her perfume gently filled the air
Her red dress joined the evening sky

When she turned and smiled at me
I was helpless as can be
I found the courage for a smile
But I was shaking all the while

Chorus

I met the queen of the night
We sat and talked for just a while
A treasured moment held in time
So, I could make believe she's mine
I met the queen of the night
And then I kissed her hand goodbye
My cherished memory for all time
I met the queen of the night

G.I. Rock 'n' Roll

Verse One
C'mon everybody and listen to me
There's no squares allowed
When you're pulling 'KP'
You gotta go go go to the G.I. rock 'n' roll

Private Jimmy has got the blues
Cause' they won't let him march
In his blue suede shoes
But he go go go's to the G.I. rock 'n' roll

Chorus
The G.I. rock 'n' roll they sing
Early in the morning to reveille
They're shining those buckles and boots all night
Standing up straight and getting into line
It all adds up to one big marching show
You gotta go go go to the G.I. rock 'n' roll

A wash in cold water can give you a thrill
Like a running up and down
Oh blueberry hill
You gotta go go go to the G.I. rock 'n' roll

Big boy bloaters in the canteen
Eating twenty-six pies
Yu' know what I mean
But he go go go's to the G.I. rock 'n' roll

Repeat Chorus

You gotta go go go go
You gotta go go go go
You gotta go go go to the G.I. rock 'n' roll

Swing Me Baby

Swing me baby
Swing me baby
Swing me baby

Verse One
Swing me baby to and fro
Knock me flat like a domino
Pick me up and start again
Oh boy my baby really swings

Swing me baby left and right
Oh I'll be seeing stars tonight
And if she sees me start to sway
My baby swings me round again

Chorus
Swing me baby
Swing me baby
Swing me baby

Swing me baby around the clock
A keep on going just don't stop
Monday Tuesday bop and stroll
A Wednesday Thursday go man go

Friday night it's time to swing
Saturday it's all those things
Sunday morning got the blues
Monday morning need new shoes

Repeat Chorus

Swing me baby
You gotta swing me baby
You gotta Swing me baby swing

Anne Marie Valentine

Verse One
All my dreams had come true
Every time you walked in the room
With your hair shining like the sun
I knew right there that you were the one

I was lost in a world
That was filled, filled with love
Time stood still it was just us two
To ask your name was all I could do

Chorus
Anne Marie Valentine
Anne Marie Valentine
Bells were ringing in my mind
For Anne Marie Valentine
Anne Marie Valentine
Anne Marie Valentine
Bells were ringing in my mi -i – ind
For Anne Marie Valentine

I used to think it was down to guys to ask will you be mine
Never thought I would fall so deep till I met
Anne Marie Valentine

So there we were
In each other's eyes
She asked me to dance
Oh to my surprise

Oh I was there
Mind body and soul
Except my heart
Was kind of out of control

Blue Eyes and Pink Lips

Verse One
Blue eyes and pink lips
She's some kind of lady
Always wears tight jeans
Especially on pay day

Now I've gone and fallen
For that girl that I adore
Some friends say I'm so foolish
But my heart can't take no more

An arrow through my heart I've invited
All the way right to my front door
But I don't mind as long as we're together
For blue eyes and pink lips I adore

She Wants It All

Verse One

Yes she wants it all
She wants it all right now
I guess she wants it all
I guess she wants it all right now
I tell her take it easy
She doesn't want to know
She only wants to rock
So I guess I'd better roll

She's born a wild tiger
I ain't never ever gonna tame
Beauty is her curse
But I love her just the same
She looks like Cleopatra
And she dresses like Monroe
Atomic kitten baby
With a Lindy Boppin' soul

Blue Suede Dreams

Verse One
Take a stroll now take a listen
There's a place where lovers meet
There you'll find what you've been missing
A paradise oh so sweet
I have been there my eyes are closed but I still see
I have found a love forever in the land of make believe

Chorus
In a blue suede dream that's where she stole my heart
In a blue suede dream we vowed we would never be apart
In a blue suede dream, a blue suede dream

I love the way that she kisses
I love the way she holds me tight
Now I've found what I've been missing
Gonna' have some fun tonight
I have been there my eyes are closed but I still see
I have found a love forever in the land of make believe

Now I have the answer
It's all so clear to me
I see it written in the stars
I belong - In a blue suede dream

20

JOHNNY EARL DISCOGRAPHY

45rpm SINGLES

1986: You Left Me Last Night/Your Cheatin' Heart

Released in 1986 and mainly for the purpose of having something other than photos and cassettes to be sold at live performances and shows. Only 1,000 copies were pressed by a pressing plant in Hayes, Middlesex, called Damont, with 4 different colour sleeves, blue, yellow, orange and white - 250 of each. This was to be my first record label (Lasso records); why I chose that name I have not a clue. The label was owned by manager Kevin Smith and myself. I was elated as it was going to have an original song that I wrote for the A side, and a classic for the B side so at least 50% of the music publishing would be kept in house. It was a very simple pressing, I mean the record sleeves came as flat pieces of card which meant each corner needed folding then they had to be individually stuck together. These were the early days for me and my manager Kevin Smith (who later became Kevin Allen) and we both stuck all the 1,000 record sleeves together, one of the first of many in house productions. Chris Emo who was my previous manager helped with the promotion. The front cover design was done by a guy called Nick Chennells who was also a singer in the very first line up of the British Doo wop vocal group, 'The Roommates' who I performed with in those early days.

The very day I received this 45rpm single my heart was pounding - it was a fabulous feeling. I wanted to tell the world, so my mind worked overtime and off I went to Capital radio, (one of London's biggest radio stations of the day) which was based on the Western Avenue just past Baker Street tube station. I dropped it into the reception, not addressed to any DJ in particular. I told the lady at reception it was my first release and it would mean the world to me if they would be able to play it. The receptionist smiled and said she would try her very best. Incredibly when I got home a couple of hours later a friend phoned me saying they were sure they had just heard my name being mentioned on Capital Radio and the song they played sounded really like me.

I informed Kevin my manager how easy it was to get promotion done when you do it yourself. From that day on, that was pretty much the only way we worked (not having any money is also a very good reason for doing it all yourself).

1990: Let the Boogie Woogie Roll/In A Modern World

Jive Records was the first major record label that took a serious interest in my career. Kevin Allen and I were called into the Jive record company office to have a meeting with chief artiste and relations guru Steven Howard. We had done some research and found out he was the guy who was a major force in the success of Zomba Music Publishing. He had already signed artists like The Thompson Twins, The Boomtown Rats, Billy Ocean and soon the likes of The Stone Roses, so we knew he was the guy who could make everything a lot brighter. He liked what we had done up to date and thought the idea of doing a single with The Jordanaires was pretty cool, but like any man in his position he was not always around to overlook the project and passed us on to A & R manager Neil Watson. I knew the writing was on the wall after the first meeting. Kevin was not the easiest guy to get along with and Steven Howard was not going to listen to someone else saying what they thought was the right direction for Johnny's career; or not with their money.

Steven Howard not long after was involved with four major number one singles: Britney Spears, *"Baby One More Time"*, Boyzone *"When The Going Gets Tough"*, Backstreet Boys *"I Want It That Way"* and Westlife *"If I Let You Go"* guiding these songs to Zomba. If you threw in the pot a couple of other classics Steve also guided to Zomba - Brian Adams *"Everything I Do"* and Bruce Springsteen's *"Born In The USA"* it proved to me one thing, there are times in the music business where you wish you could turn back the hands of time and start the whole meeting all over again, and that first meeting with Steve Howard is THE one first meeting I would like to be teleported back to.

Kevin Allen got pretty disenchanted with the whole Jive Record situation and it ended up that Jive records gave us all the studio time we needed to record the song *"Let the Boogie Woogie Roll"* with The Jordanaires and then gave us all the total rights to it.

So after nearly being signed and promoted by one of the most successful music companies on the planet, my third single was now going to be released as KAMA 001. To be precise this was the release number which was short for Kevin Allen Management - 001 (the first and last single release) and good old 'Pride Of Devon' being the record label (no Blue Peter badges for guessing who thought of that name), and of course the B side being a self-penned song *"In A Modern World"* and this time I gave the publishing away as we now joined forces with the world famous music publishers Acuff Rose/ Opryland Music.

To sum it up with this single release, we sold a few thousand copies and it brings it home to me when I said to Kevin at the time 'Why is it every time as soon as I have a new record release it becomes a collector's item?'

1990: Pocketful of Rainbows, Medley - Stuck on You, King of The Whole Wide World, Please Don't Drag That String Around.
Released by Rockhouse records, a Dutch record label that joined forces with my manager Kevin Allen to coincide with a Dutch tour featuring myself and the Jordanaires. Rockhouse had already released the album *"The Presley style of Johnny Earl"* and this was the 45rpm single that came from that album and would you believe it, I was informed this was to be my first and last number one single - in Holland that is (..Get that Orange on the Union Jack).

1991: The Girl of My Best Friend/Love Letters
Johnny Earl & The Jordanaires, again released on Rockhouse records. This 45rpm release was the single that came from the second Rockhouse album release Johnny Earl and The Jordanaires, *"My Way"*.

2019: Swing Me Baby/Anne Marie Valentine
Double A side 45rpm on that British legendary record label Fury Records.

VINYL ALBUM RELEASES

1990: The Concert Sessions

My first album. The format was to release an album that could be sold at the shows with the soundtrack containing most of what the audience was listening to at live performances. A very basic cover design, (you have to start somewhere) using one of the publicity shots used at the time by Kevin Allen Management. This album was on the Pride of Devon label catalogue number - KAMA002 the second and final release for Pride of Devon records.

1991: The Presley Style of Johnny Earl, Pocketful of Memories

The first album to be released by Rockhouse records, track listing being all Elvis songs that I performed at my shows.

1991: My Way - Johnny Earl & The Jordanaires

A 16-track album with 14 tracks performed with the Jordanaires. As a Dutch tour was soon on the cards Rockhouse started pressing once again, and this album along with the first release sold quite well for them all throughout the Dutch tour.

1994: Johnny Earl - The American Dream

My only ever picture disc, a 12-inch album in a clear plastic sleeve that was released by Fury records. I knew both the owners of the record label very well, Del Richardson and Steve Chapman. Unfortunately for them, in 1994 rockers were getting ready to spend their hard-earned bucks on a brand-new music format - the CD. This album has become a collector's item in recent years, a twenty-year investment campaign. The soundtrack compromised of 14 tracks. *"You're the One"* was the only track with the Jordanaires but was an original song written by Neal Matthews Jr. from the Jordanaires and myself.

The song writing team who wrote Shaking Stevens hit *"I Might"* Leathwood/Sulsh joined the bandwagon, a right couple of characters who were a great laugh to be with. We all went for a meal one night with the Jordanaires and my manager Kevin Allen along with Shakin' Stevens in London's West End. After the Jordanaires had left, I cried with laughter when it came to paying the bill as it took 30 minutes to decide who was actually going to contribute. Another songwriter who I co-wrote 2 songs with on this album was writer/composer Barrie Guard who wrote the ITV theme for *"Darling Buds of May"* and informed me in his early days he was the string arranger for a lot of Billy Fury's major hits. I knew I was now writing with r 'n' r royalty. A new songwriter aboard the ship was a man called Ronnie Bond who wrote the Cadbury's Flake advert jingle, so a large part of this album brought a new team of songwriters to the party. As well as my cover versions of Eddie Cochran's *"Jeanie Jeanie Jeanie"*, Little Richard's *"Lucille"* and a Hank William's song, this album was a melting pot of old and new directions.

The above four album releases were proper registered releases; the only other vinyl pressing was a 12-inch white label promo of *'Johnny Earl & All the Kings Men'* pressed by Bill Kimber with a 12-inch black sleeve which never got released. Only 250 were pressed and a lot were disposed of as it was never to be released on vinyl. It eventually got released on the hugely successful Party Megamix CD compilations.

2018: Blue Suede Dreams

Yes, the vinyl demand is back! and to coincide with the book release of 'Blue Suede Dreams' what better way to celebrate this momentous occasion. This fabulous twelve inch was released in blue vinyl and the track listing includes a mixture of up to date songs along with great tracks throughout my years with the Jordanaires. One song never released and only available on this release *'Sleeping Names'*.

CD'S

There have been various CD releases from the 1990's up to date, one fabulous release was notably *Elvis In Paris* which had a lot of the movie soundtrack *Private Elvis*.

From the years 1994-1999, I had my own independent record label and music publishing company called JEMusic. I released the album *"The Singerman"*, country songs all self and co-written. Also released during this period *With Elvis In Mind...* all three releases were on JEM Records. Today I have my own independent label in conjunction with a business partner and friend Allan Denny – this label is aptly called Patricia Records (my mother's name) with 5 CD releases from 2011-2018.

The three latest releases are a double CD *'Blue Suede Dreams'* to also coincide with the book release, and a great new release with my German band called *'She Wants It All'* (Johnny Earl and the Dukes). My most recent release *'Rockin' Mo'*, consisting of 10 original songs and 4 cover versions, this CD release was produced by one of the UK's top guitarists John O'Mally.

All future releases and information will be at:
www.bluesuededreams.com

21

THE WORLD OF THEATRE

In the world of UK theatre, as I experienced it, you will very quickly come to find out if it's really a direction that's best for one's career. There are definitely different ideas of what theatre means from the general public's point of view, or even people in the music and entertainment business.

I will take you behind the theatre curtains and show you a little of what I experienced. Although my few years were in a musical, when you stand behind those curtains and are propelled centre stage at the very start of the show, and you are the first person the audience sets their eyes on, it is quite an emotion: Thrilling, scary but sensational all in one. When those giant set of curtains start to separate as if Moses is parting the waves, bang! It hits you, and if you can get through that you are on the first rung to being able to hold an audience. To be a part of, or belong to the theatre way of life, you do not have to be a main artiste. Being a musician, a member of the band or a dancer are all equally important. All I can say is it takes a lot of courage.

A very good way of seeing a lot of what the theatre world has to offer is take a look at the theatre guides. Those little booklets which inform you of what's on and when. Go to as many different shows as possible, you might not like everything you see but you will certainly be well entertained. I found the experience of joining the theatre amazing, coming from pubs, clubs and town village halls, then entering a totally new surrounding where the audiences actually sat down for two hours and more to appreciate what was put before them, was quite a learning curve for me. I was astonished in one way because compared to my previous touring experiences, on the theatre circuit the different kind of shows and performances one can expect to see ranges weekly, or even daily. Musicals of all types.. rock, rock 'n' roll, country, opera, plays, drama's, comedies, ballet to a big orchestra. Then the next night could be a whodunnit play. Of course, do not forget the seasonal yelling of 'it's behind you' 'oh yes, it is - oh no it isn't'. What a different world this was!

I came from the world of rock 'n' roll clubs and dance halls, but when embarking on the theatre circuit I felt it was like joining the army. I am all for a bit of discipline in order to get the best results but straight away I was on a treadmill of rehearsal after rehearsal after rehearsal until YOU GOT IT RIGHT! I learned very quickly the discipline required for a theatre show. This was a whole new ball game to me; a totally different kind of rehearsal than what I had previously encountered.

If you played the wrong chord or sang the wrong word in a normal band rehearsal the general response was 'That's the wrong note (or word) but just make sure you get it right for the gig Saturday night', but in the theatre, if a song is ruined or incorrectly performed in rehearsal by any member of the band or cast, or even the dance crew, then back to the start you would go, thirty times if necessary until you all got it right, and I'm not joking!

As regimented as this might sound, look at it from the other end of the scale. A couple of years earlier I played a rock 'n' roll show at the South Harrow Borough Football Club one Saturday night with The Louisiana Hayriders. My manager Kevin Allen had put this event on and he always wanted to get one of his friends from the successful and well-known rocka-billy band "The Deltas" to perform with us. His buddy was the guitarist of the Deltas, 'Captain Pat Marvel', and so Kevin worked it for Pat to appear with us on this show. Pat was a lovely guy whom I got on really well with, we had the same sort of humour.

Now when I mentioned to Pat a couple of weeks before the show it might be a good idea to at least have a couple of rehearsals Captain Pat said, 'This is rock 'n' roll, let's just get up there and play it man', and that is exactly what we did – except Captain Pat was in a different key on a lot of the songs than the rest of the band. The sound that resulted from that performance I can only say is exactly what you get from having no rehearsals whatsoever, es-pecially when you have two 45-minute sets to perform. Some songs we just about got through and others were sounding like an orchestra tuning up. One of the worst stage moments I have ever experienced.

So, to have 3 years of theatre experience was quite sobering to say the very least. Should any artiste, dancer or musician get the chance to experience even a short spell in a theatre production, it can be a lot of fun and who knows you might meet the love of your life, you might even become a big film star. You will certainly learn stage etiquette, so let me share with you the joys and wonders I had while in the touring musical "Forever Elvis" which was to be my world of theatre.

FOREVER ELVIS THE MUSICAL

In my early days of touring and gigging, shows were frequent and lots of fun and just like with many an artist, the word gets out to the music world when you are getting more noticed, and then you get that phone call that changes everything (Well in my case my manager at the time, Kevin Allen got the call.) A phrase I often say to people even today is that in the music and entertainment business it takes one phone call to change your life and this call was no exception. On the line was the producer of a UK touring and soon-to-be West End musical called *Forever Elvis*.

Kevin was quite pleased because he thought maybe Johnny is going to walk the same path as Shaking Stevens did, especially as Shaky was the young Elvis in the West End musical called *Elvis*, and that show shot to fame performing at London's Astoria theatre (ironically where *Forever Elvis* was bound). I was apprehensive at first because I was used to halls and clubs and I couldn't stop thinking of how once Tommy Steele was a great rock 'n' roller with some great rocking tracks like *"Rock with The Caveman"*, *"Elevator Rock"*, brilliant rockin' tracks, then for whatever reason threw himself into the world of theatre and ending up singing *"The Little White Bull"*. To me that was a frightening thought, but sometimes you have to grab that little white bull by the horns, and after all, in my situation at least I would be performing Elvis's early years ..brilliant songs like *"Mystery Train"* and *"Heartbreak Hotel"* ending with *"G.I. Blues"*. After a few little chats with Kevin and personal one to ones with the *Forever Elvis* producer, contracts were exchanged, I was theatre bound so from now on at my performances wooden seats were out and velvet seats were in.

My first taste of what the theatre world was like was very sobering to say the least. Very quickly I had to adapt from my up-to-now Louisiana Hayride gigs, which were audiences of a few dozen and sometimes over a couple of hundred, compared to a now seated audience of well over a thousand or two or more!

This time though there was a little bit of acting to be administered, which to me was going to be a challenge. I loved the idea that there would be beautiful girl dancers all around me(!) along with an 8-piece band which included a brass section who were all mainly from Manchester and Oldham. (I say this from the heart, what a great bunch of characters they were).

Paul Forcus was the bass player and eventually became the musical director. A great guy with a wonderful family who I met a couple of times and went to his house. He lived in Oldham and on one occasion I remember looking out of one of his windows (looking down Coronation Street, the actual one in the TV series).

On another very memorable occasion we all performed a show near Manchester and unfortunately that night it was not very well attended. My manager Kevin Allen told me after this show we should go to Paul's house before setting off to London. While having a cup of tea at Paul's home we met his lovely wife and bubbly little daughter Faye, but something was on Kevin's mind that was troubling him. He then broke the news to Paul, we had no petrol money to get back to London and could Paul help us financially (I think the show Kevin had put on lost money and after paying all the band members etc., he was skint, and even Paul's wages were not enough to get the van back to London). The only money in the house was sitting on the mantelpiece, in Paul's little daughter Faye's piggy bank. As the piggy bank was one of those you can only retrieve the money by smashing it when it was full, Faye agreed Kevin could have all her lifelong savings as long as he did not break her piggy bank.

While I, musical director Paul, his wife and little Faye were drinking our cups of tea, we watched intently as Kevin, sitting at the table using a knife to get the coins out of the piggy bank, one and two coins at a time. It took ages and was very embarrassing to say the least! I do not think Kevin telling Paul's wife the show was quite successful really, except for on this occasion, while emptying all her little daughter's wealth onto the living room table was the best idea, however I reminded Kevin even Colonel Tom Parker started at the very bottom. Kevin was not interested in my jibes; just getting the coins out of the pig for enough petrol to get back to London was the order of the day. I made sure after a couple of days Faye was rewarded financially for her kind-hearted gesture.

I must tell you that all the band members were just great guys along with the female backing vocalists who were a pleasure to perform with. One member of the band was Mick the lead guitarist, who I had many a drinking session with, and on one occasion I accidentally turned around quickly the same time as he did and administered to him a big black eye - what do you expect when I'm introduced to all that lovely northern bitter!

One of the other Elvis's in the musical production was Big Jim White from Manchester and he was not called that for nothing. When it came to the finale of a performance we all had to link hands standing in a line at the front of the stage while dry ice crept around our ankles, and then altogether hopefully (and all at the same time) everybody took a bow. I couldn't help but always notice Big Jim White made the rest of us look like a cast of dwarfs. All joking aside his Vegas show of the Elvis era was awesome as the queues of ladies would prove each time he handed out a scarf. Even when Jim gave out his scarves it was great to watch from the side curtains. His partner sometimes would be seated at or near the front row making sure he did not get too familiar with the female members of the audience!

Another of the Elvis's to perform was a lovely guy named Kenny G from Portsmouth who played the King through the movie years to the 68-come-back period. Now Kenny was not the closest of Elvis singers, but his quality shone in being a great performer and entertainer. To me he was a great laugh and comical to be around, but not always seeing eye to eye were him and Big Jim White. This came to the fore when the show had arrived in St Albans and unfortunately Big Jim White had a throat infection and was unable to perform, so plan B was immediately put into place. I put more songs into my section of the show and Kenny G had to perform as much of Jim's Vegas show as possible. As we had very little time the band quickly set up and sound checked, and then went straight into serious rehearsing for that evening's performance.

Fortunately, because of my previous touring years with an endless rock 'n' roll repertoire which became second nature to me, I pretty much sailed through my extra numbers. I promptly left the stage to sit about 10 rows back from the front of the stage and worked my way to the middle of the row, so I could watch Kenny G. Very eagerly I rested my arms across the seat in front of me, I then noticed Big Jim White with the producer both leaning on the front of the stage at the right-hand side so as to get the full Kenny G experience and believe me that is exactly what they got 'both barrels'.

Time was of the essence (so hopefully it's a once through each number). Straight away the band played the full 2001 Elvis intro and when the drums propelled into full rhythm on came Kenny. Instead of walking straight to the microphone and starting to sing, he walked on as if the house was full, and in an Elvis strut walked straight to the front of the stage, took a bow then walked to the left hand side, took another bow and then all the way across to the other side where Big Jim and the producer were positioned, whereupon he knelt down on one knee and put his hand out to shake the producers and Jim's hand and I think I heard in a Manchester accent 'Just ******* get on with it'. Kenny walked back to the mic and started performing Jim's Las Vegas set. The only way I can explain what ensued was Kenny started performing in a kind of Elvis mumble as I do not think he knew lyrically all the songs properly, so more humming than singing, and occasionally if you listened closely you could distinguish a word or two. It was at this point I thought to myself, I wonder how Jim's taking this. Then I noticed Jim cowered his body onto the front of the stage, bowed his head into his hands and I actually witnessed this mountain of a man physically break down and cry at his disappointment of not being able to perform the Las Vegas part of the show, along with the frustration of listening to how it was now going to be performed. It was at this point I realized I was the only person in the auditorium, so I decided it was best to gradually sink lower in my seat until all you could see was a pair of eye brows and a quiff. Because I witnessed the scenario before me and just like Big Jim White, but for different reasons, I started to cry as well. I did feel for Kenny as he was trying his best and from what I can remember we did get through the show, ending in a standing ovation.

From breakfast time to bed time Forever Elvis was like being in a real life carry on film. At the time, there was no internet, so people enjoyed one another's company and this production had its love affairs and short-term romances and back stage arguments were plentiful. Joining the tour was a lady with a fabulous persona, Annette Day who co-starred with Elvis in the 1967 film *"Double Trouble"*. Elvis came up against European criminals in the movie and if you think of the thousands of American films all clamouring for prime position, this was the 58th best gross earning movie of the year which was not bad going. Annette Day was only 18 years of age, working in her mother's shop which was an antique store on Portobello road and film producer Judd Bernard (while on a shopping spree) saw the fiery red headed Annette and did not pay her much attention. While Judd was casting a little while later for the film *"Double Trouble"* he remembered Annette and gave her an out-of-the-blue phone call and came straight to the point 'Do you want to be an actress?'

This all led to a screen test for Annette in Hollywood and she satisfied the producers enough to give her the role next to Elvis. When the filming had finished, Elvis gave Annette a white Mustang convertible as a remembrance of her first film experience. I was working alongside Annette in Forever Elvis where she shared her memories and fabulous times with the King with the audiences, and they loved the fact Annette was a home-grown girl and a wonderful person as well. I got on well with Annette and her husband Mike and of course the laughs would carry on after the show, then back to the hotel until the early hours. All this theatre partying takes its toll I can assure you and I enjoyed plenty of it, which led to me consuming 60 cigarettes a day and lord knows how many pints of beer after each performance. The devil in disguise crept very stealthily into my life at that point and on many occasions, I was the one left propping up the hotel bar until 5 or 6am. No wonder I was always the first to breakfast, I just walked into the next room.

One problem with long touring theatre shows is the days become pretty much the same. I was getting used to a hearty breakfast every morning (not much wrong with that until you find you have run out of cigarettes). I would often meet the milkman or paper boy to ask directions for the way to the nearest shop while trying to forget I had not been to bed yet. Straight back to the hotel, normally the lounge to read the daily paper, because now with breakfast all done and dusted, I loved being one of, or the first, for a Forever Elvis cast awakening, as pretty soon one by one the previous night's party animals would appear, some knowing it was time for the walk of shame. In general, the bar/lounge area was the usual congregation point (especially if there was any naughty news from the previous night's capers) and also just in case there was going to be any news regarding the show. Like an identity parade in they came, some with embarrassed faces, others exclaiming 'Has he or she appeared yet!' Of course, some decided it was better to not show at all (I dare not tell of those reasons).

Come 2.30pm in the afternoon all would be squashed into mini buses ready for the afternoon sound check and rehearsal. Should there be any telling offs then this was the time you would receive them. I recall the whole cast lined across the stage and the producer exclaimed to a 1970's Elvis act from America "Liberty Mounten", 'Why have you come to the stage with a bushido samurai sword?' (and to everyone's amazement Liberty Mounten took a thrusting step forward sword in hand, exhaling 'haaaaaaaa' in a samurai warrior fashion). For about five seconds a stunned silence came over the stage, so I thought it would be a good idea to break the ice. I said, 'Well he is American' and Keith, the Welsh producer bless him, burst out laughing with everyone else. Yes, Elvis acts are a species amongst themselves, and this theatre production was going to prove that to me time and time again.

The first of my new experiences in the theatre was getting used to the backstage communication which was excellent. In each dressing room, as well as through the corridors and hallways of a theatre, you have a tannoy speaker system so everybody hears the same announcements at the same time. This system generally informs all artistes of how close they are to the start of the shows performance.

In Forever Elvis, this is how I experienced a normal pre-stage countdown... 'This is your 30 minutes to stage announcement - 30 minutes to stage'... On hearing this a check of all personnel in the production was not uncommon, also this was the time for stage makeup, making sure all costumes were at hand, shoe polishing and any last-minute rehearsing or vocal warming exercises were administered. This was also the start of all kinds of noises you would hear, trumpets, guitars being tuned, scripted lines being rehearsed. '20 minutes to stage, 20 minutes to stage,'... at this point a professional cloak came over all involved in the production (we were all in it together and you were not going to let the side down) so all final costume, jewellery and dress wear was carefully put on (in some cases helped on). When it gets to the call '10 minutes to curtain everyone, 10 minutes to curtain,' (or stage) at this time everybody got their backsides into gear and started making their way to the stage, and in some of the older or big theatres the stairs go on forever it can feel like you are running down the staircase of a never-ending lighthouse.

'5 minutes to stage, this is your 5 minute to stage call,'... by now if you were in the opening half of the show, you were standing in the wings (which meant the side of the stage) and if you were in the band you were in position, dancers would be at hand stretching and bending to lubricate their joints, the stage manager had a headset for keeping in contact with the front of house in case a coach party or large crowd were late arriving which sometimes delayed the start of a show performance. It's better to start a few minutes late rather than have 30 people clambering over seats when the show has just begun. '2 minutes to stage, it's 2 minutes to the start of this evenings performance' – all the band are standing in position looking at the musical director to make sure all is okay. Everybody at the side of the stage collecting their thoughts, the odd kiss and the often spoken good luck, break a leg, are the two most common gestures exchanged, an odd pinch in odd places can sometimes be expected, especially if you were naughty at the previous night's party.

The girl backing vocalists were always good fun and I often had a pre-stage laugh with. They were two Scottish sisters, both were lovely and most importantly always in tune. They tried their best not to get too distracted by listening to my jokes 'One minute to show time everyone, one minute to show time,'... some of the cast had a rabbit in the headlights expression on their face, this was when the tummy rumbling started, and nerves could get the better of you (It's too late now for going to the toilet). Rarely, but sometimes and it does happen, a machine gun sound of running feet echoing down the staircase and rushing to the stage then you would catch in the corner of your eye a musician or a dancer for whatever reason, clambering to their position, take a deep breath, composing themselves at the very last second. Then the stage manager announced, 'Lights down in the main hall in 5 seconds - 5, 4, 3, 2, 1,' ...as the lights were dimmed a vocal introduction introduced the show... 'Elvis, the boy who dared to rock!'

The curtains opened to an explosion of flashing lights and a great rock 'n' roll song for the opening number called *"The Boy Who Dared to Rock"* which I sang from the side of the stage wings behind the curtain while the guy on stage mimed to it. Kenny and Emma who were two of the dancers who were brilliant; they jived and danced to this opening tune like they were made of elastic throwing each other in the air then over each other's backs, it was amazing to watch. Then the song would finish to rapturous applause, the lights would dim to an almost total blackness, I would make my way to a platform centre stage where I stood alone and a small piece of narration would introduce the beginning of Elvis's music career along the lines of 'This was a recording he himself paid for, which he then gave as a present to his mother', I would then strum an E chord, a red spot light would turn on me from the waist up and I would play a vocal and acoustic guitar version of the first two verses of the song *"My Happiness"* (the show had begun).

Forever Elvis was the first and last theatre production I performed in, I performed in many theatres after this but as a solo artiste with my own bands. I had gained pretty good experience in the theatre and I learned a lot of stagecraft. I was on occasions offered parts in a pantomime but to me that was a whole different ball game 'Oh no it isn't, oh yes, it is', and anyway that was a way of life that was not rock 'n' roll enough for me.

I do thank all the theatre staff and musicians and artists I had met and worked with, especially through my Forever Elvis years. I know there has been lots of touring Elvis musicals, it's rumoured that Forever Elvis was the longest running UK Elvis musical ever.

I had a ball while performing the Kings early years and most of the people involved in the production I am sure would say the same. Along with all who were involved with the musical, I will never forget how we rocked those theatres throughout Great Britain and I am sure all the tens of thousands of people who attended the shows, will agree that musically Elvis blessed our lives and deserves the title of this musical – "Forever Elvis".

Today in theatres all over the world the curtains still open, the lights still flash, musical productions still perform the hits of the King to all the millions of fans who will never forget the boy who dared to rock.

22

ELVIS IMPERSONATORS

BE AWARE! VERY AWARE! This is a worldwide industry.... Just the name alone makes a bold statement. Generally an Elvis Impersonator means a character in a glitzy costume trying to dance and sing the hits of the King. If you put into the mix that a lot of Elvis impersonators are going to get paid for the honour and do it for a living, this opens the door to a world some would say of often failing self-indulgent people trying in vain to capture all the essence but never as good as the real Mr. Elvis Presley. In my experience the general concept, especially from the press and media I'm sad to say, is that they love to negatively report the impersonator as being off-key, grossly over gyrating and hip swivelling, for what can only be called an unconvincing mediocre portrayal of Mr. Presley.

An Elvis impersonator can be a man or a woman, boy or girl, but one thing most of these people will have in common is they will dress in Elvis attire which can be child sized, adult sized, ranging from a gold lame suit or a wing collared romper-looking Vegas styled jump suit that will have hundreds of stuck on multi coloured beads. Some Vegas styled costumes will cost you thousands and at the other end of the scale I have seen a guy turn up to an Elvis contest with a white painter and decorator's boiler suit with the collar turned up with blue trainers.

Before I go any further here is a factual statistic I read from the Guardian newspaper: 'The number of Elvis Presley impersonators has reached an all-time high. There are now at least 85,000 Elvis's around the world, compared to only 170 in 1977 when the King died. At this rate of growth experts predict that by 2019 Elvis impersonators will make up a third of the world population'.

You have all types of Elvis impersonators, some good, some not so good. I myself on the one hand feel if you are having fun and not hurting anyone then go ahead and shake rattle and roll your life away, but on the other hand Elvis Presley to me is the best entertainer to ever walk the stage and I find it hard sometimes seeing people taking the mickey out of the King. It is not uncommon at many special occasions e.g. weddings, stag nights, hen nights, or even world-famous darts tournaments to see men and women with stuck on and often falling off sideburns, topping a rubber quiff and jumbo-sized gold and silver rimmed glasses, and that is just the headgear! You then have the oversized and very tight-fitting jump suits, along with footwear being anything from work boots to trainers because not everyone can afford blue suede shoes.

All that I have mentioned is just the 1970's Elvis impersonator! But in most circumstances, it is all done in good spirits. As I have said, all this fun time Elvis mimicking is a bit hard for me to actually take in, as it's being done to a man who in my mind will always be number one in the music and entertainment business. I have over the years come to realize that the general public's poor perception of the Elvis Impersonator, is unfortunately largely due to the media's need to be unkind towards even Elvis himself. That is why it has become very popular to celebrate an Elvis cheesy burger wedding in Las Vegas, and as soon as the vows have been said by the bride and groom you can be pretty sure at the end you will hear something like 'I now proclaim you man and wife, and can you now please carry on through the drive through where you can order your cheesy burger and fries, uh uh uh'.

In most towns and cities, there are fancy dress shops where you can hire your party outfit, and there will always usually be a very cheaply made Elvis jump suit, which can normally be seen parading in the front window and you rarely see a quality made Elvis outfit.

Staggeringly some Elvis impersonators that I have witnessed will be wearing badly made outfits and even they can charge a lot of money for their Elvis performance. You do have the other end of the Elvis impersonator world where it will cost thousands of dollars, pounds and euros for a costume which can look quite spectacular. I have yet to be convinced by any Elvis impersonator to be as good as Elvis himself, but some do perform a brilliant Elvis tribute show.

ELVIS IMPERSONATORS

I have certainly noticed that a lot of people who try to be an Elvis impersonator will, just to be on the safe side, tend to lean towards performing the 1970's era with all the big musical arrangements, as this can help to disguise a weaker sounding Elvis voice. By contrast when performing the 1950's and 1960's years of the Kings repertoire you tend to need to be not only looking a little fitter, you will soon be noted if you cannot sing very well as it is a lot harder to disguise a not so good sounding Elvis voice. I certainly have always had an Elvis style but always kept my own identity when performing and this has definitely worked in my favour with the audiences, no matter how they were thinking when walking into my shows... by the time they leave, they know they have been to a Johnny Earl show not an Elvis impersonator performance.

Today you can search YouTube and see for yourself the world of Elvis impersonators. A good one to watch is Ben Portsmouth, who's best performance is very close to the 1971 *'That's the Way It Is'* styled Elvis. I have Elvis impersonator friends, Marty Tempest being one, who I think is a top-drawer Elvis act from Ireland, and from Wales Lee Memphis King is fabulous.

Earlier in my career while treading the boards a very well-known UK Elvis act was a guy called Rupert and do not let me forget the Elvis acts I performed with in the musical 'Forever Elvis'.. 'Big Jim White', 'Liberty Mounten', 'Kenny G', 'Ian McKaye' (It's all good fun). Agents as well as members of the public often ask me for a reliable top-drawer Elvis act normally because they have recently gone to see one and have been very disappointed by what they saw. If I had to sum up a bad Elvis impersonators performance, one can only say although they might not be the best singer in the world, or be able to perform on stage very well, neither move or communicate with the audience at all, the one thing that remains is what I call the 'Elvis Impersonator Bible.'

This bible is not written in script but is more a code of honour. Throughout a not so good Elvis act you must firstly never forget, in the mind of the impersonator there is only one thing that counts... when they walk onto that stage or platform or pallet, it's as if they have been teleported from Star Ship Graceland by Scotty, to appear before your very eyes. And no matter how you the public might view it, in the performers mind, "behold all before me, the spirit of the King resides in my soul", and no one will dissuade them otherwise. Even if their performance was not the best (from the public's point of view that is), in which case the public is mostly wrong and should understand to be polite enough to sit all the way through the entire performance until that crescendo ending..., yes that eternal anthem *"The American Trilogy"* and only then as the performer drops onto one knee with arms stretched out as if about to be hung drawn and quartered, then you will hear that machine gun drum roll of that legendary Elvis outro *"See See Rider"*. Only then may you attempt to leave the building, but not before the Elvis act has got up and left the stage first of course.

The problem with a not so good Elvis Impersonator performance is when the act goes to collect their wages, it's usually at this stage it becomes apparent that the person who enjoyed the show the most is normally the performer themselves. The club or venue owner might have an unhappy or disgruntled look about them and usually say something like 'Why am I paying you wages when all you have managed to do is empty the place'. 'That's your point of view' is all the performer would normally reply, along with something like 'The other night I did exactly the same show and got a standing ovation... now where's my wages!' Be aware club owners, their Elvis impersonation might go all the way, like Elvis, they themselves could be a black belt in Karate. As funny as this all sounds, these types of situations happen day in and day out in the Elvis tribute world.

Two great Elvis styled acts I grew up listening to were Ral Donner and Jimmy Ellis aka Orion. Ral Donner was a brilliant artiste in his own right. He released a wonderful version of the Elvis hit *"Girl of My Best Friend"* but he is mostly known for his hit recording *"You Don't Know What You Got"* reaching no 4 in the U.S. charts and 25 in the UK charts. Jimmy Ellis on the other hand gave you the real sense Elvis was still in the building, he really did. He was also known as Orion and was the person who basically started all the 'is Elvis still alive' debate with his release of *"Save The Last Dance for Me"* which was followed up by a very clever media campaign making Orion certainly one of, if not the best known Elvis performers of his time.

To close the Graceland gates on this worldwide industry, you will never stop the gimmicky side of it – that I'm afraid will be with us for an eternity – and as ironic as it sounds, you could say it is this tacky portrayal of the King that keeps the media motivated which in turn, keeps him on everyone's mind. The good side of Elvis however is not brought to the public's attention often enough; he is not called the King of rock 'n' roll for nothing.

So, in the end I suppose it is down to you the individual and whether you take Elvis Presley impersonators seriously or not. I can proudly say I am one of the millions of people who will always maintain, the music of the real Elvis Presley will last forever, and so I will stand alongside all the Elvis impersonators worldwide, let us all link arms and together in harmony exclaim... LONG LIVE THE KING!!!!

23

THE PRESS & MEDIA

Better the Devil you know! In this instance, he or she will appear in many guises, they will greet you with a smile and befriend you only to re-appear to bite you in the ass. That is one way of looking at the press. I remember very well Boy George being asked by a journalist what was his biggest regret in his career and he replied, 'Being too kind and trustworthy to the press'. A question I was once asked by a reporter was 'Why is it Johnny that when you played locally at the Beck Theatre in Hayes, on stage you mentioned you would hopefully return with the King of rock 'n' rolls band. Now that the dream has come true why choose Wembley as one of your top West London venues', I replied 'Simply because of ticket sales, the Beck theatre holds 600 people and the Wembley Conference centre holds 4,000 people and the tour was very expensive to put on'.

I thought that was a pretty straight forward question and answer until in all the local tabloids the following week in print 'Johnny says he is too big now to perform at the Beck Theatre and is now off to bigger greener turfs and Wembley is where he is glad he is now heading'. Thanks a bunch I thought!.. I trusted you and now I have the biggest head in West London. Of course it is a double-edged sword; without the press you will always be an unknown unless you are in the very fortunate financial position to pay tens of thousands of pounds to be represented by a top PR company whose sole job is to create a scenario to be press and media friendly. The problem with that is any good PR company costs a fortune.

For those of you with little showbiz experience if you are trying to get on in the music world then a good PR company is essential. (PR meaning 'Public relations'). A top PR company will have in their armoury all the direct contacts and access to a list of top TV and radio shows and programmes, along with a network for you to tour and extensively promote everything you are trying to promote, with national as well as independent newspaper and magazine journalists. You must understand I am now talking about the same people who represent the stars and celebrities who are the vogue of the day, so basically money talks, bull**** walks. On one of my album releases which was going to be released alongside a nationwide tour, my manager Kevin Allen decided enough was enough. After personally phoning radio stations to hunt down the various producers of the right kind of radio show that would suit my tour, it just took forever; and as for the press, trying to track down the editor or reporter and finally pinning them down to speak to them was immensely laborious.

The bitter truth is spending sixteen hours a day on the phone to different newspapers and hundreds of radio stations does take its toll. The time had come for paid assistance to help undertake this gargantuan task, so into the world of who's who of the PR kingdom we delved and we actually got through to one of – if not the top – PR and media companies in the UK that deal solely in the music and entertainment business. After a brief conversation with Kevin they were pretty confident they could put me in the top ten of the UK charts, which of course for Kevin meant a good financial return from sales and the publicity would pretty much guarantee that I would be a household name. Well at least we had found the next couple of rungs of the showbiz ladder to climb, which to us seemed the right way to continue on our road to fame (..or wherever we were heading).

First rung, for this situation to actually happen of course, it was explained there would need to be a three to six month campaign minimum. This was all understandable for me and Kevin Allen as we'd gained experience from previous tours and I suppose you could liken it to an American presidential campaign; once you are on the scene, keeping the campaign rolling in the right direction takes an extensive and well thought out operation that will hopefully lead to the right destination you were hoping for. We now realized if we were aiming for the top then this was the next rung of the ladder, so the mountain will hopefully start becoming mole hill. As this PR company were working with the best stars of the day, they obviously had to see if they could actually fit our project into their busy schedule, at the specific time we were putting on our tour, so as to coincide with an album release.

Very importantly we needed to sort out our finances (Uh oh) so Kevin told them he will call them back in an hour. A very important discussion between myself and Kevin ensued: Kevin was willing to do overtime on the taxi driving and the buses and I would do a few more performances. Of course we also agreed to cut out the takeaways and pub visits as every penny was needed for this PR pot, and we knew the bank manager very well and he liked us, so a little bank loan would come in handy as well. All was good, Kevin was gleaming and I knew with this PR company on our side, everything should now start taking shape ...the stars in the sky are becoming within arm's reach?

Kevin totted up what we could afford and one hour later a very confident Kevin called the UK's foremost PR company. A couple of seconds into the phone conversation and I was shocked as a stuttering Kevin said, 'Would you be interested in buying shares into Johnny's career'. I watched his face stretch downwards with an unhappy expression, then with a low tone he mumbled 'I see, so for the first three months it would be £30,000 a month and we would negotiate thereafter'.

I could see where this conversation was going. My heart rate and pulse soon went back to being normal, Kevin thanked them for their time and slowly put down the phone. I said 'Welcome Mr. Kevin Allen to the top end of the music business', so it was back to square one, back out of the bin came the ripped out diary pages of all the press and radio contacts, yes I'm afraid after that very sobering phone call we were just going to have to do it all ourselves, ouch! This was a tough lesson learnt by the both of us because we had used lesser PR companies who could get the odd major tabloid interested and local BBC or independent radio stations on board but we now realized the real world of showbiz comes at a huge financial price. Whether you like it or not the people who have been in the business for a long, long, time are always saying things like, talent has very little to do with it..., being in the right place right time..., strike while the iron is hot... These are not worthless sayings, they are just a few of the accumulated expressions needed for success in the music business – although they can become tiresome on the ear.

The press and media world can be fickle and it's best to make personal contacts of them, try and give them a call now and then because knowing them personally is the best format, but even that comes at a price (lots of beer and wine comes to mind), and when doing the phone calls yourself you have to keep trying to come up with a new sensational story that has mileage to it. We did manage on a few occasions to create a buzz for the press and media, one time being when the German Elvis Presley Museum actually loaned me Elvis's army uniform to wear on my UK and European tour where the Jordanaires, Scotty Moore and D.J. Fontana were appearing.

Most of the major press and Reuters were informed and it is always convenient to try and use somewhere central in London's West End for interviews. So where better than the Rock Island Diner in Piccadilly Circus where the staff would jump up on the tables and do a 1950's dance while you dined eating American styled hot dogs and burgers. Kevin personally went to Germany to collect the Kings uniform and on his return flight he mentioned to the cabin crew that he had Elvis's army uniform in his possession so as he was leaving the plane the cabin crew formed an orderly queue just so they could touch the package containing the Kings uniform.

At the press conference I put on the Kings uniform stood staring straight into a large mirror and felt like a million dollars. I just could not help myself; I put my guitar over my shoulders, walked into the dining area and I heard a gasp of admiration from the awaiting crowd that had formed, and never before had I seen such a gathering of major press in my life.

Thames News with all their cameras and lights turned up as well. Joseph's Technicolor Dream Coat was again jumble sale material compared to the coat of the King of rock 'n' roll. I started strumming away singing *G.I. Blues* and the whole euphoria of this event started setting in. I was feeling great, so I knew we would get some fabulous photo's which would be out in the following day's major tabloids.

There were so many press attending and I couldn't help but notice that they were all strewn with cameras dangling off every shoulder along with bags full of accessories. I remember one reporter had five different cameras hanging off him then all of a sudden, a photographer yelled 'Everybody follow me, I have just the place for a great photo shoot'! He was very clever as everyone thought he was given authority by Kevin to somehow be in charge and he just turned around and led the way through the doors and started trotting down the stairway. Kevin looked at me 'Go on then follow him', so guitar in hand I did, and like a cavalry charge, there must have been twenty people or more, ran out the doors, down the stairs then out of the Trocadero onto Coventry Street and then paraded down the Haymarket. I can remember it now the sound of jangling cameras and heavy breathing and 'Wait for me', being yelled – the whole scene not unfamiliar to a cross country army slog with full kit. I also noticed all the public stopping in amazement beholding loads of press following this G.I. with a guitar wrapped around him until the photographer who orchestrated all this, and who was at the helm of this charge of the light Fleet street brigade, suddenly came to a halt. Unfortunately, some of the press at the back crashed into the ones in front of them and 'Be careful of the King's uniform', was shouted by a couple of reporters. Everybody came to this sudden halt, some even gasping for air (as a good old army slog around London's West End was not on the to do list for this normally free-of-charge wine-drinking and canapés journalist legionaries). 'Thank Christ for that', I heard someone say. Then everybody looked at the instigator of this expedition and watched as he candidly put his hand in his pocket pulled out some coins and started putting them into a parking meter. 'Made it just in time', he exclaimed then turned to everyone and announced, 'Right then where are we all going', I never saw so many reporters gathered in one place with an expression of knowing they had been duped by one of their own. You have to bear in mind to pay to have a half page in a major tabloid cost in excess of £10,000 and we did make the major tabloids, half a page in some and three-quarter pages in others the very next day, there were some great shots, army slog or not it, was worth it. For once it came off 'Big Time'.

I had a girlfriend who was a lady reporter and we speak even today, and I have found reporters in general are very colourful people, good to have on your side. I also had a friend who has now sadly passed away called Lez Gazeke (I think that's how you spell it) who had a wooden leg, and once he had a corker of a press party and held it at his flat which was a couple of floors up in Uxbridge, Middlesex. Things got a little heated at his party and somehow someone threw his leg out of the window and it was not until the next morning the postman knocked and kept banging on Lez's front door. With a terrible hangover Lez quickly searched but he could not find his leg, so hopped as fast as he could to the front door upon which the postman handed him his post and said 'I think this belongs to you', and gave him his leg back. Lez gave me an insight into the world of Fleet Street and showed me the sort of genius you need to be as well as informing me, 'Unfortunately Johnny you have to be a rat at the same time in order to survive in my world', because Lez also informed me he was part of the paparazzi and some of the antics he got up to I am certainly not going to write about in this book. Though maybe in the next one!

He did tell me of how a bomb went off in London's West End and the police cordoned off the whole street and nobody, not even the press, could get through. Thinking quickly Lez saw a lorry driver frantically trying to get through the gathered crowd, his job being to start clearing the debris. Lez managed to get to him showing the driver his press card along with giving him £50, then hid in the back of the truck under the canvas and 30 seconds later appeared like a jack in the box from the back of the lorry. Lez stood up and snapped as many shots as possible then legged it to the Daily Mirror and nearly all the photos that he took pretty much covered the tabloids over the following days.

I took Lez for a drink once and arriving at his flat he took the time to show me his personal and best unpublished photo's that he had in a folder. I could see he was biding his time with this collection, a photographer's trove, and I remember among them pictures of a teenage Lady Diana. On these alone Lez was flown around the world first class to show the photos personally to some of the world's top editors. They would then decide whether to act on them or not. I will never forget one of the most amazing stage shots I have ever seen that was in Lez's collection: It was of Mick Jagger live on stage, in a kind of statue of liberty pose, arm stretched high wrapped in a life size Union Jack. It was amazing.

Although Lez is no longer with us, I learnt so much from him regarding the press and media and never forgot what he once said to me, 'Johnny no matter what really happens in a situation, especially when it comes to relationships, when you become a celebrity some of the press will get hold of your now ex-partner and sit them down and say to them', "With what you are telling us we will pay you £1,000, but think back very carefully because if this happened or that happened in any way then we would pay you £10,000 plus, depending on the public response". That sent a chill down my spine for I now realized the higher up the ladder you go in the entertainment world, you have to be prepared for your life to be destroyed at any moment, even overnight.

The last time I saw Lez it was over lunch at the Harvester in Ruislip,

West London. He informed me he was in some sort of stake-out regarding Gary Lineker and the net was closing in and he had to be very careful as Mr. Lineker was a much loved character and ardent proof was needed. I told him 'Can't you leave him alone Lez, Gary Lineker is a soccer legend and I like him, can't you pick on someone else?', but I was forgetting that as much as I liked Lez, when it comes to getting the story, a long tail appears and Lez will head camera-in-hand towards the nearest gutter. As we left the Harvester I noticed he started filling his leather satchel with all the cutlery he had used along with the salt and pepper pots. I later went back to pay for the items, but the manager knew of me and said, 'This happens all the time, but thanks for the gesture'. Yes, I can honestly say I have associated with the press and media at all levels (..but that's a book in itself).

24

BECOMING LONDONISED

When we embark on any big move or change of direction in our lives, it is usually in gradual steps, one leading to another, to an eventual life changing decision. That was definitely the case for me, and my London life (I have named it becoming Londonised) which is now 34 years, was instigated by meeting a young man who was to become my very good friend, Sean Thomas. He first moved to Devon from London with his family in the early 1980's and they moved to a lovely house in a little place called Holcombe, which is in-between Dawlish and Teignmouth. He was the first rockabilly mate I had, before then the only music fraternity I met were mostly teddy boys, and Sean's friends from London, who regularly came down on holiday, were all London rockabillies. I remember Paul Maitland who called himself a Hep Cat, had dark hair at the sides with a blonde peroxide quiff (this was my introduction to hep cats). Also, in the London gang was Chris, and the Devonshire women loved him even though he had his girlfriend Sharon with him, because he looked a lot like Elvis. Another was a guy nicknamed Hedgehog who had tattoos around his neck (I never saw anyone have that before). He became a good friend and I was pleased I got him a job on the trawlers.

Another cool looking rockabilly was Dennis, who had a girlfriend Yaz who he adored. It ended up 8 or 10 rockabillies would come down to visit and tour the Devon rocking clubs. Of course, it took a bit of getting used to their London attitude, but hey I get on with anybody, and I found out even at that early stage, once you've bonded with Londoners they are the best friends any one could have. They all kept on about my singing – Paul Mait-land suggested I visited London and it was not a problem for digs as I could dwell at all their houses, starting with his. He lived with his mum, brother and sister in South Harrow.

On one occasion I stayed with a guitarist called Chris Sharp who lived with his parents in Chiswick, West London. This led to a couple of small gigs and I knew from my first visits to London, this was my destiny. I was 18 and buzzing with vibrancy (enjoying the company of my new Bow-Bell and jellied eel friends) and when it came to me being very naive they turned a blind eye and gave me encouragement rather than taking the micky and mocking me, or so I thought. Then again knowing Londoners now as I do, I was being ribbed left right and centre without having a clue it was even hap-pening, (orrriiight buys).

That was the cockney acorn sewn. It was now decided a life of rock and roll was my destiny so when Chris the guitarist said, 'Johnny you can live at my house for a while, until you get properly sorted', it meant the move was inevitable, just a case of when. I was 18 when I met all the London rockers and by the time I was 19, I was on my way. Years later this obviously gave me the idea for a country song I wrote called *"London Town"*.

Line one - *'It was London town that stole my heart'*

Chris Sharp the guitarist was true to his word: First port of call Chiswick, London. I arrived in London like the 'Ready Brek Kid' with a red glowing ring all around me ready to take on the world. My first abode was sorted thanks to Chris and it was in Rothschild Road, Chiswick, which was around the corner from Chiswick tube station. Just up the road in Chiswick High Road was a brilliant record shop called 'The Spinning Disc' which only had rock 'n' roll and rockabilly records. Terry was the guy who owned the shop and one of the most decent guys I have ever met. Now the band was formed.. 'The Louisiana Hayriders': Chris Sharp on guitar, Paul Maitland on slap double bass, and I played a bit of rhythm guitar with lead vocals. Also, at Chris's home was his Dad, Ted who was a big jazz fan and still played 78rpm records and his mum who was a lovely lady who smiled all the time. This meant that Paul Maitland, Chris and I, had somewhere to do our first re-cordings (like most rockabillies of the day). We could not afford rehearsal rooms or recording studios, so the bedroom became our Sun recording stu-dios. We were excited and ready to rock.

Just like any new musical group, the teething problems started on the first day of the third week. There was I sitting at the breakfast table, Chris's mum says 'Johnny won't your mum be worried about you? This is your third week', I replied 'Oh don't worry, I told my mum you are all lovely people and I could not think of anywhere better to live'. She exclaimed 'What!' I looked at Chris and she left the room very upset. Ted followed her, telling Chris 'you should have said something'. A few minutes later they both returned and said I could stay until I found somewhere more permanent. Chris and I could not thank them both enough and told them if we became famous they would reap the rewards. I think at first, they laughed with us, then at us – either way The Louisiana Hayriders were now firmly on the road. I lived with Chris and his parents for three months and we recorded some kicking rockabilly on Chris's 8 track reel to reel recorders (I hope he has not lost them). On those very early gigs the three of us had no car, so we would carry all instruments, amps and speakers on the tube, which meant Chiswick tube platform was where we would sometimes have a quick rehearsal. We did not intend it that way but the first time we played on the platform, although being a rehearsal, passers-by asked us where they could put the money. Very shortly after that occasion we made it a regular thing to spend an hour at the tube platform to at least get enough money for a drink or two prior to the gig. After a couple of small gigs, it became came very apparent a bigger sound was needed so a drummer was required.

A lovely fella called Paul Moxam came to the fore, the trio became a band and now we were playing venues all over London that were hip on the rockin' circuit. I was getting Londonised very quickly; the shock of seeing row after row of homeless people at such places as Kings Cross train station late at night was a constant reminder of how close one can be to living that way when life turns sour. This was a big eye opener for me and after some late night rockin' gigs, I visited what was called a squat, which were buildings inhabited by the forgotten and the less fortunate people of London. I never saw any of this in such abundance while living in Devon, and at these squats they would have a little sing song and tell a few jokes, which for me looking at their plight was humbling.

A lot of things shocked me through my early days in London, little things like when I was meeting bass player Paul Maitland from work one night. As we walked back to his house to rehearse I noticed his toes coming out from under his shoes, so I asked him if he was okay and he just gave me a funny look. Today I would not have even mentioned it, I would have just gone out and bought him a new pair. When we got back to his house during a tea break Paul passed the biscuit tin around and another band member took the tin from him, twiddled his finger inside and pointed out there was not a sign of any chocolate on any of them, so they were thereafter called poverty biscuits. I have to give it to Paul, on the one hand he did not have a bean to his name yet would give you all he had, and thinking about it, we all had that attitude in the Hayriders.

I had to get used to London mannerisms. For example in Devon after you have made someone happy with a job or a bit of work you'd done for them, or even when you had done them a good turn, if they said to you, 'That's brilliant Johnny, the next time I see you I will see you alright', that would normally mean the next time they caught up with you they would most likely come up to you and reward you financially in some way. Now, being in London what I had to get used to was when someone said I'll see you alright mate, unless you got it there and then, you could ask them monthly for the next twenty years, and the only thing you'd eventually get back is to be told 'Are you still keeping on about it!'

After living at Chris's house, I stayed with Paul for a week before moving into a house in Doncaster Gardens in Northolt, with 6 other rockabillies. We would all give the landlady her rent on the Friday so by the time we came back from a rockin' club in London on the Saturday, we all knew she would have filled the freezer up with sirloin steaks. You can imagine with 6 rockabillies it was on a first come, first serve basis, so by Sunday afternoon the cupboards and freezer were bare. There was usually a kitchen fire, caused when instead of watching your steak cook slowly under the grill, you would be distracted by hearing songs being played in the living room upstairs, leaving the steak under the grill to burn. I'm not joking, someone would jump up after the latest King Federal or Ace record or Mercury rockabilly album was on the turntable and shout 'Bo***cks my steak'! We would all leg it downstairs to be greeted by smoke pluming upwards, then we'd all bundle into the kitchen, eyes closed, to try our best to put out the fire from under the grill. All the windows would be opened and finally we would ask the neighbours not call the fire brigade AGAIN!

Among my rockabilly mates living there, was Brian Dukes who was the third drummer in The Louisiana Hayriders, and who also drove us to the gigs, bundling everything into his Humber – a sturdy car. On the roof went the double bass and the drums were stuffed into the boot. Dave and Steve Flint and Paul Taylor were all good guys; it was helpful the landlady's sons were rockabillies as well. Great times were had but thinking back I do feel a little bit sorry for the neighbours though – rock 'n' roll and rockabilly very loud at all hours whether they liked it or not. When I did not go to the clubs with the guys, I was lucky enough to go with the rockin' girls who would let me join them. Sue, Deidre (who was one of my jiving partners), her sister Debbie and Fran, Sue Mason, Kate, and Sandra Brooker and Elaine, both good jivers, and I must say Elaine's boyfriend Glenn and the other guys did not mind me jiving with their girlfriends, as I pretty much danced all night long. I never really left the dance floor. They all were a great bunch, and I was lucky to have met good London people.

After living in Northolt, I moved to Chatsworth Road in Hayes for about a year with my first manager's mum Barbara. Then moving back to Northolt, I lived in a flat in Willsmere Drive that I shared with lifelong friends Sue and Darren Moxam, and I was still living with them when they had their first son Dario. This is where I learned how mothers had to get up every 3 hours through the night, all through a baby's first year (Mums you are all saints and deserve a ruddy medal!). Lastly I moved to Sue's parent's (Ros and Tom's) house in Victoria Road, Ruislip Manor, where I continued to live for 12 years. I think by then I was well and truly Londonised.

25

NASHVILLE, TENNESSEE
- MUSIC CITY U.S.A.

Nashville, Tennessee. The name is as beautiful as is the place. I have been travelling to Nashville since 1990, and although changing over the years, the one thing that never changes is the city's melodic heartbeat. Still today it's as strong as ever, which is why the world-over, Nashville, Tennessee is known as Music City U.S.A.

With my first footsteps on Nashville soil, I had mixed emotions. Is this really the music kingdom the rest of the world has been told about? All the country albums Nashville this... Nashville that... The sounds of etc., etc., or will I actually be disappointed in what lies ahead of me.

I was full of ambition and like most entertainers or singer/songwriters I wanted to know if anyone was interested in what I had to offer. Boy was I in for a shock! (At that moment I had no idea there were most probably 2,000 others starting off their day like me, trying to climb the ladder). In the early 1990's, looking back at it now I believed and took on board what most people had to say, and because everyone was climbing the ladder for one reason or another, I ended up a little lost and confused in the end just as to what Kevin and I were really trying to achieve. I quickly came to the conclusion expect nothing, just take what comes your way and create as many good contacts as you can. Once I'd fully absorbed that attitude my Nashville puzzle started becoming a lot easier to piece together. After a couple of visits to Nashville my attitude had totally changed, and I became a little bit more acclimatised to Music City U.S.A. and the way of life. This enabled me to enjoy this music heaven and sail with her, rather than against the tide …Mind you I had to tell Kevin to row a little harder. Fame and fortune: Well that would just have to take a backseat for the moment.

Walking the streets of Nashville, which I did a lot, would always lead me to downtown Broadway at night. There each night, 7 days a week you would behold a thriving music scene, mainly country and blues, in every bar and club. Foremost for me was watching and learning from the professionalism along with the presentation, which was all a learning curve. One night I was watching a guy – he was in his 40's, and he was a brilliant guitarist and singer. As he chatted with his captivated audience, he gave some good advice to the Nashville novices which definitely included Kevin and I. He said, 'If you are coming to Nashville to become rich, think again my friends. I have been playing in Music City for 25 years and I have learned it is much better to make friends and build your business associates; then you will find you have become a lot healthier and wealthier in your country music attitude'. One side of me was saying have I heard him right?.. forget trying to become famous.. or is he right? Because if he is, there isn't enough time or money in our pot to hang around to build an everlasting bridge of contacts. Unless you are going to live here for quite a while to make that happen. Oh dear, my manager Kevin Allen might need another two jobs to go with the two he already has, and I'm going to join him. Eight jobs between us just for starters.

Certain realities kick in quite quickly when you are trying to get ahead in Nashville. I was taken aback on one occasion: There was a guy called Rob who stood on the street corner with his acoustic guitar, just up from Shoney's Hotel where I was staying on Music Row. I chatted with him more than once; he played songs that he wrote and played guitar better than any European player I had ever heard, but he could not even get a gig in the local bar. This told me that without the right representation you have not got a hope in hell in progressing in this business. When returning to my hotel, I picked up the quite thick Nashville local phone book and looked at the musicians that were available from song arrangers to guitarists and so on. There were thousands and this book was the same thickness as our yellow pages of the time. To think, back in the UK we would all have our little diaries of maybe fifty, sixty to a hundred contacts – well hello! Come and have a look at this lot!

Kevin and I had a meeting arranged at a world-famous music publisher's office, Acuff Rose. We sat down with a very enthusiastic and cheerful guy who was very happy to see us, as we had strong connections with the London Acuff Rose office. At the time cassettes were all the rage of the day, and you could have 10 to 20 songs on each cassette. After all the niceties, Kevin pulled out a cassette with some demo songs I had written. All of a sudden the publishers face went very serious and he told us 'Guys don't give me songs! Hold it right there, look at this'. He stood up and pushed a 6-foot high sliding door back to reveal over a thousand cassettes all with demos on including a lot written by the biggest names in the business. He carried on 'If you're looking for hit records then you have come to the right place, but I have to be honest with you, I have not got any room for new songs at the moment'.

It became quite clear after that meeting how far down the ladder Kevin and I were, and with all the new American country artistes becoming sensations around the world at that time, our attempts at making any sort of impact here were fast becoming futile.

Some rockabilly friends of mine also took a trip to Nashville to try and make some headway, and as the drummer informed me, they went to see what it was all about. After their first night touring most of the venues down town I think they got the wakeup call. The very next day the drummer told the rest of the members he no longer wanted to be in the band, explaining that as far as he was concerned all the acts they had seen the night prior were so talented, he did not want to waste his or their time in going around record companies trying to get interest. He just wanted to spend the rest of his time in Nashville enjoying a holiday. You might say (trouble amongst the ranks), the other band members were upset at first, but eventually they ended up agreeing with him. It turned out everyone was now on holiday.

I feel in any band situation, try to eradicate politics as soon as you can and let diplomacy have the biggest voice, especially when you visit Nashville as a budding singer or musician. I would strongly advise anyone, unless you are already famous (world famous), have a good long look around Music City – there is no better way to decide your way forward.

On another note, the southern food I liked very much, which earned me the wrong kind of pounds. You have traditional cafés and little restaurants with local delights, although even to this day I could not get on with grits, but I adored the pancakes and loved the ribs, chicken and burgers. Some people call it junk food ...I call it tasty, eat-until-your-stomachs-full food! Yummy yummy! Followed by a wonderful southern peanut butter or chocolate cookie milkshake – maybe it is a good job I did not stay there too long?

On one occasion another budding U.K. rock 'n' roll entertainer was visiting Nashville, Mark Keeley with his partner. I had performed with his band back in the U.K. so we enjoyed a meal and visiting a couple of honky tonks, and I enjoyed his views on Nashville life. A previous partner of Marks was Karen Keeley who has become a top-drawer Nashville DJ, whom I met and got on well with. I liked them both a lot, seeing a productive and good side to British entertainment.

The Country Music Hall of Fame was a humbling visit for me as they had a room with bronze framed pictures of the musical legends that had made Nashville or Music City U.S.A. the place it was. I think there were 50 of these plaques, among them The Jordanaires and Carl Perkins. I had to pinch myself to take it in, that in musical terms these people had become friends and working associates of mine.

Then in a little sectioned off booth in the corner was a glass case with a 78rpm record of the song *"Gone"* by Ferlin Huskey and if you pressed a little button a recording of this country music classic would play.

Straight away you would hear the haunting but angelic background voice of Millie Kirkham. I stood there loving the whole experience and understood why Elvis when first hearing this record asked the Jordanaires, 'Who's the lady singing?' to which they replied, 'That's Millie', which led to a phone call to Millie and although 6 months pregnant, in 1957 recorded her first session with the King. *"Blue Christmas"* was the first of many she would record with Elvis.

A few years later on a future project, I was recording a gospel album and Millie Kirkham was featured on 10 of the songs, along with The Jordanaires, I can say without doubt, Millie sure had the voice of an angel.

Nashville has many musical wonders; wonders that will amaze any person that goes there. You do not have to be a musician or related to the music industry in any way, everyone will find their own wonders. For me, to get the real feel of Nashville with all it has to offer you need go no further than 'The Ryman Auditorium'. Also known as the Mother Church of Country Music, this is where The Grand Ole Opry Show was performed live to radio listeners from 1943 right up until 1974. The ambiance of this historic venue was amazing, from the wooden bench seating to the stage area, you could feel the magic. I visited the Ryman during the daytime with the sun shining through those big colourful stained glass windows, as if straight from the gates of heaven. With its encased museum pieces, which at the time had letters written by soldiers from the American Civil War and uniforms, there was the Confederate Gallery which was constructed in 1897 for the Confederate Veterans Association reunion, thus increasing the seating capacity to 6,000.

Early days of the Ryman had Charlie Chaplin speaking from the stage along with Bob Hope and Doris Day, even Harry Houdini performed. Just some of the stellar list of country legends.. Hank Williams senior, Little Jimmy Dickens (who I saw perform there on several occasions). He was 4 feet 11 inches tall and took full advantage of the fact should he fall, his guitar would save him. One of my all-time country music moments was seeing with my own eyes George Jones performing *"He stopped Loving Her Today"*. Unbelievable! ..for me an historic moment in time. The Ryman was where Elvis performed a one and only stage appearance, with very little applause (I think he was told to go back to truck driving). Obviously the King vowed never to return. I loved every time I went to the Ryman Auditorium, and on one occasion it really hit home. When one of the best Bluegrass bands that I had ever seen, The Del McCoury Band, were performing the auditorium was full, the ambiance was electric. I took a good look around the auditorium at the audience where I saw children with their parents, along with older relations some of which must have been the ripe old age of 90.

All were loving and living the songs that were being performed, and it dawned on me, some of the older aged people will remember coming here with their aunts and uncles who would have actually fought in the American Civil War. I thought for a moment and felt like thanking all 6,000 people individually for such a warming and wonderful experience. I felt like one of the family.

I went a couple of times to The Grand Ole Opry, when it moved to Opryland Drive in Nashville. These were big events with 8 to 10 acts performing live to thousands of people with the biggest stars of the day, and the whole show is broadcast by WSM, which now can be heard all over the globe.

I have had remarkable experiences in Music City U.S.A, and I know I will soon return and cherish all it has to offer. With all the music culture from Bluegrass to the Appalachian sounds, to the country and rockabilly beats, I can see why some people who are lucky enough in life to reside there, never want to leave. If like me, one day you feel compelled to visit, you too will come under the spell of guitars and singers and take home the memories of a lifetime. You too will become entwined, with no regrets I promise you, in Music City U.S.A.

Play it again and you'll
Strike it rich!

LOTTO BINGO

It's coming soon, folks SEE PAGE 13

A RAVE FROM THE GRAVE

LEGEND: Elvis

Lawdy! Johnny sounds so like Presley

By TONY PURNELL

SHIVERS went down the spines of Elvis Presley's old backing group the Jordanaires when they heard the voice of Johnny Dumper.

They were sent a tape of 24-year-old Johnny singing classic Presley hits like Blue Suede Shoes, Heartbreak Hotel and Jailhouse Rock.

And it sounded so eerily like Elvis, they had to keep telling themselves that the King died twelve years ago.

"It was like hearing a voice from the grave," Jordonaires' leader Gordon Stoker said yesterday.

The American quartet jumped at the chance of teaming up with the British singer tonight in Kentish Town, North London.

Memories

It will be the first time since Presley's death that the Jordanaires have sung his hits on stage.

During a break in rehearsals Gordon said: "If we close our eyes, it's as if Elvis is back on stage with us.

"Singing with Johnny brings back so many memories. His enthusiasm for Elvis just bubbles over.

"He has all the moves and can sing all the songs. But the good thing is, he does not try to impersonate Elvis.

"We stay clear of singers like that — we've seen hundreds of lookalikes who even dye their hair to try to look like him."

Dream

Devon-born Johnny, a former painter and decorator, has been touring Britain in his own show, called The Definitive Elvis Experience.

But tonight's appearance with his hero's original backing group has him all shook up.

He said: "It's my wildest dream come true."

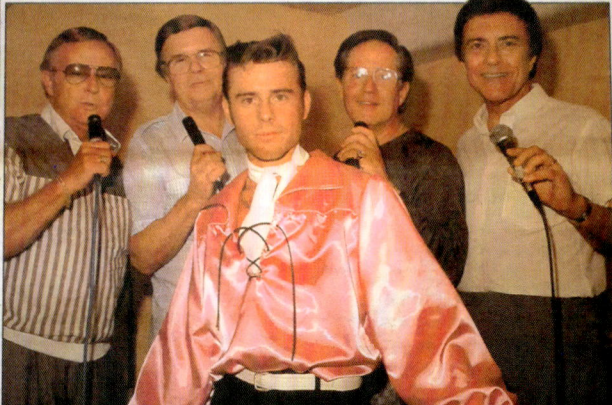
IT'S NOW OR NEVER: And thrilled Johnny won't be lonesome tonight as he teams up with the Jordonaires   Picture: SIMON LEIBOWITZ

GOLDEN OLDIES: The Jordanaires backing Elvis in their Fifties heyday

Fan's all shook up

PRESLEY fan Mike Buckingham was left "gutted" yesterday after three rare records were stolen from his office.

Mike, of Langley, Berks., bought the limited-edition RCA gold discs — worth around £1,000 — in the States.

They were the singles Fools Rush In and Can't Help Falling in Love, and an LP of great hits.

COREY'S FIRST IN THE RACE

By MIRROR REPORTER

STABLE lad Corey Roberts is set to become Britain's first black jockey. And as he donned his racing silks for a practice gallop yesterday he said: "This is like a dream come true."

Corey, 17, started as a YTS trainee just 18 months ago. The Jockey Club is now processing his application for an apprentice's licence and he expects to ride in his first flat race for Captain J.R. Wilson's famous stables near Preston, Lancs, within a month.

It was Captain Wilson's daughter Geraldine Rees — the only woman to complete the gruelling Grand National course — who spotted his potential.

She bought him a pony and taught him to ride. Now full of confidence, he is thundering along the gallops on thoroughbreds which dwarf his 4ft 8in frame. Geraldine said: "He's a natural."

His foster mum Kathleen Adamson said at her home in Wallasey, Merseyside: "We're all bursting with pride."

JOCKEY: Corey, 17

JOHNNY EARLE The Singer Man

He is probably Britain's best exponent of 'New Country'. Had this 1997 album been issued by an American major with millions of dollars of promotion I have little doubt that Johnny Earle would have become one of the scene's biggest stars.

As it happens this 14-track album has been issued on Earle's own label: a smart move, in one way, for it means he controls his business destiny (what Elvis Presley would have given for *that*!), which may not mean fame & riches, but it does mean freedom and independence. This album may not have made any charts, but that doesn't make it a flop. On the contrary, it acts as a powerful showcase for Earle's songwriting talents: any number of songs here could be picked up by a major act and become a hit. Recognition of Earle as a top drawer performer in his own right has yet to come.

The material here is varied: tender ballads alongside strong, kickin' movers. A sampling of titles: Wherever Love Can Be Found (so beautiful and human, *and* commercial! A smash hit waiting to happen!); Born A Country Boy (just dig that voice! Sounds like he's from Tennessee, not Devon!); Daddy's Leaving Home; The Power In Me (a powerhouse ballad: another smash waiting to happen).

Sold usually for £11.99; check it out at **£6.99 ($13)**.

JOHNNY EARLE WITH THE JORDANAIRES Elvis In Paris

This beautifully packaged – like a slim long box – 27-track compilation from JEM Records focuses on Presley's army period, and *includes CD Rom film footage of Presley himself in Paris in 1959*, footage which apparently is unobtainable elsewhere (but note this can only be accessed through a computer).

But you don't need a computer to relish the music on offer here. The songs are split between Presley and Earle originals. About the tracks: A Fool Such As I – wow! Sounds like a '59 out take (but if only out takes were usually *this* good!). How on earth does Earle do it? There's absolutely nothing to betray it as a 90s' recording! Soldier Boy: I have always loved Presley's version of The 4 Fellows' hit but *this* version – wow! Earle draws on Presley's own hidden depths to deliver a performance that Presley perhaps himself would have preferred! (Now this is getting ridiculous!)

The track that really slays me is Is It So Strange? I've always been a sucker for what I call 'Deep Elvis': the atmospheric 50s' ballads on which his voice trembles & tenses. What makes Johnny Earle the No.1 Presley interpreter (as opposed to mere imitator: there is a subtle but keen difference) is his handling of this aspect of Presley. There are several 'different Elvises' you can seek to copy, but this core 'mystic' Elvis is the hardest of all to emulate. Earle not only emulates Presley but even surpasses him! This is *crazy*! I can't believe that I'm saying this, but then I can't believe what I'm hearing.

Doin' The Best I Can is another Earle showstopper, as he conjures all Presley's delicacy and depth. If Presley had lived I don't think he would have believed his ears.

Up-tempo Earle originals like G.I. Rock'n'Roll, You're In The Army Now, Going Home To The USA, & Private Elvis all sound like they could have come from the G.I. Blues album. Private Elvis is a particular gas, featuring a catchy Jordanaires' chorus behind an infectious bass voice which keeps repeating 'Private Elvis'. One might think that this bass belongs to a Jordanaire, but I believe that the voice again belongs to Earle.

Other tracks include: The Girl I Adore (if a time machine was at hand and Johnny could have delivered this Earle original to Elvis in person it would have resulted in yet another Presley million-seller); Lonely Soldier Boy (a very touching tune which acknowledges Presley's sadness and isolation).

We know that Presley was an ardent Ral Donner fan: what would he have made of Johnny Earle? I can guess. Get this £15.99 set for only **£11.99 ($21)**.

Johnny Earle
& The Jordanaires
WITH ELVIS IN MIND

James Cullinan, owner of Finbarr, writes:
Why does Johnny Earle need to be Elvis Presley? The reason is to be found in our need to hear someone who's like him. However, such a need presents its problems: a thousand Presley imitators can be a nightmare, particularly those sad souls who do the 70s' Vegas version. But I am ready to go through 999 if the 1000th turns out to be Johnny Earle.

Earle is nothing if not sensational. Prior to discovering him my all-time favourite Presley sound-a-like was Ral Donner. I couldn't get enough of Donner. In 1962 he gave us the badly needed consolation for Presley's own descent into the bland. I cannot describe my reaction to first hearing Earle. Disbelief. Astonishment. And joy. All I've ever wanted is someone to be as good as Donner, let alone Presley. But, for God's sake, this guy is *better*.

This 20-track CD consists mainly of Presley tributes, featuring both Presley hits & original songs, penned by Earle himself. The Presley tunes are staggering. Fame & Fortune typically sounds like an *out take* from Presley's own 1960 session. The Earle originals are what floor me, for you could swear they were written by Pomus & Shuman, Leiber & Stoller, or whomever, in 1960 with Presley expressly in mind. Earle is sole writer of these songs – there's no collaborator to help him – so how does an English lad, 3000 miles away from Nashville and decades away from the period conceive such songs that are the *very essence* of G.I. Presley??

Listening to this disc is like listening to a lost Presley album. The songs seem familiar, but you know you haven't heard them before. You hear the unmistakable voices of The Jordanaires, and then the luscious Nashville pop sound of 1960: and then the *lead singer*.

Briefly, about the tracks: Blind Date, an Earle original, would surely have been a Presley million-seller in 1960. It should be a smash hit *today*: it's so good. Christmas Bells Ring sounds like a track missed off Presley's 1957 seasonal album. Faithful & True and Queen Of The Night are ridiculously Presley-ish.

The cover states that the sessionmen here include Carl Perkins, Scotty Moore & D.J. Fontana. Earle receives A1 endorsements all the way round, even having Stuart Colman writing the liner notes.

But it isn't the Presley sound all the way. We also get several tracks showcasing Johnny Earle *as Johnny Earle*. We get his own songs again, and one is at a loss to understand why he isn't one of the most famous ballad singer-writers of our day. Note in particular I Have A Dream: a ballad of towering beauty and humanity. Usually I have no interest in contemporary music, but I find it impossible not to be struck by the compelling power of Earle's artistry.

This release on JEM Records sells usually for £11.99. Get it now for **£7.99 ($15)**. You won't be disappointed.

SKIFF-A-BILLY (FEATURING JOHNNY EARLE) Skiff-A-Billy. 'Skiff-A-Billy is a new music made up from skiffle, country, r&r and r&b', say the notes from JEM Records. The six-piece group include Tom Donegan (son of Lonnie), Terry Peaker (ex-Emile Ford bassist), & Johnny Earle, who handles lead vocals. 20 songs, including: My Dixie Darling; Have A Drink On Me; You Are The One; Hillbilly Rock; Putting On The Style; Wig Wam Bam; Blue Bayou. **Only £6.99 ($13).**

ROY 'BOOGIE BOY' PERKINS Roy 'Boogie Boy' Perkins With Bobby Page & The Riff Raffs. 1958-61 sides cut for the South Louisiana label Ram. 25 tracks, shared between Perkins & Page. Both are white, but in a black groove. The Riff Raffs are a 7-piece band with a black sound. The style is r&r & r&b with inevitable New Orleans' & swamp overtones. Raw exciting music. Drop Top; Ba Da; Ginnin'; Hey Lawdy, Mama; etc. 25 tracks on Ace. **£7.99 ($14).**

Maggie's Blue Suede News

£1

Rock 'n' Roll Magazine

Issue 90   £1.00   December 2004

Established Since 1997

Beat The Blues, Get Maggie's News!

Johnny Earle & Friends at Lea Hall

Review: Stevie Brookes, Wolverhampton. Photos: Maggie Sampford, Coventry.

Show: Public exhibition; theatrical or other entertainment; Showman: Man skilled at presenting anything spectacularly. Where does all this lead? Well I'll tell you! On Friday 5th November, Lea Hall Miners Welfare Centre. played host to The Spitfires and Mark Keeley's Good Rockin' Tonight.

This night's entertainment held concern for all as October bought a poor crowd and of late poor JD's Record Hop has seen diminishing door sales, largely due to other venues being on at the same time.

This night proved to be a 'break in the clouds'. I arrived at the club at 7pm only to see people there, already more than last month. The Spitfires were sounding good and that was only the sound-check with Mark Keeley being their anchor man on the mixing desk. By 9pm the room had packed out with visitors from all over. As far as Wales, Northants, Worcestershire and Warwickshire, (thanks Maggie). So nice to see you all.

Music of the night by JD's Record Hop consisted of a good mix of ever popular jivers, boppers and strollers. The dance floor remained full through all the tracks and JD's wealth of knowledge kept the rapport sweet. The Spitfires were first on stage and started with 'Red Hot'. Young Alan as we old 'uns call him, has improved vocally and accompanied by Keith (Lucas), played excellently, the Haley numbers being my favourites. They were loud and mighty and rocked through every song with an unusual rendition of 'Rag Mop' - you had to have been there to see it!

Mark Keeley's Good Rockin' Tonight played the second set. Now what can I say good about them? Well, nothing that hasn't already been said this year, always good, I've seen Mark and GRT so many times this year I defy anyone to say differently. Again, they played brilliantly to the highest quality. Maybe the repertoire could do with a change buddy.

And finally! If you're brave enough to read the first sentence again, the finale of this fantastic evening was down to Mr. Johnny Earle, as billed. However, Johnny introduced himself as 'The Jive Time Show!' Not a problem though. To those of you who have seen Johnny then no explanations are necessary. To those of you who haven't, then go and see him and you decide. My view; a showman - truly entertaining in his line of show. He has a brilliant voice, not unlike the King but you also see Johnny, the solo entertainer.

Now I know he has his cynics and say what you must but this particular night he did a show and he was loved by everyone. If you like Elvis, go and see an Elvis impersonator or tribute. There's only one Johnny Earle, and yeah, he did swing me baby!!

southern country £1

THE SOUTH'S No. 1 BRITISH COUNTRY MUSIC MAGAZINE

Issue 213 November 1996

18th Year of Publication

Johnny Earle

SILVER DOLLAR MARK II

KINSON

September brought the return of some fine missing from this club for more than a year. First BORDERLINE MUSIC COMPANY's special sound with the full time fiddle and Tom's lovely voice which is so good to hear. A wide selection of songs from "The Cowboy Rides Away" to "Blue Wing", "Birmingham Turnaround" and the final sing-along medley of oldies, not forgetting the instrumentals, particularly "San Antonio Rose" featuring the fiddle and an assortment of sounds from the guitar.

Next CHRIS RAINBOW BAND. A late start due to transport problems (broken fuel pump, replacement van to the rescue). No time wasted, breaks cut down to just a few minutes and an amazing number of songs fitted into the time available. Special for me were "There Goes My Heart", "If Tomorrow Never Comes" and "Under The Sun" with some lovely lead guitar. A really good show which more than made up for the late start.

Highlight of the month was surely the return (at last!) of JOHNNY EARLE with ideal backing from SOUTHERN STAR. (photo below: *Johnny Earle photo by Roger Sealy*.)

A professional to his fingertips, thoroughly at home on stage, Johnny certainly knows how to keep an audience entertained. The performance tonight had everything - life, humour, movement and a wide ranging selection of songs which suited Johnny's great voice to perfection. "Alibis", "Statue of a Fool", his own song "The Next Time I See You I Will Cry" (a brief sample of the forthcoming CD with all originals) I loved every one, but the best for me was Collin Raye's "Angel of No Mercy". At the end of a great evening there was no way to follow Johnny's outstanding version of "I Swear" so only two encores.

Poster for 'Private Elvis'

Chapter 2
ARRIVAL

When Elvis disembarked at Bremerhaven on October 1, 1958, he was greeted by hundreds of cheering German fans and the same kind of media circus as the one he had left ten days ago in Brooklyn. Military police had cordoned off the whole area and blocked railway lines because there were so many fans on the tracks. Press reports about girls climbing over barbed wire fences and bursting through military police cordons were gross exaggerations. Access to the quayside at Bremerhaven was not substantially restricted and the scenes of near riot described by some newspapers occurred only in the imaginations of reporters desperate for sensational copy. The German teenagers were far more reserved than their American counterparts and had not experienced the Elvis phenomenon to anything approaching the same extent as youngsters in the US.

Above: *A young fan stands ready to greet Elvis with a cinema poster for* Loving You, *retitled in German* Gold aus heisser Kehle - Gold From A Hot Throat.

THE JORDANAIRES

I have a lot of great memories of Elvis during the years of his Army tenure in Germany.

After he completed eight weeks of basic training at Ft. Hood, Texas, Elvis was granted a two week leave. On June 10-11, 1958 The Jordanaires, along with musicians hank Garland, Chet Atkins, Bob Moore, Floyd Cramer, Buddy Harman and D. J. Fontana joined Elvis at RCA's Nashville studio to record the five songs that were to be his last of the 1950s - *I Need Your Love Tonight, A Big Hunk O' Love, Ain't That Lovin' You Baby, A Fool Such As I* and *I Got Stung.* Elvis was always concerned about his fans, but now he wondered if he would have any fans left when he returned.

I saw him one more time before he left for Germany. My wife, Jean, and I were visiting at Graceland in Memphis and he asked us to go with him to the Reserve Headquarters where he had to take care of some last minute details. During these last moments we spent with Elvis, it was obvious that he was afraid his career was over. WE ASSURED HIM IT WASN'T.

I give Colonel Parker a lot of credit for keeping ELvis's name in front of the public while he was in the service.

We kept in close touch with him the eighteen months he was in Germany. Among other things, I sent him an album by the black spiritual group *The Harmonizing Four.* When I finally saw him after his return, I asked him if he liked it. He said, "Are you kidding? I wore it out!"

The only other time I saw him while he was in the service was when his mother died in August 1958. D. J. Fontana, Neal Matthews and I drove to Memphis the day of her funeral. I'll never forget entering Graceland and seeing Elvis sitting on the steps in the entry hall crying his heart out. It was one of the saddest things I'd ever seen.

I know Elvis enjoyed the Army, basically he liked the German people. He enjoyed being with German girls and, of course, it was while he was in Germany that he met Priscilla, who was stationed there with her father.

There's one thing we shall always treasure of the fifteen years we worked with Elvis . . . we were sitting around eating during a recording session at Radio Recorders in Hollywood. He looked at us and said, "if there had not been The Jordanaires, I guess there would not have been a *me.*" We said, "What . . . you can't mean that." He said, "Yep, you guys took an interest in me and when I didn't care, you helped me with bad material (*referring to the movie songs*) and just when I did not want to record." We did it because of our love for him.

Gordon Stoker

UXBRIDGE & HILLINGDON

Also serving Eastcote, Hayes, No

Leader

No 274   Wednesday, August 24, 1988   AFN

It's now or never!

'Elvis' hopes for the big time

■ Left: Johnny Dumper as he appeared in the Mirror

■ Right: Local boy made good... nationwide tour for Elvis impersonator Johnny Dumper

by Sheila Bannister

ELVIS impersonator Johnny Dumper hopes to make the big time.

The 23-year-old Hayes man has hit the headlines, appearing at theatres and in newspapers, and now he hopes to break into television.

Johnny appeared at the Beck Theatre, Hayes, last week, in a tribute to Elvis Priesley to mark the 11th anniversary of the death of the king of rock and roll last week.

It marked the start of his nationwide tour at venues including the 2,000 seater Dominion Theatre in London's Tottenham Court Road, where Elvis's backing group, The Jordanaires, may be making a special guest appearance.

Recently, Mr Dumper, who appeared in the West End musical Forever Elvis, bared his muscular chest to appear as a Page Three Fella in the Mirror.

Now the former painter and decorator is negotiating a television appearance on the Last Resort show.

He writes and sings his own songs — a cross between Roger Whittaker and Elvis, he says.

Born in Devon, Johnny was brought up on the music of Elvis, and Eddie Cochran whom he also impersonates. As a teenager he entered an Elvis competition, and won, singing "Hound Dog".

"I don't look particularly like Elvis but I sound and perform like him. It comes naturally," says the singer, model and actor.

And he adds: "I remember seeing my father cry for the first time when we heard of Elvis's death."

The tall, dark, handsome entertainer, who used to live in Chatsworth Road, Hayes, has no girlfriend. He still lives in the Hayes area, but is keeping his new address a secret from admirers.

"I haven't got a girlfriend. How could I be faithful to her when there are girls waiting for me at every corner.," he says.

•Headline note for non-Elvis fans: 'It's now or never' was a Presley hit record.

DAILY STAR

BRITAIN'S BRIGHTEST NEWSPAPER

WEDNESDAY, AUGUST 12, 1992   **25p** (26p Cls)

KING'S MAN: Johnny Earl has been picked to sing Elvis hits with backing musicians including The Jordanaires (above)

Johnny is King of Elvis revival

BY MADELEINE PALLAS

★ THE KING lives on . . . in Ruislip, Middlesex! Elvis Presley's old rock 'n' roll mates have picked young British singer Johnny Earl to let the legend's music live on.

★ Former painter and decorator Johnny, 27, flew to Tennessee last month to meet the Pelvis's old backing musicians, including guitarist Scotty Moore and vocal group The Jordanaires.

★ They cut a single, Long Live The King, to be released on August 17. The following night Johnny and the band — called All The King's Men — kick off a 15-night nationwide tour.

★ Excited Johnny said last night: "I still can't believe this is happening to me. Last time these guys played together was back in 1960."

informer

The ENTERTAINER

INSIDE THIS WEEK	FILM FILE	ART FACTS	GIG GUIDE	COMPETITION
	A flick through the screen scene - page 10	The curtain's up on the theatre - page 11	Check out the hot local gigs - page 11	Win tickets to a West End show - page 14

PLUS ▪ Weekend TV Guide ▪ Mega Byte - the latest computer game round-up ▪ Prize crossword

SWAPPING THE CROWN FOR A STETSON!

Andrew Balkin talks to The King soundalike hoping to make it big in America

SMOKING 60 cigarettes a day is not good for anyone - let alone a singer - so it's a good job Johnny Earle packed in the habit!

But he has come a long way since those smoking days, doing Elvis interpretations, NOT impersonations, and is about to launch a career as a country rock singer Stateside.

Although it is the Elvis 'thing' that's about to bring the former Exeter man bucketloads of fame and fortune.

Johnny has just finished a five-song soundtrack for a new video called *Private Elvis*, released next Monday. The video traces Elvis' lost years in the army serving in Germany, and holds a few surprises in store.

Johnny said: "I wrote and sang the songs for the video. The people at Gracelands heard some of my stuff and they didn't believe that it wasn't really Elvis; that's flattering. This should come as no surprise to him - he was voted across Europe as the closest soundalike to The King, and he has built up a massive following, especially in Germany.

Estate Agents • Sur

See Johnny in concert

WE HAVE tickets to give away to Johnny Earle's last UK concert. Just write, by Wednesday, September 29, telling us who Johnny Earle was previously known as, and name one of Elvis Presley's first four movies.

Answers on a postcard to: Johnny Competition, the Informer, Lawrence House, 45 High Street, Egham, Surrey TW20 9DP.

Singing for our boys in the Gulf

By Audrey Downes

RUISLIP'S up-and-coming singing star Johnny Earl has been called out to the Middle East to entertain our troops during the Gulf crisis.

The Elvis soundalike of Victoria Road, has agreed to fly out to Bahrain for a 10 day tour next month.

And the action has prompted a big career boost for the singer — formerly known as Johnny Dumper — as he performed on TV AM yesterday and has now been invited to appear on Wogan.

His manager Kevin Allen was contacted by the multi-national forces' morale officer of the US Navy last week, who requested Johnny and his band fly out on September 18.

Kevin said: "Johnny was a little bit apprehensive at first, but now he is feeling very honoured that he's been asked to go.

"He will be the first entertainer out there and will do two shows a night for both the Brit-

■ Johnny Earl in his GI gear

ish and American forces."

Johnny plans to adapt his usual rock and roll show to appeal to his audience more specifically, by including plenty of Elvis' army songs. And he's even got himself a GI-style uniform so he looks the part.

His open-air performances are each expected to attract crowds of about 10,000.

Kevin added: "If war breaks out before September the 18th, we won't be going and if it breaks out while we're out

Local singer picked to entertain the troops

there, they've promised us we'll be airlifted straight out to a place of safety."

Last time Johnny Earl played locally was at the Beck Theatre earlier this month, and the Hayes venue was packed for the show.

The former painter and decorator turned to showbiz six years ago. He played the starring role in the West End musical Elvis for two years, and supported Jerry Lee Lewis on his ill-fated tour in April.

His next big effort will be a UK tour with Elvis' old backing group The Jordanaires, next year. He is the first Elvis impersonator the Jordanaires have ever agreed to sing with.

130 Poster for Rock 'n' Roll Summer All-dayer

131 Publicity photo, 1990

Music & Merchandise

Blue Suede Dreams
CD & Blue Vinyl LP

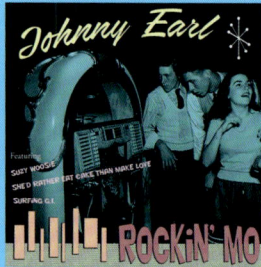

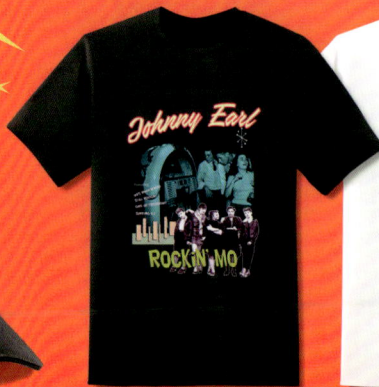

21 Great Jivers & Strollers
Swing Me Baby

I Rockin' Mo

She Wants It All
WITH JOHNNY EARL AND THE DUKES

Even Poppy says it looks cool!

All items available from
BLUESUEDEDREAMS.COM

26

TESCO

Elvis Presley was once a truck driver and then became a rock 'n' roll singer; I'm just doing it the other way around. Okay, you may well ask what's rock 'n' roll about Tesco. I can tell you one thing, when I deliver to customers it is amazing how many customers have pictures of rock 'n' roll, country, and swing music legends adorning their walls, along with statuettes on their shelves. It proves again and again that this era of music has a long lifespan and means so much to so many people and will be with us a long way into the future.

I work a few days a week for Tesco (Dot.Com) delivering groceries to online shoppers. Yes that's right, I'm one of the guys who walks up six flights of stairs with no lifts, five or six trips with trays full of goodies (I've never been so fit, no gym subscriptions needed here). There is never a dull day and I have a lot of laughs with the guys and girls who are also part of the dot.com delivery team. Here's just a little taster of some of my customer experiences...

Part of our duties is to ask for carrier bags that the customer no longer has use for, and on one occasion I asked a lady 'Do you have any carrier bags you do not want as we recycle them'? 'No sorry I use them for nappies', so I remarked 'That's a clever idea, I suppose you make two holes in the bottom of the bag for the legs and use the handles to slip over the baby's shoulders', 'No' she replied, 'I use the bags to put the nappies in'. At first, I looked at her a bit puzzled, then realization kicked in of what she really meant, I said 'Oh I see, now I get what you mean'. I suppose never having any children myself, I have very little experience in this field! I'm sure she thought I was crackers.

Now when you are a delivery man in south west London you become pretty open-minded, especially when you deliver to all nationalities of people. I was finishing my round one day and one of my last lady customers was a very nice South African lady, and as usual I finished my delivery by asking if everything was okay. 'Yes thanks, certainly better than last week' she remarked, 'Why is that'? I said, 'Well I had a lot trouble with the papers'. I replied, 'Well in that case it's best not to read them, as these days they are always full of depressing and bad news'. She then looked at me quite angrily and in a louder tone of voice blurted out 'No I'm telling you the papers were really very bad'. I smiled and said, 'I can only advise you not to read them'. 'The papers, the papers!' and with that she bent down and pulled out of the tray a red and a yellow pepper and exclaimed 'The papers' 'Ahh', I replied 'Peppers', and I could not help but burst out laughing. She did not find it very amusing but I'm sure as she closed her door she must have been thinking English humour is very strange.

I couldn't help but share the experience I'd had with the next customer. This customer told me of a similar experience she had had with her English teacher at college who was called Mr. Peg, but a South African student always called him Mr. Pig... What a colourful place London is.

Don't think it's always women us drivers have unusual experiences with. I must have delivered to the real Mr. Bean. No, not Rowan Atkinson – this man was called John; slim build, around 5 feet ten and well into his 60's. As I drove the Tesco's van into his narrow driveway, he came waltzing out of his front door, came to my driver's side window and tapped on it which I thought was a bit unusual. I lowered the window ready for anything that was about to happen whereupon he said, 'Hi I'm John, and I have a military way of having my groceries delivered'. 'Okay', I said 'Fire away'. He then told me to take all the trays that belonged to him off the van, and then I must proceed to take all the items out one by one and line them up down the side of his house and then carry on into the garden, which I did. After this parade of groceries was all lined up he then went through his three order sheets and ticked off each item one by one which took ages. With my sense of humour, when he finally said, 'Looks like everything's here', I just could not help myself and said, 'All present and correct sir'. He smiled, signed my machine and said he was happy with the delivery. Just when I thought it could not get any more ridiculous he marched down the driveway, climbed onto a three-foot high wall and stood on the flat pillar and said, 'I will safely direct you back out of my driveway onto the main road'.

I got into my van, looked in my wing mirror at a Mr. Bean-like character frantically waving me back out of his drive, whilst balancing on his garden wall. I was in tears of laughter throughout the reversing stage and by the time I reached the end of the drive I could not even look at him and drove off, noticing as I did so in my wing mirror that he was waving goodbye while still standing on his brick wall. He was obviously over the moon with my marvellous G.I. military precision in delivering his groceries; you see it's not boring at Dot.Com. Thank you to Tesco's and all the people I have met, for a great laugh while working with good people. With thirty years in the music/entertainment business it's sometimes nice to work and meet non-show business people.

27

PAGE 7 FELLA

I was having a lot of tabloid publicity and Kevin Alan my manager at the time put it to me, why not try and become a page 7 fella? 'Just give it a go'. We already sold photos at the shows where some did not look not too dissimilar from the pose that a page 7 fella looked like. At the photo session I will never forget the photographer, as he was taking the picture, said 'Johnny keep that smile but take a deep breath and hold your stomach in'. That takes getting used to I can tell you, but when he did snap away it was like a machine gun, so a lot of photos were either going to turn out brilliant or else there was a strong possibility I would become page 67 fella! When I saw the photo in the Daily Mirror, it dawned on me 'I don't look like that every day'. All the preparation that went in to get this to happen I can now see how difficult the fashion world must be day after day.

I visited Sid Shaw's shop Elvisly Yours the day this was released in the major tabloid and one of the guys working there said, if that was him as page 7 fella, he would walk down the high street with it pinned on his back. It was not apparent to me how people really reacted to page 7 fella but thereafter when mentioning it in my publicity, it got a good review rather than bad, so a job well done in the end. The picture that was on the 45rpm single of *"Let the Boogie Woogie Roll"* was from the same photo session, so we certainly made good use of the one day in my life when I was - page 7 fella.

28

FOLLOW THAT DREAM
(WHEREVER THAT DREAM MAY LEAD)

Will I ever wake up, I doubt it!

When you have experienced a life of rock 'n' roll and have entertained audiences all over the world, you never lose that mystical feeling of I wonder what's going to happen next. The music gods point their finger and can smile on you at any moment, but as for fame and fortune I am afraid you never can tell when either is upon you. You might never get that phone call; you know the one – the one that can change your life forever.

In the writing of this book Blue Suede Dreams, what a journey I have had! A good rewind in assessing one's life, it has had me crying with laughter along with tears of sadness, I have literally creased up on the floor with un-controllable lunacy. Would I have changed anything, could I have changed anything, impossible to say. The Devil has shown himself on more than one occasion and that has led me to believe God always triumphs in the end (I'm still here aren't I). I am where I am today because of all that has happened to me. I have been a fool, on occasions very green to say the least, and you can throw in I have also been a little bit of a drunk. I've had a lot of girlfriends but mostly good women relationships and today I can honestly say, if I have learnt anything from my past, then I will definitely never be a drunk again!

On my journey, what I have enjoyed the most is meeting so many people who themselves are lovers of life. My love of music has enabled me to travel the world, so I have met all levels of society. Still today I get on a plane and perform on foreign shores when called upon, and today in my life I feel the cherry on the cake is I get to see my mum a lot more than I used to. If I turn to the next page of my music career, I would not have a clue what would be written – I suppose that is the intrigue that makes entertainers just keep on going. Writing this book has certainly made me realize how lucky I was to walk alongside legends in the world of music and I never had a clue that all the while I was living 'The Blue Suede Dream'.

29

ACKNOWLEDGEMENTS

As I started to understand the music world, it made me stand outside the guitar shaped goldfish bowl in order to take a good look in. My acknowledgements are mostly to the ones who to me, make the music world's heart beat, and without them there is no music world at all. They are the reason I still write and perform today, and they include not just my friends but also members of the general public.

My first acknowledgement goes to the person who was the first to stand with me before I even drew my very first breath, my darling mother. She is very Devonshire and found it hard to understand why I even bother performing and writing songs with the kind of people the music business produces, with all its setbacks and knock-backs. She sees a brighter glow in me today as one of my best achievements so far was to bring her to live in London, 90 seconds away from me, so I can see her every day and know she is safe.

My late father Stuart sadly passed away at the young age of 38, (I was only 16) and I was too young to understand the technicalities of life at that tender age. I loved him very much but could never work out or understand how he lost his love for my mother. He was a very busy man which I understood after one day visiting his yard (really it was more of a field) full of JCB diggers, HYMACs, low loaders and all the plant machinery you could think of. I counted over 30 machines belonging to him. I blessed the ground he walked on and at the age of 15, I told him how proud I was of him and of what he had achieved. He gave me a fatherly hug that I will never forget, but unfortunately this was to be my last. To this day, I have never visited his grave, as I have never come to terms with losing him. I feel, although passed on, his strength of character is way too strong to leave my life, so he walks with me now and again until I join him on the other side. (I'm not going mad, it's just life has a strange way of building and bonding its bridges).

My brother David who also had a big strength of character (as anyone who knew him would tell you). Known as the Josey Wales of Exeter, he fought for what he thought was right, a tough nut to say the least, and definitely would have been a contender on today's programme 'Britain's Hardest Man'. I loved my brother even though we were so different. While I learned how to look after myself, through judo and karate he did it the hard way and became a brawling street fighter at every opportunity that came his way. I never understood this way of life, but he felt it was his destiny (although many might not agree; among them the Devonshire police). He fought my father as well as the school teachers and all the bullies whom he encountered. It was not unusual of odds being 4-1 stacked against him (sometimes you gotta' fight to be a man).

He finally found solace in his body building, entering competitions in which he would eventually reign over the other contenders, a very hard world to do so in. Unfortunately, steroids and body mass substances got the better of him. He once said to me 'John to live life the way I do, I know I will never reach the age of 40', I never replied as Dave said this so meaningfully, I found it hard to take. I got a phone call while living in London that he passed away, the cause being an inflamed heart at the age of 32. As he was being lowered into the ground, I held my mum, telling her as he was laid to rest in the same grave as my father, that we now had to be strong and we both would go on in life and fight the world together.

It is funny that even at this sad occasion, a family member from my father's side waited for the right moment (as soon as my brother was finally lowered into the ground), to come up and ask me if I knew the whereabouts of two very expensive antique chairs my brother had borrowed from my nan and granddad. (Orright buy, my beauties, ow be doin)!

My sister, who never understood the path I walked and why should she! (Each to their own). We never really saw eye to eye on anything, but I wish her and her family the very best in all that life brings them.

Tom and Ros (Ros is sadly no longer with us). A massive thank you to the both of them for putting a roof over my head for most of my London years, adopting this Devon lad and helping him grow up in a London environment.

(Gone but not forgotten Pat) and Marie, Lorraine, Roy and Nita and all the family, Janet and all the Stanley's.

My now departed Nans and Granddads, aunt and uncles and all family members who are no longer with us. God bless you all (as well as all the living of course).

A big thank you to my partner Sue who gives me the love and support to enjoy life to the full. My thanks also to my friend Frances who has helped with the release of this book. To DJ Annie who now has found her happiness with husband Vinnie who is an out and out Punk Rocker but tells me even he is a Johnny Earl fan, you can't beat good rock 'n' roll music I keep reminding him!!!!

I thank all my school friends (especially girlfriends) from Devon for a wonderful and energetic childhood. Melville Thomas among them, one of my best and trustworthy friends, who one weekend decided to borrow my boat, without asking - and SINKING IT! (Orright buuuy!). Never forgetting Neil Leggett and his family – we started rocking and rolling together right from the start. The school teachers who bought all the fish I could sell them and helped me finance my rock 'n' roll lifestyle. Devon's own rock 'n' roll D.J. Eddie Falcon, and all the Devonshire rockers whom I shared the dance floors with, not forgetting the people who transported me to all these venues (Chris and Wendy, Steve Palfrey).

My fishing buddy Trevor Hall, and his dad, never forgetting when we all went fishing in his dad's boat and while trying to fix the outboard engine to the back Trevor and I fumbled and dropped the engine in 3 feet of salt water. (Game over as far as going out fishing went!). Fortunately, his father did not witness our stupidity, so we sat there pulling the starting chord for about 20 minutes while crying with tears of laughter saying to his father we had not got a clue why it did not work! Hello to Dobsie (Trevor's mum).

Gerald and Peter from the old boy records club, and this club has more attitude than the Masonic gatherings. It has three life-time members and I am the third. Let's not forget their wives and families who put up with us. Maureen who still jives the night away, along with Kenny and Donna.

Bob and Shelia Thomas (my great friend Sean's parents) and all of their family who employed all us teenage rockers to work in the takeaway kiosk at the Riverside Hotel, down on Teignmouth seafront. It was a great laugh and when I worked with Sean in the kiosk someone would ask for fish and chips and without Sean knowing it, I would wrap a frozen piece of fish in with the chips, wrap it quickly then give it to him to give to the customer and then say I'm off to the toilet (Oh the commotion I would return to).

I would like to give a big thank you to 'Big Jem Newman', a friend who was like a brother to me. He made me get off my backside and put pen to paper, because I can tell people until the cows come home 'I'm going to write a book!' but just like anybody who has embarked on such a massive endeavour, they know the main battle is to actually get writing. And even then realizing it takes a long, long time. I thought this book of my magical journey would only take a couple of months. Throw in London life, working and touring, shows and moving my mum to London etc. etc., it has now taken me nearly 4 years. So, thank you Jem and his girlfriend lovely Leigh (who was his rock of Gibraltar) for igniting the flame (I say this with the heaviest of hearts as only a few months ago dear Jem sadly passed away. Gone but never forgotten, loved by so many he will be very sadly missed). I thank Steve Edwards for introducing me to Jem.

I thank all the guys and girls I first met when coming to London moving from house to house, room to room, flat to flat - Sue, Deirdre, Debbie and Fran, Kate, Sharon, my dance partner, Sandra Brooker, all the Moxam brothers and sisters along with Dave, gone but never ever forgotten, their lovely mum Jean, the Colwell brothers and Webb brothers, Nick Kennedy, Dennis, Chris, John and Sharon Henderson, Lee, Dave Flint and brothers Steve and Phil, Jim, Colin (Shepherds Bush), Brian Dukes, Sammy, Paul Taylor, Steve Horner and sister Sue, Steve Chapman and his sister Sue, Sue Mason, (I seem to know a lot of Sue's), Ginger Joe, Jackie and Danny, lovely Ali still my Jive partner and Shirley from the Isle of White and her now sadly departed husband Dave, a Rock 'n' Roll DJ Legend.

Thanks to all the rockers that went to the London Rockin' clubs 'Silks', 'The Phoenix, Oxford Circus', 'Pink Elephant' 'The Fox', 'The Clay Pigeon', Liverpool Street all-nighters, Noel and Caroline (true rockers with a big heart) and to all who went to the Caister Holiday Park rock 'n' roll weekenders at Great Yarmouth and that is to mention but a few. My German friends of course, the Schroer family Annie, Andy and Lisa and Dominic with their beautiful baby daughter Juliana, Toby the Hawaiian shirt legend, Michael, Oscar, and my favourite German bands 'Danny and the Wonderbras', along with all the "Dukes" my Dutch friends Yohan, Cherrie, and son Kevin, Ellen, Petra, Ario, Elonka and Paul, Mark, gone but never forgotten

Margie, and of course Trudy along with all the Explosion Rockets. Ben Ball and Sally along with their family and Alan and Pat, Anne and Dave.

Vanessa and Adrian and I give Vanessa my medal of honour for raising so much money and supporting various charities which she has worked for and I was honoured to perform to help her causes.

True rockers Jane Austin, Jerry Richards, Pam Gregory, Len and Sherri, another long time jive partner Daphne, and my rock 'n' roll DJ buddy George.

My long-time friend Tom Keen and Richard his father (my fishing buddies).

All my Anglo-Indian friends amongst them Shirley and Pride, Lynn and Glenn, Richard and Di, and of course Alan and Denise Fernandes all great Rock 'n' Rollers.

Nobby and Barbara for all their support along with Eddie and Caroline and all the Harefield crew.

Siful and Bobby and Akik and Rob for all their friendship over the years.

All the musicians, from the Louisiana Hayriders to all the rock 'n' roll band members over the years, not forgetting all the 'Skiffabillys' and musicians and friends not only from the UK but also abroad.

All the crew from 'Forever Elvis' and the cast and musicians, all the thousands of people I met when living the British country music scene. (That means nearly every village hall in England).

I must thank all the band of Jive Street from Gosport: Inge, John, Kevin, Dixie, and Mick and Sandy (thanks for all the laughs we have had and still do). I think it is only fair to share Micks taxman episode with all you readers, which went something like this. There stood lead guitarist Mick before the taxman after being summoned to his office, 'Mick did you bring all your accounts and paperwork with you?' 'I've got it right here', so Mick pulled out of his pocket half a folded cornflake packet and written on the back was all his sums and figures, 'ear u r'. 'I find this most irregular', said the taxman at which point his phone rang and to the taxman's horror it was Mick's missus Inge on the phone. The taxman said despondently 'I'm sorry but this is the tax office. I do not believe this, Mick it's your partner asking me to remind you not to forget to bring home a bottle of milk and loaf of bread!' Welcome to the music business Mr. Taxman!

Oh, and let's not forget the national insurance people who went around to Mick's house, made themselves at home and sat down looking very serious. Mick asked them if they would like a cup tea and a biscuit and the lady told Mick he should be taking this situation a little bit more seriously. Mick told the two N.I. representatives in no uncertain terms, 'It's as simple as this, there is no need for a long meeting as I have calculated everything five times and came up with the exact same figures every time. Once I have paid all the bills and then for all the food there is nothing left for you!' And it did not matter how much they divulged with Mick regarding his finances, they just did not get it – the rock 'n' roll pot was dry. Good old Mick (you gotta love him).

Peter Hart and Dorothy Porter. Peters father was war correspondent to Sir Winston Churchill and Dorothy could have been a Judge. They are two of my close friends who look after their cats and dogs better than most, but most of all prove to me the values of Great Britain still exists! (We will fight them on the beaches).

I thank from the music, TV and entertainment world... The Jordanaires for bringing me into their fold and I cherish all the great moments on and off stage we shared, TV music producer John Hawkins who was fabulous to work with, Carl Perkins who I totally agree deserves the title 'The King Of Rockabilly', Jerry Lee Lewis (for turning up), Gary Shoefield always there with his foresight and encouragement and Ray Santilli who proved to me you do not need talent to succeed in this business. Scottish Harry (Ray's second in command) who needs a Blue Peter badge to put up with what he did.

I thank the following presenters because I thought they were brilliant at their job and I enjoyed being in their company: Richard Madeley and Judy Finnigan, every interview was great fun. Really wonderful couple. Lorraine Kelly (one of the best!) – Lorraine interviewed me a couple of times live on TV and to be honest I think I ended up fancying her, (we are all allowed to have our dreams). Gloria Hunniford who just made you feel you were in her living room, The Jordanaires all thought she was fab! Derek Jameson (brilliant host), Jonathan Ross and little brother Paul – talented boys, Michael Parkinson Jnr, Paul Gambaccini, Paula Yates (sadly no longer with us), Spike Milligan (I wonder what the heavens are gonna make of good old Spike), Gyles Brandreth, Tom Bell, Willie Morgan, Geoff Barker, Del Richardson, Mark Lamar (I never had an interview with Mark but growing up we met at rock 'n' roll weekenders and he is a good ambassador for the rock 'n' roll world), Randall Lee Rose (America could not send us Alan Freed so we got Randall instead, he's done a good job in my book). There are a lot of presenters I have not mentioned, forgive me for that but thanks for taking the time to have me on your show!

Rick Blaskey, Steven Howard, Olav and Carolynn Wiper, Bill Kimber for opening the door just a little.

Music Publishers: David Paramor, Tony and Mick from Acuff Rose UK for their guidance.

Musicians: Chris Skornia, Barry Guard, Steve Oakman, Dave Hayward and all the guys from the band Southern Country.

Producer, Stuart Coleman – When you have been produced by Mr. Coleman as I had on many occasions, you find out he is the master of getting the best out of any artiste or musician, always making sure the end result is worth all the boot camp production he endorses. If you want the best you have to work very hard for it, especially when your production is procured by the master. This is a very sad time for the music world for on the 19th April 2018 Stuart sadly passed away in Cheltenham, England. In my mind Stuart was Britain's answer to America's Alan Freed. Certainly the best music producer I had the fortunate pleasure to meet and work with. Another star glows very brightly in the rock 'n' roll heavens.

DJ Annie, a brilliant DJ but one of my best friends who has also helped me with my diction, as well as to leave out all the jibber jabber throughout the writing of this book. Blessed to have met and become part of her family, Matt, Siobhan and all of Siobhan's family, Lisa, Chloe and Ellis, my good buddy her son Dave and wife Caz and their daughter Molly.

Tommy and Heather, Brad and Laura. Tony and Alex, along with Jill and Dave, and Babs, Chris and Sherrie – all good supportive friends.

Gone but not forgotten, Terry from The Spinning Disc record shop, Chiswick.

Great record shops I still buy collectibles from are friends Paul Green from Sounds Original record shop and Chris Giles, The Elvis Shop.

Charities I am proud to have been associated with:

UNICEF, Help for Heroes, Breakthrough (breast cancer for women), Chain of Hope for Harefield Hospital. They are all very worthy causes I have worked closely with, along with others, and I will carry on in the future doing all I can.

ACKNOWLEDGEMENTS

I would like to acknowledge the people that I see every day while delivering. The unseen heroes. These are the people who work with the elderly and give them comfort and affection, the people who work with children with special needs and children who are not lucky enough to have parents who can care for them. Let's not forget the boys and girls and men and women of our armed forces who strive to keep us safe in this turbulent world, and the people who give their time to the homeless and weak. All the people who tirelessly help stray and injured animals. These people are in their thousands throughout Great Britain and abroad, God bless them all!

If I have forgotten anyone or someone feels they have been left out I apologize. Who knows when 'Blue Suede Dreams' The Sequel will emerge? All I have written so far is only a percentage of the laughs that I wish to share with you, which leaves me to say:

'WATCH THIS BLUE SUEDE SPACE...'

TV & RADIO APPEARANCES

TV Appearances

TV AM - 3 appearances

This Morning - 5 appearances

The Jonathan Ross Show

The James Whale TV Show

ITV Motormouth (My first TV appearance)

The Derek Jameson Show

ITV Perfect Scoundrels

Sky News

BBC Pebble Mill

35 UK TV appearances.

Holland - 2 national TV appearances.

U.S.A. (The Voice of Elvis singing on the Pepsi ad campaign)

Radio Shows

BBC Radio 1 Newsbeat

LBC

BBC Radio 2, The Drive Time Show - 2x1 hour live performances with Johnny Earl, Jordanaires, Scotty Moore, D.J. Fontana in my home town Exeter.

BBC Radio 2, Gloria Hunniford Show x 2

Other Radio performances - BBC and regional over 100 UK live and pre-recorded.

Holland to promote Jordanaires tour

Germany to promote Jordanaires tour

Sri Lanka to promote Coca Cola

Australia to promote concert

ACKNOWLEDGEMENTS

PRESS

Regional and major tabloids & magazines
The Sun
The Mirror (Page 7 Fella)
The Daily Star
News of The World
The Independent
Daily Mail
Daily Express
Daily Record
Regional press - over 100 articles
Time Out
Woman's Own
(In most of the major tabloids on 3 or 4 different occasions)
With regional press, mainly relating to live theatre or show performances when in their area.
Germany: Der Spiegel, Der Stern, Der Welt, Der Zeit, Focus - plus all various tabloids and magazines that coincide where shows and tours were performed.
Holland, Denmark, Finland, Australia, Sri Lanka: All major and regional tabloids to coincide with tour.

30

EPILOGUE

The best way for me to look back over what I have done up to now in my career and all I have experienced is in two ways. Firstly, my views on the positive side, and all I have achieved in a pretty much cut-throat business, and secondly the not so glamorous side.

The Sunny Side...

I have lived the dream I never thought in my wildest imagination could ever become a reality and still today I am rockin' 'n' rollin'. I have the best memories any rocker could have wished for, and a lot of what I am about to say will certainly help any new budding entertainer. We never stop learning in the music world. For example, I read in one of Johnny Cash's books that after one of his performances at the Louisiana Hayride, the owner told Mr. Cash 'Johnny in this business the higher you climb the ladder, the more yer ass shines'. Boy is that true.

The role you are to play in the music business will dictate or certainly play a large part with your health, wealth and sanity. I am what they call a front man; centre stage, loving the thrill, the accolade of an enthused audience (95% of the time), the meeting and greeting after performances to all the people e.g. fans (well I like to call them friends and music lovers). I never took for granted the ability to command an audience; it was a gift that only few are fortunate to have. Having this gift gave me the opportunity to travel most of the world. I got to meet all fellow rock 'n' rollers worldwide. I found it amazing; the stigma attached to people in the music and entertainment world. To a lot of people it means they are in positions of power to dictate politics and have their finger on the pulse with important world affairs. It is unbelievable the power of fame and all it commands.

I also found you are treated very differently depending on which country you are in. When I was in America just mentioning I was an entertainer lit every conversation; they love people in the music business. I can also say I have always had this very positive response in Holland and in Germany even today. The people just love singers and performers.

The press and media need entertainers to brighten up the tabloids; they thrive on entertainer's lives. They can certainly make or break you. Overnight it can feel is as if a cloak of importance has been bestowed upon you. I performed at a Royal Air Force base and I and the entire band walked through the officers' quarters as they were having their salmon and champagne canapés and they greeted us as friends. I realized being in the music business opens many a door that in normal circumstances would just never happen.

Of course, touring and recording with The Jordanaires, Scotty Moore, D.J. Fontana, Carl Perkins, Brian Connolly from The Sweet, and many others, as well as meeting their families and working with so many fellow entertainers, in most cases have been a blessing. There is a lot of fun to be had when you spend time on tour. It can be like a never ending 'carry on' film, and when you get to travel to different countries it's wonderful... the sights and scenery along with the different foods. Still today when I tour I enjoy the thrill of different towns and cities and festivals. I guess when it's in your blood, it's there till your very last breath.

I never get tired of listening to Elvis, rock 'n' roll, country and doo wop and blues music which keeps the thrill when writing songs – that will be part of my existence eternally. I know the world is certainly a different place than it was 30 years ago. One gets the feeling today that the world is a lot smaller but a lot more dangerous... anything can happen at any time. I used to enjoy catching up with the world news, not so much these days. Now you never know what horrors are going to be announced. A blessing I have today is I get to see my darling mum a lot more and we enjoy each other's company.

I am an avid 78rpm record collector. My latest two little gems, my old friend Carl Perkins ("Glad All Over") on London (cracking track) and the Del-Vikings - ("Whispering Bells") also on London... FAB!!!

Unfortunately, a lot of fellow friends and musicians have gone to rock 'n' roll heaven. We all have loved ones we will miss as the years pass by, family and friends being the most important. To some, they find that people that live their lives always dancing and playing music are a little strange, especially when there are more important matters in the world today, but I am one of those blue suede souls who have been so influenced by the music of the 1950's, 1960's and 1970's, I'm kind of stuck in the vinyl groove and it's too late to change now….

We all have milestones in life where we look back and a sentiment in time is never forgotten, but in musical terms, would I have changed a thing? Well when you read the next bit about the downside of the entertainment business that will enlighten you on my thoughts.

I learned my trade so to speak by listening and watching the likes of Elvis, Buddy Holly, Bobby Darrin, Billy Fury, Johnny Cash, and I believe there is always a place in music for this style of artiste.

Another moment in time that changed my course of thinking and direction was when I drove home one year on Christmas Eve. I drove late through the night and arrived at my Mothers down in Dawlish, Devon around 1am. I knocked quietly, and it took a little while for my mum to answer, then she opened the door, gave a gleaming smile, hugged me and said, 'Darling I must not lose my thread'. I followed her through the passage into the kitchen and she told me 'I am writing a letter and must finish it'. I never saw my Mother so intense about something, so I asked her what an earth was so important to be finished on the computer at 1am on Christmas morning… She told me 'I am writing to Simon Cowell and letting him know it's appalling the way Rhydian (who was thought to have been unfairly mistreated in the votes and talked to badly by Mr. Cowell from what I remember on the X factor show), has been treated and I am going to make sure he gets treated just and fairly'. At that very moment I stood there stunned… the penny had finally dropped: The power that the X factor had over the public was astounding. Right there and then I knew that how I saw the music and entertainment business world had changed forever.

Little did I know that the birth of the World Wide Web would influence such a massive change in the way future music would be listened to. Why pay for music when you can listen to it for free!

Yes, the world has changed so much. Not so long ago if anybody was looking for talent they would go to a live performance, whereas today if you are looking for new talent you just simply go on the internet and can see hundreds of acts the world over. Vinyl has made a big come back in the UK and recently sold more than digital sales for the first time since CDs were upon us.

So, to sum up the positive side to all my years in the music and entertainment business, I am still alive and still living the dream. I've learned how to laugh soberly, and my wants in life are good friends and a happy heart, and I say that wholeheartedly, especially as we are living in such a mixed-up world.

I see things a lot clearer now and understand the pitfalls of the music world and I have come out the other side pretty much unscathed. You learn to embark on a couple of projects you can make work, rather than a full scale out of control mess. That frequently occurs when you take on far too much that you were never going to be able make a success of, in any shape or form.

I recently went to a country music festival in Germany, a rock 'n' roll night in Holland, and one here in the UK in Kingston upon Thames and they were all as popular as ever. This year I am going to release a new album with my German band The Dukes (see releases) along with my latest release *"Rockin' Mo"*.

So, I still bless the music gods and in this year of our lord 2019 it will be the birth of my book and here's hoping it's a Blue Suede Dream of a year … A wop bop a loo bop a lop bam boom!

Okay folks, it's time for the not so sunny side of the music and entertainment business...

I am only telling you this from my personal point of view. You will always get people in the music and entertainment business saying 'I don't see it like that... he's just over-reacting'. Performers will always have their own view from what they have experienced – they're entitled to their opinion of course. So here is mine...

It's not so easy to write this section as anyone who knows me will confirm, I am always pretty positive and I like to think there is a good side to everyone and any situation. If you have any form of talent, no matter how small, when you try to fulfil your potential people will only want to help you reach your aspiring entertainment goals...

WILL SOMEONE GET ME A GENIE IN A BOTTLE AND LET ME HAVE ONE WISH: TO BECOME THE GHOST OF SHOWBIZ PAST SO I CAN FLY TO DAWLISH TRAIN STATION ON THAT COLD AND WINTERY THURSDAY NIGHT BACK IN 1984...

I could take that Devonshire rocker sitting there pondering what the future holds, take him by the hand and fly him through the air to the wonders of his future, starting with the bright lights of London's West End theatres that he is to star and will perform on... The many romances, good and bad... The music legends he will become friends with... walking the streets of Nashville, Tennessee... and as always, and most importantly, a caring and loving mum throughout... along with meeting some lifelong friends. At least that will keep him a little bit sane and realise there are goals and achievements worth fighting for. Now show him the reality of the business he has chosen, and the way people would approach and advise him on the right way forward, hoping only that he would fail at every corner. Yes, that's right... you are now in a world where as long as you're paying you will have the best friends in the world.

Let me give you an example. From the very beginnings, my manager and I were forever on tenterhooks trying to find finances to book theatres and tours to keep the band in work, and I wholeheartedly trusted them. We would give them all fuel expenses per performance as they told us they were all coming in separate vehicles... then after one performance we saw them on the way home at a petrol station, all in one vehicle, thereby pocketing £80 out of every £100 we gave them. So they had lied and cheated us at every performance they could.

Now I know it might seem petty but that was the sort of thing that happened all the time. I quickly came to the conclusion this is a very selfish business. I would later learn you have to be a HARD, HARD, HARD person in this business if you want to climb the ladder, let alone make any financial gains. You also come to understand that you can enjoy the music business a lot better if you don't constantly concentrate on trying to make a fortune – that is mainly for the business people. In every country that has music awards each year, the artistes change but not so much the business people. The general public's perception of the music business is much, much more glamorous than it really is.

The music business has changed beyond belief and I certainly do not take it as seriously as I once did. The biggest stumbling block is having any form of talent and thinking it will be a stroll in the park ...well that's what the thousands of hopefuls think who join this industry year after year and believe me when I say, I feel for them. The years of torment of being told how good you are by unscrupulous manipulators, unfortunately ends up being the biggest financial and emotional cost a performer will ever have to pay.

Now that's enough of all that......!

You enjoy your read and your own personal dedication. We will put the world to rights together and brighten up the musical airwaves. Hopefully you can tell that the positive side of the music and entertainment business far outweighs the negative side, so it's onwards and upwards for this rock 'n' roller. Keep rockin' and I'll do the same.

31

THE STORY OF ROCK AND ROLL

Not too long ago I put a lot of time and effort into writing a script for a live show called "The Story of Rock and Roll". It had all the ingredients of being a small theatre production as it had narration in-between the songs explaining the birth of rock and roll and portraying that how in 1954 the first ever British rock and roll chart entry was Bill Haley's *"Shake Rattle and Roll"*. The production was followed by a chronological order of events with the songs that this new world-wide craze of the 1950's had spawned. New styles of singing sensations, Elvis Presley among them, who to the senior citizen of the 1950's society, shocked them into endless nightmares thinking the decency of their youth was being corrupted by this demonic music.

It was all put to script and professionally bound, then I sent a copy to none other than the UK's leading rock and roll promoter Paul Franklyn "Legs" Barrett who I got on quite well with and let's not forget he was the manager and pretty much created the success of Shaking Stevens, so credit where it's due. I liked the way Paul worked and was quite elated with his very positive response to my new production and he wanted to get to work with it straight away. I will never forget that phone call to Mr Barrett, and I laugh about it now because basically a script was all I had, and I froze with shock and horror when I realised I was selling a show with no physical element whatsoever. When he asked "When is the first performance", I kind of replied "It's still in the rehearsal stage". That's when it comes home to roost... "Mr Earl" where is all the financing coming from for a well-rehearsed and professional production which can take months to formulate and thousands of pounds for the standard of show you are aiming for. I told Mr Barrett I would contact him further down the line when the project was fully functional. Yes, you got it, the show never surfaced, simply due to not only the finances but also the time it would take to put this mega production together. Today for me, it's a kind of blessing in disguise, for I now know the full extent of what I was really trying to procure.

The good outcome to how I first scripted the story of rock and roll is although it had all the makings of a brilliant show, it was definitely lacking in musical depth. Today I feel it would be a fuller story with the DNA embodiment of rock and roll, especially now that I have become more educated with my diversity and understanding of the many music genres involved. This enables me to portray the story of rock and roll with greater allure, with the origins combined with the true story of its roots; not just a Bill Haley or an Elvis Presley song that started the rock and roll phenomenon, but you have got to get to the core of how they came to be.

What indeed were the musical events that caused this sensation? I feel this is a very apt way to finish my "Blue Suede Dreams" book – a much more in-depth look at rock and roll. And as I'm not actually performing this show live, I'm able to put into writing a more bang up-to-date editorial, so that younger rock and rollers and all the people that ask me, "Why do people love rock and roll so much?" can understand. So here it is… "The Story of Rock and Roll".

Rock and roll music is a fusion of musical styles; it's main components being rhythm and blues, country music, boogie woogie, jazz, gospel and jump blues, …you can also throw in some western swing. All these styles originated in the United States of America.

The Blues is certainly a large element of rock and roll which evolves from African musical traditions, the blues lyrics were a reality of life. Workers created a music style based on the bad working conditions and the hardships slavery endorsed. They sang songs to tackle their misery and pain, singing the blues was pretty much their only way to release their frustration. They often sang to remind themselves of their homeland which was a land far away and knowing they were never really going to see it again. "The Blues" says exactly what it does on the tin: It would be very hard to believe say, a multimillionaire singing the blues. What is for sure, is that without the blues it's very unlikely there would have been an Elvis Presley.

I have read and heard many an argument on what started rock and roll. I remember a situation where one guy said it's definitely *"That's Alright Mama"* by Elvis Presley, whereupon the other person said, "But what made him perform that song in the way that he did?"

I'm going to start by transporting us back to 1928 to a song called *"Bulldoze Blues"* performed by Henry Thomas who was born in 1874. This is as good an example as any, the lyrics tell you the terrible situation he was in, working his fingers to the bone, wishing he could up sticks and leave to go to Tennessee for a better way of life and of course be with the woman he loved. When you think of the way we use our phones today, we press a button and someone from the other side of the planet will instantly speak to you in real time, that's how we get our message across or even download a track from music cyberspace in a nanosecond.

Back in 1928, putting your message across on a recording was as 'Star Trek' as it got. This Henry Thomas release was one of the earliest and barest forms of rhythm and blues. He's playing a rhythm guitar and when not singing he uses "Quills" which are very similar to panpipes and they are a rare instrument from the American South, and you can hear the reminisces of the same feel that the native American Indians would have used or even the earliest Mayan civilisations. He performs the song with intense emotion, you hear the cry for freedom, he certainly gets his message over, the listener would have got the full extent of his performance.

This recording was released on a record made of shellac not vinyl, as vinyl never came into use until thirty years later. Shellac was a very brittle material and was the main material used for all the record releases of that era which started being made around 1898 right up until the late 1950's. I could cry when I think of the record gems dropped and broken carelessly as the owners of the time did not really have any idea of the collectable value of those gems.

It was record collector's that coined the phrase 78rpm records which means 78 revolutions per minute. I have a record player that plays 78's as I actually collect 78rpm records and have done so for 45 years, as I love the rawness and only being able to hear one track at a time thus giving the recording the listening it deserves. It is also quite interesting to realise that before 1925 the artiste would sing and record straight into a horn, these were called "acoustic" recordings, after this artistes sang into a microphone which gave the licence for a wider range of sounds to be recorded, which became the "electrical recording era". So I think Henry Thomas's 1928 version of *"Bulldoze Blues"* has a valid right to be the very first rung on the ladder and start the musical DNA to "The Story of Rock and Roll".

In the 1920's the radio was invented, which gave gospel music a much wider audience and gospel certainly has a cog in the rock and roll machine. Western Swing in the late 1920's with an up-tempo beat bringing big crowds to the local dance halls and clubs throughout Texas, Oklahoma as well as California was formulating a music culture. Western Swing is different from what was known more commonly as just Swing which was more like the big band brass sound. Western Swing has a steel guitar which being electronically amplified gave it a unique sound. Bob Wills was a mentor along with Spade Cooley; they both were at the forefront of the Western Swing movement. Boogie Woogie was very popular in the 1920's with its piano thumping rhythm, this sound paved the way for Blues legends like Lead Belly, so really the 1920's embedded sounds and rhythms structuring the birth of what we were going to term rock and roll.

Emerging into the 1930's and the 1940's the underbelly of rock and roll was simmering to the surface. Bands were now performing with electric guitars, piano, bass and drums with vocals. Now the 1940's became the era where we have not one or two but a few contenders for what can be crowned the first commercial rock and roll record. I'm not going to say there is a definitive first rock and roll song or recording simply because I bet there is a demo or an acetate recording somewhere in a dark secluded basement that has never seen the light of day written ten, twenty or thirty years prior to the 1950's.

Certainly, the mid to late 1940's gave birth to what you could say are the very first rock and roll songs. You could call them rock and roll's version of the ten commandments but in no particular order when it comes to which song sounds the best. 1946 heralded a stunning and fantastic performance of the song *"That's All Right Mama"* written and performed by Arthur "Big Boy" Crudup. Some would say this was the first rock and roll record and later on in Crudup's career due to this fact he would be labelled 'The Father of Rock and Roll'. I personally love this song and in my early years visiting London venues this song was often played and the dance floors were packed.

A definite leading contender for the first commercial rock and roll record, Crudup wrote not only *"That's All Right Mama"* but also *"My Baby Left Me"* along with a song I have always wanted to release and is now on the *Blue*

Suede Dreams double CD *"So Glad You're Mine"*. All three were recorded by Elvis and these were at the start of Crudup's writing career, but unfortunately like so many artists of the day, Crudup was robbed of all his royalties so he stopped recording in the 1950's and he quoted "I realised I was making everybody else rich and here I was poor".

You can't get a more creative artiste of the day than Crudup and he was just a forebear of the many artistes to follow that the business people of the music industry would take advantage of at every turn, but you have to give it to Crudup when you think he started as a street singer living in a packing crate until an RCA record producer found him and got him signed. Any accolade awarded to this guy, as far as I'm concerned, he has earned a million times over.

Move up a year and 1947 gave us another contender for the title, Roy Brown's self-penned *"Good Rocking Tonight"*. Wow what a tune, he did a good version and it reached number 13 of the Billboard R&B chart. Roy Brown originally offered the song to a very well-known singer who previously had a number 1 r&b hit in 1945 with the jump jive rendition of *"Who Threw the Whiskey in the Well"*, Wynonie Harris. He at first refused to record *"Good Rocking Tonight"* but when seeing the success Roy had with it he recorded a version a year later and his version of *"Good Rocking Tonight"*, took a new lease of life. This version was jumpin' and to this day it still fills the dance floor, I absolutely love it… no wonder in 1948 it went to number 1 on the R&B chart.

In 1949 three songs that prove to me rock and roll was just around the corner, were *"Rock the Joint"*, Jimmy Preston …what a rocker! and *"Saturday Night Fish Fry"* by Louis Jordan and as well in 1949 a recording by the future rock and roll legend Fats Domino belting out *"The Fat Man"*. Still in 1949 a terrific candidate for the first rock and roll recording Goree Carter with the song *"Rock A While"*, and for the record to me this has to be one of, if not THE first rock and roll record. He was 18 years of age when he recorded this awesome track and what a brilliant name for his backing band "The Hep Cats". If anyone had told me this song was recorded mid 1950's I would have believed them. Let's put it this way, to me what makes a classic rock and roll song is Chuck Berry styled guitar, Fats Domino boogie woogie piano, throw in a wailing saxophone, with a backbeat, so you can't lose it! Lyrically getting the message over Goree Carter starts the song with "Feeling good this morning, so I wanna rock a while…" so to me, *"Rock A While"* has all those ingredients. Others can have their thoughts on the first rock and roll record; I have to say, this is pretty much mine.

Now, 1951 saw a milestone for me in the story of rock and roll because whenever I see a documentary or a 1950's music based film, the one song normally played is *"Rocket 88"* performed by "Jackie Brenston and his Delta Cats". Where was it recorded - Memphis, Tennessee, produced by none other than the legendary "Sam Philips" on that fabulous blue and white "Chess" label. Add all this up and it tells any rocker, the rock and roll carpet was now being unfurled, music history was certainly in the making because *"Rocket 88"* was not only classed as a rhythm and blues song, but today you can definitely say "Hold on this sounds like rock and roll". Reaching number one on the Billboard R&B chart I know a lot of musical historians will say this was the first rock and roll record and I can understand why, with all the lyrical references to a fabulous car and the rhythm to back it up for sure. *"Rocket 88"* was another footstep on the rock and roll ladder.

Let's make way for a R&B masterpiece reaching the number one spot for 7 weeks in 1952 selling nearly 2 million copies. Another R&B class act, Willie Mae "Big Mama" Thornton unleashing *"Hound Dog"* – you only have to listen to her mannerisms and the feeling of how she expresses every word that she's singing to understand why the R&B stars and songs of the 1950's were a force to be reckoned with. You can also understand how the establishment would try their damnedest to quash this style of music, for what they thought were ethical and moral reasons, judging by the popularity of this monstrous sound. "You said you were high classed, but I can see through that".

In 1953 R&B female singer Ruth Brown released *"(Mama) He Treats Your Daughter Mean"*, this was her third R&B chart number 1, although classed as R&B you certainly get the vibes of rock and roll. At the start of the 1950's there was a significant cultural change in American society and not only were the rhythm & blues stars coming to the fore, who were obviously mainly black artistes, but just like R&B music, country music had been evolving. It too was finding a lot of its earliest roots from the 1920's weaving the sounds of folk music with Appalachian and Western music and it is worth noting the U.S. congress actually recognised Bristol, Tennessee as the "Birthplace of Country Music". It was there where recording sessions had marked the commercial debuts of Jimmie Rodgers and the Carter Family.

Country music was predominantly white performers and really came to the fore in the 1940's, brewing a melting pot of Hillbilly, Western music and it's from all these fusions we get Rockabilly, a very integral part of rock and roll. The Great Depression in America had resulted in a decline in record sales, which in turn, meant most country music fans were now tuning into the radio. This gave rise to the "barn dance" shows, featuring artists of the day and these were being aired all over the Southern States and North as far as Chicago, and West as far as sunny California.

This gave birth to the most important show aired, *The Grand Old Opry*, starting way back in 1925 by WSM in Nashville and is still aired today. I have been to some of these performances and sat in the audience and watched how the acts intertwine with the dancers, all good fun. An early star of the Hayride was Roy Acuff known as "King of Country". He created Acuff-Rose Music Publishing, whom I have actually worked with on occasions. They signed artists like Hank Williams, Roy Orbison and the most famous commercial rock and roll duo, The Everly Brothers. As I have said, a major part of rock and roll is Rockabilly: A mixture of Hillbilly, Western Swing and Country Music along with some Bluegrass and I can go along with the first Rockabilly song being *"Birmingham Bounce"* by Hardrock Gunter and the Pebbles, released in 1950.

You listen to the record and straight away the intro is very similar to *"Jungle Rock"* by Hank Mizell and that reverbing echo on the lead vocal with a good rockin' rhythm gives you that feeling this is a great forbearer of Rockabilly. These are some of the legendary rock and roll artists that widely used a large ingredient of Rockabilly in their career... Wanda Jackson, Bill Hayley, Buddy Holly, Carl Perkins, Elvis Presley and Jerry Lee Lewis.

Imagine there you are back in 1954 America, slumped back in the chair then you decide to turn the radio dial looking for something to satisfy your listening and as clear as day a voice comes across "All ready to rock, it's Saturday night, this is Alan Freed with my late-night show "Rock 'n' Roll Party". You would be listening to the man that coined the phrase 'rock n roll' and promoted the first rock and roll concert. Through his radio shows he drew upon white and black listeners, and this of course caused a lot of controversy. Alan Freed was colour blind; he just loved the music and the fact that they were black artistes, he did not give two hoots. He not only opened the ears of the United States with his radio shows but Europe as well, playing the songs of real artistes that expressed energy and rhythm that really rocked, not the subdued second-hand cover versions, mostly by white artistes, aimed at being government and public friendly.

He was a mentor to me as I recounted earlier in this book. My growing up in Devon watching the film *"Rock, Rock, Rock"*, in which he introduced all the acts, basically enlightened me to see that rockabilly, doo wop and R&B are really what generates the music that is rock and roll. Alan Freed did so much in spearheading rock and roll for the general public. 1954 was the year great songs began to surface... *"Goodnight Sweetheart Goodnight"* by The Spaniels, *"I'm Your Hoochie Coochie Man"* by Muddy Waters and the brilliant *"Shake Rattle and Roll"* by Big Joe Turner. They were just a few of the good tunes on the R&B charts compared to the safer sounds of Doris Day and Perry Como who were topping the U.S. hit singles chart.

1955 is the year the Billboards Best Sellers in-stores charts were all topped by Perez Prado performing *"Cherry Pink and Apple Blossom White"* – a lovely melodic cruise ship piece of trumpet playing, which you have to remember was very much the theme of the day. To stand the slightest chance of having the same impact or chart success with anything slightly obscure, would quite literally take something like real aliens being captured and brought to the public's attention. But in 1955 they did land!.. for it was Billboards second best-selling tune that really cements rock and roll to the ears of the whole wide world, *"Rock Around the Clock"* by Bill Haley & His Comets. Okay it might have been Billboards second best-selling record of 1955 but worldwide it was THE BIGGEST SELLING RECORD. Helping the song take off into rock and roll orbit was the alignment of *"Rock Around the Clock"* being used under the opening credits of the film *"Blackboard Jungle"*, which years later was selected for preservation in the United States "National Film Registry by the "Library of Congress" as being "culturally, historically significant". Now the fuse was lit; *"Rock Around the Clock"* became number one in the U.S.A. as well as the U.K., and even Australia.

"Rock Around the Clock" was the song more than any other previously to give the whole music business a good shake down, because unfortunately for the safer side of the mainstream music world, rock and roll was now upon you. Not only was it going to fill the airwaves and fill the dance halls, the raw youth would be unleashed in their millions. "Wop bop a loo bop a lop bom boom" ..and spearheading all this vulgarity, imposing this new demonic music craze, would be a man dressed in gold lame, exhibiting sexual

232

connotations on stage. Yes all you mainstream music lovers of "How Much Is That Doggie In The Window" and "Hot diggity, dog ziggety, boom what you do to me" will cringe with fear and hatred when endlessly the echoing haunts of "Well, since my baby's left me, I found a new place to dwell". Oh yes, to all the squares of music society you'll feel so lonely you could die i.e. it's time for all you squares to step aside and welcome onto the dance-floor the newly bred "rockers" and let them express their inner most emotions! And with open arms, reach out and welcome the year 1956.

Now, I'm British and I can personally testify WE DON'T LIKE CHANGE. In Britain for hundreds of years teenagers wore pretty much the same attire as their parents did but the early 1950's gave rise to the Teddy Boy, a new defined style for the youth of the 1950's. With an approach to society of self-being, being able to think for themselves, and not being dictated to – whether the upper social structure of the UK liked it or not. When the film *Blackboard Jungle* came to the UK and was on show at the cinema in Elephant and Castle, South London in 1956, not only was the odd soda and snack devoured by the youth of the day but dancing in the aisles and ripping up the seats were administered. "That's no way for youngsters to behave in the land of manners and decency" so as far as the press, media and general public were concerned bedlam was afoot to the swinging tones of *"Rock Around the Clock"*.

Teddy Boys and Teddy Girls adopted this film and rock and roll music as their identity. I have given you a lot of events leading up to 1956 but it is this year that rock and roll puts on its blue suede shoes and kicks aside a lot of the safe mainstream songs, and deservedly stomps right to the front end of most pop charts in the world. *"Blue Suede Shoes"* released February 1956, was written and performed by Carl Perkins and anyone who has worked with or met Carl would agree being called "The King of Rockabilly" is no small achievement. Carl was inducted into the Rock and Roll Hall of Fame, the Rockabilly Hall of Fame, the Memphis Music Hall of Fame and the Nashville Songwriters Hall of Fame as well as being awarded a Grammy Hall of Fame Award.

I mention all of this because for starters this book "Blue Suede Dreams" for one, would never have been given the title if it was not for Carl's song, and the list of people who have covered this iconic rock and roll anthem is endless. I doubt when Carl wrote it he ever thought this would be the most commonly known phrase and footwear relating to the 1950's and rock and roll.

America 1956: The rock and roll cake was baked. We know most of the ingredients, one was the solid body electric guitar which had been around for three years, and appearing through the speakers in millions of households was a piano pumping, big stature of a man – Fats Domino, who introduced himself to the world with *"Blueberry Hill"*.

No one artist in the music and entertainment business will ever make the impact that Elvis Presley did in 1956. Elvis was well known in the Southern States of America and on Sam Philips' Sun record label, releasing 5 records with *"That's Alright Mama"* being his first, giving birth to the music of the King. Some would say this was the first rock and roll record. Elvis became very popular, but it was on the signing of a managerial contract with Colonel Tom Parker who got Elvis signed through Steve Sholes to RCA Victor Records, that the guided rock and roll missile was about to hit. In April of 1956 Elvis topped the U.S. charts with his first single release, *"Heartbreak Hotel"*. Along with network and television appearances he was at the spearhead of all that was rock and roll.

Head to toe he was a threat to the youth of not only American society but the world! Most male teenagers wanted to be him, and most female teenagers wanted to love him. Jerry Lee Lewis was on record as saying, "Any guy that looks that good of course you're gonna hate him". Elvis gave the youth of the world what they'd been longing for, their own identity. The floodgates were now opened for the "King of Rock and Roll". *"Hound Dog/Don't Be Cruel"*, the power ballad *"I Want You, I Need you, I Love You"* were all hit records that year.

The King would sell over one million copies of his single *"Love Me Tender"* – the first for a single to do so – and this caused a ripple effect for he was performing his first acting roll in a movie titled *"The Reno Brothers"*. The title soon had to be changed due to the success of his million-seller and so Elvis's first movie was aptly re-named *"Love Me Tender"*.

If you are now a new devoted follower of rock and roll, what a year you are going to have! For starters get straight on down to the local or nearest cinema or take your car to a drive-in movie theatre and before your very eyes watch *"Rock, Rock, Rock"*. Like an early Top of the Pops you'll hear songs from Chuck Berry, LaVern Baker, Frankie Lymon and the Teenagers, The Flamingos, The Moonglows and the brilliant Johnny Burnette trio. The film that stamped rock and roll is unwanted onto most squares foreheads, *"Rock*

Around the Clock" – well I can tell you, if you've been looking for the dance beat to fill any dance hall this is it. Look at the terrific song list: *"Rock Around The Clock"*, *"See You Later Alligator"*, *"Razzle Dazzle"* all by Bill Haley and His Comets, *"Teach You To Rock"*, Freddy Bell and the Bellboys, in "Amazing Technicolor" you will get to see and hear the amazing Platters performing *"The Great Pretender"*. You get to see Alan Freed as himself and for the first time a lot of viewers will have seen white musicians performing in the same venues as black and Hispanic performers and then all sharing the stage at the end.

If you have seen these two films you'll be first in the queue to watch *"The Girl Can't Help It"*, a brilliant soundtrack and artists: Little Richard, Eddie Cochran, Gene Vincent and His Bluecaps, Fats Domino. The storyline could have come straight out of the Carry On film sense of humour, starring female bombshell Jayne Mansfield, you even get to see a couple seconds of Sgt. Bilko as a milkman, but it's the music of this influential rock and roll film that really hits home. *"Twenty Flight Rock"*, *"Be Bop a Lula"*, *"The Girl Can't Help It"*, all just amazing tracks and Johnny Olenn performing a favourite ballad of mine *"My Idea of Love"* with the rockabilly feel of Eddie Fontaine's *"Cool It Baby"* not forgetting The Treniers, *"Rockin' Is Our Business"*.

The film, *Don't Knock the Rock*, (again a Bill Haley and the Comets, and The Treniers) is a good dance film along with Alan Freed appearing. Another great release *Shake, Rattle and Rock* which had the brilliant Joe Turner appearing in and the film *Rock Pretty Baby* – if you had seen these five films in 1956 you had to be a fully-fledged rock and roller. There's still time to party, with musical adrenaline running through your veins, it's off to the diner for a milk shake and a hot dog while putting a quarter into that musical maestro, the Jukebox.

In 1956 Jukeboxes were all the rage originating as a nickel-in-the-slot phonograph, dating as far back as 1890 and evolving into the 1950's Jukebox. These were outstanding in appearance and caused an emotional euphoria jiving away in front of colourful glass tubes – for me the Wurlitzer took some beating in appearance and sound. This enabled a person to play a tune of their choice and here's some of the most played on the Jukeboxes of 1956... *"Hound Dog"*, *"Don't Be Cruel"* by the King that will get you dancing in the café aisles, and if the owner lets you get a little romantic *"My Prayer"* by the Platters, *"Why Do Fools Fall In Love"* by Frankie Lymon and the Teenagers, now that must get the taste buds going because this was only the beginning, as 1957 is a paradise of songs for any rock and roller.

It's 1957 and "Just let me hear some of that rock 'n' roll music". Yes that music that has been bubbling away for the last 30 years now comes home to roost. Chuck Berry wrote the song *"Rock and Roll Music"* and then bestowed upon us *"Johnny B. Goode"* – these chugging guitar classics gave rock and roll direction lyrically and melodically, a far cry from "You must go and play with your own ding a ling". The most popular dance craze associated with rock and roll is the Jive, but you also had The Bop and The Stroll but most commonly, especially in the USA, they called it the jive but also the "Rock 'n' Roll". The stars kept coming and although making his first appearance on local television in 1952 (as well as in 1955 opening a show for Elvis), welcome to the club of best-selling records of the year, from Lubbock, Texas, Mr Buddy Holly and his "Chirping" Crickets – with one of rock and rolls defining songs *"That'll Be the Day"*. You also had the softer side of rock and roll portrayed perfectly by a song written and performed by Paul Anka, the classic *"Diana"*, a number one hit in many countries for this Canadian born singer.

Now through many diverse entertainment and music channels came the rock 'n' rollers and it was a radio and television series called *"The Adventures of Ozzie and Harriet"* starring a cool looking, seventeen year old dude, Rick Nelson that released on the Imperial record label *"Be-Bop Baby"*.

The guitar was the most recognised rock and roll instrument until a wild man who let loose on the piano, and even set fire to one on stage, started his career at the legendary Sun Records (boy we owe Sam Philips so much) – the formidable Jerry Lee Lewis; a true pioneer of rock and roll, it was time for him to stamp his authority on the music world. Talk about making an impact... *"Whole Lotta Shakin' Going On"*, only followed by *"Great Balls of Fire"*, *"Breathless"* and *"High School Confidential"*. Welcome to the party Mr. Lewis and let's not forget, not only the U.S. single charts had rock and roll filling the ranks, the U.S. R&B chart in 1957 was bursting at the seams with rock and roll: *"Jim Dandy"* by LaVern Baker, *"Long Tall Sally"* by Little Richard! No stopping this bus.

The women of rock and roll were now among us and in 1957, although only given as a nickname "Little Miss Dynamite", Brenda Lee, gave us a wonderful rendition of the song *"Dynamite"*. She only stood at 4 ft 9 inches, and was a brilliant addition to the rock and roll hit parade. Another top drawer act Janis Martin known as the female Elvis, toured Europe in 1957 giving us a taste of *"My Boy Elvis"* and her own composition *"Drugstore Rock 'n Roll"*. We also had the great *"Fujiyama Mama"* and *"Honey Bop"* performed by Wanda Jackson. Although a little less known chart-wise both these ladies became a very important cog in the story of rock and roll.

The 1957 Chevrolet Bel Air can be called the most iconic car of the rock and roll era but there are a whole host of amazing rock and roll cars. The "Chevrolet Corvette Convertible", the "Ford Ranchero" ...just take a look at the 1957 "Oldsmobile Starfire" or the "Super 88", these were the chariots of the day and don't forget the 1950's Hot Rod cars bringing to the public the following year the film *"Hot Rod Gang"*. As it said on the poster 'Crazy Kids… Living to a wild rock 'n' roll beat'. What a fabulous soundtrack featuring the brilliant Gene Vincent, *"Dance To The Bop"*. What a sight it must have been seeing all these fantastic cars taking you to the local dance hop. 1957 saw the release of the film *"Mister Rock and Roll"*, starring Alan Freed with a whole host of now household name rock and roll stars, but the film that landmarked everything rock and roll, was distributed by Metro-Goldwyn-Mayer... *"Jailhouse Rock"*. On the movie poster it stated, "Elvis Presley At His Greatest" and he certainly was.

The song *"Jailhouse Rock"*, written by Mike Stoller and Jerry Leiber is as fundamental to the cementing of rock and roll music as is *"Rock Around the Clock"*. *Jailhouse Rock* the movie itself had Elvis performing a role as a young man sentenced to prison and there he finds his innermost talent as a singer. Just as in real life, Elvis looks mean and cool all at the same time and shows the world his array of dance moves throughout his performance of the song *Jailhouse Rock*. We also see Elvis the balladeer, oozing with the brilliant renditions of *"Don't Leave Me Now"* and *"Young And Beautiful"*, that rocketed in the charts like most of Elvis's single releases. After you were blown away with the A-side – in this case being *"Jailhouse Rock"* – you just flipped the record over to the B side and listened to *"Treat Me Nice"*. Equally fantastic!

Let's take a look at how in 1957 the story of rock and roll was being received through the eyes of rest of the world. Here in the UK the BBC came to the fore and in February the *"Six-Five Special"* was aired and as television was completely live we got to see our first British rock and roll stars performing live for the first time. Marty Wilde, Wee Willie Harris, Don Lang and his Frantic Five; a pretty good introduction I thought to the world of rock and roll.

Rocking through the British charts were rock and roll songs which were creating havoc with the establishment, especially the lyrics. One of the biggest selling records world-wide was *"All Shook Up"*, which sent a shiver down the rock and roll spine, and this was Elvis Presley's first UK number one with a duet vocal of Gordon Stoker of the Jordanaires. Great Britain was loving the King, Bill Haley's *"Don't Knock the Rock"*, Buddy Holly, The Platters, even our very own Lonnie Donegan hit the turntables with his single *"Gamblin' Man/Putting on The Style"*. I know Lonnie, the King of Skiffle was not rock and roll but even as a rocker you would still go out and buy this record. *"Long Tall Sally"*, Little Richard, Jerry Lee Lewis, The Everly Brothers, Fats Domino, Charlie Gracie, Frankie Lymon, and one of my favourites "Jackie Wilson", were all making an impact on the UK charts.

As well as British rock and roll cars like the "Ford Consul", the "Ford Zephyr and Zodiac", we had brilliant motorbikes like the Harley Davidson and Triumph Bonneville roaring along the north circular road in London to the "Ace Café". This was home to the rockers, which were in their element all through the 1950's along with the Teddy boys and rock and rollers. In 1957 they'd all never had it so good.

Elsewhere in the pop world, Australia had chart toppers – mainly Johnny Ray, Perry Como, Bing Crosby and Marty Robins but in 1957 they got the rock and roll bug and rising right to the number one slot was Paul Anka's, *"Diana"*, Elvis Presley's *"All Shook Up"* and Buddy Holly and the Crickets *"That'll Be the Day"*.

I found out from an avid record collector that the letters JO on the numbering on an Elvis Presley HMV 45rpm was short for them being destined for Johannesburg, so even South Africa was on the rock and roll compass. No country in Europe or the rest of the world was now going to be untouched with the global phenomenon that was rock and roll. With its James Dean, Elvis slick-back-hair style and leather jacket and jeans, penny loafers and bobby socks, blue suede shoes and motor cycle boots, this all meant with 1958 looming it was going to be another dance floor filling, multimillion record selling, year for the story of rock and roll. One slight shock in 1957... Little Richard becomes a preacher.

1958: I don't care what people say, rock and roll was here to stay, never a truer word spoken. This was the year Danny and the Juniors gave us the song *"Rock and Roll Is Here to Stay"* but they kicked off the year in the number one slot with *"At the Hop"*, while at home in the UK Cliff Richard and The Drifters hit the top spot with *"Move It"*.

During the 1950's there was hysteria capturing the sci-fi age. Spaceship films engulfed the cinema screens... "Forbidden Planet", "The Quatermass Experiment", being a huge success and these types of films gave birth to Sheb Wooley's song, *"Purple People Eater"*, a good jiver, a lot of fun. Critics from the very beginning slated rock and roll but in this year the King released his fourth movie, *"King Creole"* and he said later, he enjoyed playing the character of Danny Fisher more than any other role throughout his movie career. "Variety" actually gave Elvis praise for the role he played, and would you believe it the "Catholic World magazine", said Elvis is showing signs he is getting the hang of acting.

Instrumentals have always made their mark in the story of rock and roll and this was the year we got the foot tapping and swinging *"Tequila"*, by The Champs, *"Rebel Rouser"*, by Duane Eddy and where would rock and roll be without it's novelty songs, *"Lollipop"* by The Chordettes, *"Short Shorts"*, by The Royal Teens, *"Witch Doctor"*, by David Seville. You had your now cemented rock and roll stars releasing hit after hit. The Platters, the Everly Brothers, Ricky Nelson, Elvis, and you also had great hit songs by artists like Don Gibson, *"Oh Lonesome Me"*, with The Teddy Bears singing, *"To Know Him Is to Love Him"* and *"Who's Sorry Now"* by Connie Francis. All these songs have become iconic in their own way.

Again, on the U.S. R&B chart of 1958, the number one slot was filled 48 weeks out of 52 with songs that could have been put on a rock and roll compilation album. Dion and the Belmonts headed the Italian-American doo wop acts with the smash hit *"Teenager in Love"*. By 1958 anyone who wanted to be a rock and roller they now knew exactly what they stood for. You had become a follower of the music that would stay with you for the rest of your life.

1958 saw Bill Haley just beginning to wane to the rise of different rock and roll stars and the King was getting ready for his "G.I. Rock and Roll" induction. By now there weren't many places in the world where rock and roll had not penetrated in one form or another, and in the UK Jack Good's *Oh Boy!* TV show saw the light of day. This was the first teenage all-music show in Britain, broadcast live from the Hackney Empire, which I performed one of my earliest theatre performances at and I loved this venue; you got a great ambience. The *Oh Boy!* show shone the starlight on Cliff Richard and Marty

Wilde, Billy Fury, Conway Twitty and the Vernon Girls along with many more of the UK and U.S. stars. *Oh Boy!* kept on rockin' right into 1959.

1959: The day the music died. On 3rd February, Buddy Holly, Richie Valens, and "The Big Bopper", were killed in a plane crash near Clear Lake, Iowa, along with the pilot Roger Peterson. They were all on the "Winter Dance Party" tour across the Midwest of America. This certainly was the beginning of the end for rock and roll music as the dominant style of popular music in the USA, losing three legends in that fateful tragedy.

The list of the Billboard top 100 number one hit singles started leaning towards *"Come Softly to Me"* by The Fleetwoods, *"Venus"* and *"Why"* by Frankie Avalon, *"The Three Bells"* by The Browns. You still had the King releasing *"A Big Hunk of Love"*, although he was away in the army, but you could feel American pop music was starting to head in another direction.

Things were a little different in the UK charts, as they were still holding on to the rock and roll coattails with the brilliant Billy Fury, who released his Decca E.P. *"Maybe Tomorrow"* which he wrote the title track of. Also released, a true British great along with Billy of course, was the song *"Please Don't Touch"*, by Johnny Kidd and The Pirates, *"I Got Stung"* by The King, *"Stagger Lee"* by Lloyd Price, *"Donna"* by Marty Wilde, *"Oh Carol"* by Neil Sedaka ...okay a bit sugar and spice but he did give us earlier in the year *"I Go Ape"* and not forgetting *"Mean Streak"* by Cliff Richard and The Drifters and another killer track by the King, *"One Night"*.

January 1960 and one of Britain's great rock and rollers Tommy Steele, who gave us *"Elevator Rock"*, *"Rock With The Caveman"*, along with *"Doomsday Rock"* (yes all titles told you "Rock") showed to one and all that times were a changing for he now started the year with a big hit record, *"Rockers, please turn the other way"*. I'm afraid we have lost the "Rock" we now have *"The Little White Bull"*.

We now see a transformed Elvis Presley – which I might add I love his recording years from 1960-1963 – but the gold lame suit was worn for the last time and thereafter became a museum piece. 1960 gave us one of the coolest rockabilly singers, Johnny Burnette, who with his rock and roll trio gave us the best rockabilly album of the 1950's, but now tamed all that rawness down and gave us *"Dreaming"*, along with *"Poetry in Motion"* by Johnny Tillotson. These styles of songs started transforming the UK charts. Like in America, it was time for the girl groups and the Bobby's of the pop world to walk into the starlight. The early 1960's was the end for rock and roll as we knew it.

Alan Freed's career was ruined by the Payola scandal but in 1960 there were still great tracks to surface. *"Shaking All Over"*, by Johnny Kidd & The Pirates was an exceptional rock and roll song, but now all roads were leading to the emergence of bands like the Rolling Stones, The Beatles. Although America blessed us through the 1950's with rock and roll, unknowingly they were about to be invaded with the British invasion of Beat Music, which the Beatles were spearheading.

Rock and roll music influenced as well as led the way for most of the 1960's new performers, plus many like Roy Orbison who started their careers off as rockers but changed their style, which led to major stardom in the 1960's.

Rock and roll re-surfaced in the 1970's along with Rockabilly. Two of the original rock and roll stars who have always been adored by British fans (me among them), are Gene Vincent and Eddie Cochran. Eddie Cochran still has a rock and roll all-day event every year to celebrate his music. Another show performing worldwide is the musical Buddy, *"The Buddy Holly Story"*, which is a musical in two acts. I went to see this show four times in London's West End, at the Victoria Palace Theatre, so I think the music we all embraced will be here for many years to come.

I've enjoyed writing it, I hope you've enjoyed reading it. Without it, there were no 'Blue Suede Dreams'. NOW PUT MY BOOK DOWN! Get up from your chair, put on that lovely 12" blue coloured vinyl *Blue Suede Dreams* album (or the double CD), don your stunning new *Swing Me Baby* t-shirt. This is the year all you readers can go to *www.bluesuededreams.com* and have a little browse!

And let's carry on with the party and live… the story of Rock and Roll.

Singing for our boys in the Gulf

By Audrey Downes

RUISLIP'S up-and-coming singing star Johnny Earl has been called out to the Middle East to entertain our troops during the Gulf crisis.

The Elvis soundalike of Victoria Road, has agreed to fly out to Bahrain for a 10 day tour next month.

And the action has prompted a big career boost for the singer — formerly known as Johnny Dumper — as he performed on TV AM yesterday and has now been invited to appear on Wogan.

His manager Kevin Allen was contacted by the multi-na...

■ Johnny Earl in his GI gear ish and American forces."

Johnny plans to adapt his usual rock and roll show to appeal to his audience more speci...

Local singer picked to entertain the troops

...there, they've promised us we'll be airlifted straight out to place of safety."

Last time Johnny Earl played locally was at the Beck Theatre earlier this month, and the Hayes venue was packed for the show.

The former painter and decorator turned to showbiz six years...

GWR RE A NER

...orld Cup hit...